Holmes's Great Metropolis Or Views And History Of London In The Nineteenth Century

HOLMES'S

GREAT METROPOLIS:

OR,

Views and History of London

IN THE NINETEENTH CENTURY.

BEING

A GRAND NATIONAL EXHIBITION

OF

THE BRITISH CAPITAL.

WITH HISTORICAL AND TOPOGRAPHICAL NOTICES OF EACH PLACE.

EDITED

BY WILLIAM GRAY FEARNSIDE, ESQ.,

AND THOMAS HARREL.

ILLUSTRATED WITH FIFTY SPLENDID STEEL ENGRAVINGS.

London:

PUBLISHED BY THOMAS HOLMES,

(Successor to Edward Lacey,)

GREAT BOOK ESTABLISHMENT,

76, ST. PAUL'S CHURCHYARD.

BIBLIOTHEQUE CANTONALE
LAUSANNE
ET UNIVERSITAIRE

ILLUSTRATIONS

TO THE "GREAT METROPOLIS."

&c. &c. &c.

INDEX.

THE NEW ROYAL EXCHANGE.

THE

GREAT METROPOLIS,

ILLUSTRATED.

Many costly, erudite, and elaborate works have been compiled descriptive of the rise and progress of the vast metropolis of England, containing much valuable and historical information, but they are principally of an early date, and so voluminous, that the reader is compelled to peruse a mass of desultory matter in order to attain the leading features of the history. Knowledge is now scattered " with so prodigal a hand" that it has become essentially requisite to condense with the utmost accuracy and perspicuity, the more material and characteristic facts, by comprising in a brief review those data, which may be considered the most important in affording interesting and useful intelligence. It has been attempted in the present work by comparative details, succinct but explanatory, to exhibit in a concise form, and to demonstrate by statistical accounts, the population, opulence, resources and magnitude of the commerce of London, the emporium of the world; making manifest the means by which the British capital has attained a zenith of grandeur and importance unparalleled in the annals of civilized nations. An effort has been thus made to concentrate the various information at present widely diffused, at the same time treating the subject more philosophically than has been hitherto essayed. The local objects deserving the attention of the antiquary or more casual observer have been minutely narrated; the manners, customs, and amusements of London at the more remote periods of history carefully described; ts civil, military, and ecclesiastical government cursorily reviewed, and the progress of literature and the advancement of the arts and sciences diligently traced.

Our ' mighty capital" and its environs possess an endless variety of ancient and modern subjects for graphic delineation, and many constituents also of beautiful landscape, which in combination with the waters of the majestic Thames, present a more diversified assemblage of picturesque objects for the pencil of the artist and the eye of the connoisseur, than any other city in Europe. In selection of the subjects for scenic illustration, every exertion has been made to depict those views, which from their individual beauty, classic association, or union with objects of an impressive character, are capable of exciting and gratifying a refined judgment or pictorial taste. The various noble structures which ornament the metropolis have been correctly pourtrayed; not isolated as they are usually represented, with merely the elevations of particular buildings; but in connexion with their respective localities, which not unfrequently identify the objects. The numerous delightful prospects created by the recent improvements in London, Westminster, and their vicinities, have communicated fresh incentive to admiration, as well as contributed to the establishment of the work; whilst the efforts of the artists have been unceasing, to blend originality of grouping, and fidelity to nature, with felicity of execution.

As prefatory to the main design, it is to be in addition remarked, that indulging in speculative theories on the origin of a name, and endeavouring to trace from sources dependant only on oral tradition, the founder of a city, occupied too zealously the attention of many writers of antiquity; who pleased with a fanciful etymology, made data subservient to their purpose, and preferring to deviate from the more beaten path, wandered in the mazy labyrinths of their own imaginations, being more pleased in gratifying their vissionary tastes, and the predilection of the age for fabulous narratives, than endeavouring to elucidate the plain " unvarnished tale;" and in order to extol the people and cities they had undertaken to describe, attempted to deduce their origin from gods, demigods, and heroes. A striking example is instanced in one of our earlier historians, the bishop of St. Asaph, styled Geoffery of Monmouth, whose intellectual capabilities and the opportunities the monastic profession possessed of obtaining by research and investigation, the most authentic information from the MSS. then extant, afforded him the facility of becoming the faithful chronicler of his own and previous eras; had not his inventive genius been too replete with fiction, disposing him to attach too much importance to marvellous and legendary lore, and inducing too ready an assumption of any new or fanciful definition, and thus from similar causes has posterity been often deprived of an irreparable opportunity of arriving at the truth of the remote annals of the kingdom.

Many historians of old have fallen into the common error of corrupting the origin of names, which has emanated from a natural propensity existing of substituting in the place of a difficult or obscure meaning, an appellation more trite and familiar, and which at times is suggested or authorized by affinity of sound. This pandering to the vitiated taste of the day, not only led the mind astray from following the path which would have conducted to the pure fount of historical truth, but distempered the imagination, by causing it to delight in the idle phantasies of romance; and in the instance of the Welsh and other monkish historians, was in the sequel of still graver import, having been the cause of eventually involving two nations in war and bloodshed; for on the assumed faith of these monkish legends of Britain, Edward I. founded his pretended right of feudal sovereignty over the kingdom of Scotland, which is especially exhibited in Edward's answer to the bull of pope Boniface the eighth. The passages of Geoffery relative to the foundation of London are intimately connected with our subject, as in the reign of Henry VI. they constituted the received opinion of the origin of our vast city, their veracity being maintained even in later days. The bishop, with the view of impressing his readers with the importance and supremacy of the British capital, indirectly traces its rise from divine origin, celebrating its *beauty* by supposing it to be founded by Brutus, a descendant of Æneas, son of Venus, the *goddess of beauty*, and daughter of "Jove omnipotent;" his words are, "Brutus considering the state of the kingdom founded a design of building a city, and carefully surveyed the country to discover a place proper for its situation. At last finding a portion of ground on the bank of the river Thames suited for his purpose, erected a city, and dignified it with the appellation of *New Troy*, by which name it was known for ages, which becoming corrupted was called Trinovant, the principal seat of the Trinobantes; and in process of time, when *Lud*, brother of Cassibelaun, obtained the government, he surrounded it with a strong and stately wall, adorned with an infinite number of towers of curious workmanship, and changed the name to *Caer-Lud*, or Lud's town, and commanding the citizens to build houses and public streets of all sorts, it soon equalled, if not exceeded, all cities at home and abroad. But some time after the new designation was again changed into *Caer-London*, and when the kingdom was afterwards conquered by foreigners, was changed into *Londres*." This tradition, perhaps originating in the poetic fiction of the Druids or bards, when history possessed no records, save those committed to the recitative powers of their memory, acquired extensive credence; and we find it amongst the archives in the Tower, as well as being noticed in ancient writings, particularly in a work called *Recordatorium civitatis*, and others entitled *Speculum*, *Liber Albus*, &c. having been formally cited by the civic authorities in petitioning the throne for further immunities in the 7th year of the reign of Henry VI. when the mayor and aldermen pleading before the king the precedence in antiquity and dignity of the city and corporation compared with Rome, commenced "*Inter nobiles urbes orbis,*

&c. or "among the noble citizens of the world rendered illustrious by fame, not any can equal the city of London, the capital of your majesty's realms, esteemed the wonder of the world, &c." *Again*, " For according to the *credit of chronicles* it is considerably older than Rome, having been founded by Brutus after the form of great Troy, *before Rome was built* by Romulus and Remus, whence to this day it enjoys the liberties, rights, and customs of that ancient city of Troy. For it retains the senatorial dignity and lesser magistrates, and its annual sheriffs supply the place of consuls." It is needless quoting other authorities of the darker ages, which have only copied this history of romance, or advanced assertions equally untenable on the ground of probability. Even Pennant appears credulous, that London was a trading port, and " a place of much resort" previous to the invasion of the Romans, about fifty-five years before the Christian era; and this belief appears the more strange, as Julius Cæsar in his Commentaries, speaking as an eye-witness, has dissipated all these visionary notions of the early grandeur of our metropolis, by minutely detailing the character and appearance of the principal settlement or town of the *Trinobantes*, and that it was merely a location of several men, with their wives and families, together with their cattle, partially defended by impassable woods, with fosses and ramparts with palisades, to prevent the sudden incursions of hostile tribes, and within which they retired when threatened with invasion. "Oppidum autem Britanni vocant, quum silvas impeditas vallo atque fossâ munierunt, quò, incursionis hostium vitandæ causâ, conveniri consueverunt." Strabo also mentions that the woods served the Britons as cities; the trees being felled, hedged them round in a large circle, wherein were constructed cabins or huts, formed also of trees, and stalls for the cattle, but which were not intended for long continuance: Herodianus gives a similar description of the primitive Germanic tribes. Diodorus Seculus is rather more minute in his description, where he says, that "the habitations of the Britons were composed of reeds and sticks interwoven in the manner of hurdles," a mode of dwelling frequently adopted by *Nomadean* people. Dion Cassius in alluding to the Mætæ, who inhabited the northern districts of our island, mentions they had neither walls nor towns, and that some of the Britons made use of trees instead of houses; and the faithful historian Tacitus distinctly asserts that the Britons lived rude and dispersed, and were first instructed by Agricola, the Roman governor, about A.D. 80, in the art of building, being unacquainted not only with brick-making, but as far as the Romans witnessed had not attempted to lay one stone above another; and we may conclude our brief extracts from the early authorities most entitled to credit, and which we have deemed essential in illustrating the facts of our native city, by making a short compilation from those authors previously noticed, and other classic writers, in reference to the original state of the ancient Britons. "Except the chiefs, who were clothed in hides and skins, the people were generally found naked, and their bodies painted with the representation of different animals, and being gifted with few if any arts, it would have been inconsistent, in contradistinction with other uncivilized nations, had they formed themselves into communities, and inhabited constantly towns, it being greatly to their advantage to wander in small parties, in order more effectually to find the means of subsistence for themselves and cattle."

In additional refutation of Geoffrey's History, the earliest British historians, Gildas, who died in 570, nearly 600 years before the bishop of St. Asaph; Nennius, the Bangor historian, who flourished in 620; the venerable Bede, whose death occurred in the year 735; and William of Malmsbury in 1140; and other authors who wrote before Geoffrey, are all silent as to the pretended foundation of the city by Brutus; and Gildas and Nennius both candidly acknowledge that their chronicles have been collected from the Roman Annals, MSS. of the primitive fathers, and other foreign historians, and doubting if their countrymen ever possessed any records, " as their greatest scholars had but little learning and no memoirs."

No doubt can be entertained of a species of barter having been carried on with our island and the shores of Gaul, previous to the expedition of Cæsar, who specifies that one of the reasons for his crossing the Channel was in order to subdue a people previously unknown to the Romans, but who during his Gallic wars " had, it was understood, furnished assistance to his enemy." From parties trading with the Britons, he obtained information of the different localities and means of defence, and from whom in return the Britons were apprised of the Roman invasion. It does not however follow that the commerce of the country was concentrated in the settlement of the Trinobantes, nor that the occasional appearance of a few travelling dealers was of sufficient consequence to have conferred upon any particular place the importance of a shipping town and port. Besides, at the period of the occupation of the country by the conquerors, *Camalodunum*, now Maldon, in Essex, was a place of more frequent than the settlement on the banks of the Thames, and which from its proximity to the sea rendered it a more convenient haven, than traversing an intricate river. It appears likewise that in Cæsar's time it ranked next in consideration to the royal seat of Cassivellaunus, at *Verulam;* and when Britain was taken possession of by Aulus Plautius, in the reign of Claudius, the Roman general established Camalodunum as a *colonia*, or colony, that is, a place governed entirely by Roman laws and customs; *Verulamium* being considered a *municipium*, in which the natives were honoured with the privileges of Roman citizens, enjoying their own laws and constitutions; *Londinium* being only styled a *præfectura*, the inhabitants a mixture of Romans and Britons, who were never suffered to enjoy more than the name of citizens of Rome, being governed by *præfects* sent annually from thence, without having either their own laws or magistrates.

We have now arrived at a period when the progress of the city of London can be described with more authenticity; but we have been anxious thus early in our undertaking to show the disposition we entertain to avoid all fabulous narrative which the ancients were too prone to substitute for fact, or to blend truth and fiction so artfully together in prose or verse, that the high-wrought imagery often led the senses captive; and the youthful mind apt to run wild and unrestrained in the airy region of romance, became embued with the feeling that the world was like a beautiful picture, glowing with a warm and sunny sky, and the scenes of life ever tinted, *avec la couleur de rose*. This perception through a false medium is generally attended with injurious effects, as the disappointment and chagrin are relatively more severe, when the *beau ideal*, the fancy world of one's own fond creation has vanished for ever from our sight, and life in dull reality deprived of its imaginary charms, seems only a bleak and desolate waste, robbed of all objects which had endeared and rendered it worth inhabiting. We doubt even that an exception should be made in favour of the mythology of the Greeks and Romans; for teeming as their fables do with poetic beauty and interest, they have a more powerful tendency to delude and alienate the ideas, than convince the understanding, or to produce incentive for useful or practical information, which can alone work out the grand desideratum we ought ever to hold as our guiding star, the attainment of that knowledge most conducive to the developement of the human mind, promoting the means for conferring *the greatest good on the greatest portion of mankind;* and though it has been said that we can understand any epoch of the world but imperfectly, if we do not examine its romance, yet we are sceptical of the corollary, that we find as much truth in the poetry of life as in the prose.

Cæsar, who, in his Commentaries, is minute in the detailed description of the principal national characteristics entitled to note, would not have omitted allusion to the capital of the *Trinobantes*, or *Tri-now-hant*, inhabitants of the *New City*, the original name, according to the authority of Baxter, of our renowned metropolis, had it been conspicuous for buildings or fortifications, especially as Cæsar appears ever anxious during his Gallic wars to represent to the Senate and the Roman people the extent and importance of his conquests. Had the principal place of resort of the Trinobantes exceeded in magnitude and consequence the fortified town of Cassivellaunus, which the Roman conqueror specifies, little doubt can exist, that the chief seat of the people, who, on his advance towards their territory on the banks of the Thames, were the first to tender homage to his power, as they had sought protection from the tyranny of Cassivellaunus, and solicited permission to appoint the young *Mandubratius* as their ruler, who had visited Cæsar in Gaul previous to his second expedition to Britain, that their town would have formed a leading feature in the enumerations of his victorious progress in our island. But after stating that the natives informed him that the town of Cassivellaunus, *Verulam*, near the site of the present St. Alban's, was fortified, and abounded with people, cattle, and provisions, Cæsar, as a context, immediately adds the passage we have before cited, describing the kind of location the Britains called a *town*. The colony of the Trinobantes were a race of Belgic-Gauls, who having effected a landing, partly under the pretext of trading, and partly with hostile intentions, had recently made a settlement on the borders of the Thames, and had established themselves among the small nations, into which England was then subdivided, and were therefore anxious to avail themselves a spot constituted by nature so eligible for their purpose, as the ground adjacent to St. Paul's, then almost an intrenched mount; having the "river of the Wells," or the *Fleta* or Fleet stream, on the west, which flowed into the Thames near Blackfriars' Bridge; a river, which some Parliamentary records preserved in the Tower of the reign of Edward the First state, had been in times past of "*such depth and bredth, that* 10 *or* 12 *shippes, navies, at once with marchandizes, were wont to come to the bridge of Fleete, and some of them to Oldborne Bridge;* having on the east a large *brook*, afterwards named Wall-brook, its course passing near and through the City's *walls*, together with the fens and marshes in the precincts of the present *Fen*-church Street and *Grass* or Grace-church Street; "Thames's mighty flood" in front, with its swamps and marshes, extending on the southern side as far as the Camberwell Hills; and on the northward, or in the rear, defended by a thick impervious forest, extending a considerable distance into the interior, which, as late as the days of Henry the Second, was infested with beasts of prey and of the chase. The place thus afforded every facility for a safe encampment, which the Belgic people had already taken advantage of; and it was not therefore to be supposed that the Romans, with their skill and experience in military tactics, would overlook so favourable a situation, which, with the assistance of art, might be readily rendered impregnable to the predatory inroads of the native tribes, while at the same time a free communication was secured with the sea.

The disposal of the feasible reasons which led to the site of our present city being fixed on is conclusively arrived at; not so, however, the designation of its name. Much antiquarian controversy has been bestowed on the subject, and derivations strenuously enforced at times as *opposite* as at others *apposite* to the probable meaning; eschewing however any prolix dissertation on this favourite theme of disputants, it may be well to notice the origin of those names which have acquired the greatest credit. The first authentic mention of the city of LONDON is found in the annals of *Tacitus* under the title of

Londinium, when recapitulating the occurrences attendant on the slaughter of the Romans and natives amounting to 70,000, in *Verulamium*, *Camalodunum*, and *Londinium*, by the forces of the heroine *Boadicea*, queen of the Iceni, a district of Britain comprising the counties of Norfolk, Suffolk, Cambridge, and Huntingdon. The learned and accurate historian asserts, that the city was so called from its *situation*, and *Augusta* from its stateliness; adding "*co ia negotiatorum et commeatu maxime celeberrimum*," noted for the number of its merchants, and the abundance of its provisions. These allusions would imply to the casual reader from Tacitus having been resident in London with his father-in-law, Agricola, governor of Britain, and wrote his history from 110 to 120 years after the first invasion of Cæsar, that if the city had not arrived at an anterior importance, it must have made almost incredible progress to have entitled it to these terms of distinction; but it is to be borne in mind, that the *Barbaric* nations subjugated by the Romans at that period, had, compared with their conquerors, made slight advances towards that envied form of organized society, ycleped civilization, a term assumed as a counter-distinguishment between the state we are living in ourselves, and that in which others are existing who have graduated less forward on the polished and slippery scale of modern refinement, a condition, which beyond the moral barrier is extremely problematical in its tendencies, and is too often erroneously and invidiously applied. Without, however, further digressing, taking the term in its popular signification, the Romans were centuries in advance, more especially compared with the inland nations; but the shores of Britain had no doubt from the remotest date been frequented by traders from different parts of the world; the Phœnicians and then the Greeks having carried on a traffic with the southern and south-western portions of the island in tin, lead, &c.; the Germans, Gauls, and Belgians, having had a commercial communication with the northern and eastern divisions in other commodities. These people, the Trinobantes, who had thus placed themselves in juxtaposition with the Romans, were doubtless more apt and experienced in mercantile affairs than the natives, who, having been insulated from communion with foreign countries, would not have attained the same extended and partially enlightened views of commerce, or of the ties and benefits of social intercourse, as a people in connexion with the continent, and who therefore only required co-operation to revive and strengthen their previously formed mercantile knowledge; and as the Romans were more versed in warfare, than the interchange of produce, they were satisfied in fostering the predilections of their allies, by granting immunities and privileges, encouraging the natives as well as confederate foreigners to cultivate those advantages emanating from trade, which have gradually produced those magnificent results which we are now witnessing, of raising London to the proud pre-eminence it maintains among the cities of the world. In later years we have however an instance strongly corroborative of the rapid rise of a city, in the example of St. Petersburg, the capital of that mighty empire, whose territories extend from the regions of ice, destitute of vegetable production, and unfit for the permanent habitation of man; to the region of the vine, the olive, and the sugar-cane, and teeming with human beings; an empire 138 times larger than the whole of Great Britain; yet in 1703 the spot was merely marked by a few humble fishing huts, erected amidst the swamps and marshes of nine small islands. Situated therefore as London was, it could not fail of becoming evident to the sagacity of the Romans, that exclusive of the strength of its military position, it comprised all the requisites for recommending it as an ***Emporium;*** seated as it was, on the banks of a river, whose waters were,

> Though deep yet clear, though gentle yet not dull,
> Strong without rage, without o'erflowing, full:—

and which after flowing through some of the most productive and pastoral districts of the country, united with the ocean, almost within view of the Continent; and thus seemed self-constituted, a mart for home and foreign traffic.

While these remarks are briefly offered in contradiction to the authorities of many respectable writers, who are worthy of much credit and attention, except on points connected with the early existence and importance of our famed city, we must in furtherance adduce, that for nearly a century after the landing of Cæsar, London, notwithstanding it was a considerable mart, was not a principal town or seat of native government; and though the reverse of this and other statements we have made is insisted upon, the erroneous impression of occurrences has in some cases arisen either from an accidental or intentional confusion of data, and in one or two particular instances, where it was necessary to the elucidation of the theory, the 55 years previous to the Christian era, when Julius Cæsar first appeared on our coast, are either merged, or made "*Anno Domini*" instead of "*Before Christ*;" it is therefore we have been more minute in our research, and where we have not offered facts, but have been forced to reason hypothetically, we have endeavoured to draw our conclusions from such just suppositional grounds that they amount almost to moral convictions. We find from Tacitus, Dion Cassius, Ammianus Marcellinus, and other early historians, that in the second year of the reign of Claudius Cæsar, A.D. 43, that the refusal of the Britons to pay the tribute levied by the founder of his dynasty, induced the emperor to send Aulus Plautius, the prætor, with a considerable army for the entire reduction of our Island. The Roman forces proving successful, the general, before his final conquests were achieved, deemed it politic to solicit the appearance of the emperor to crown his victories; Claudius arrived in Britain, forded the Thames like Julius Cæsar in the sight of the Britons, whom he routed, and marching afterwards through Essex, captured Camalodunum, the royal seat of Cinobellinus, or *Cynvelyn.* During this war which was waging near the Thames, no mention is made by Claudius of the *important* city of London, though the Britons retreated through part of Middlesex and Essex, and must have passed near the metropolis of the Triobantes; and as vanity and ostentation induced Claudius to come to Britain, it is not likely that he would have omitted noticing the reduction of this principal town; especially as *Strabo* specifies it was the custom in the triumphal pomps "to set forth in glorious scenes the places subdued."

We must here revert to the controverted subject of the place where the Romans passed the Thames, as illustrative of the false reasoning often adopted to support favourite topics of discussion. Camden and others insist that Cæsar, who mentions expressly that there was only one known ford where foot soldiers could pass, and which on his approach he found fortified by the natives with large stakes both on the banks and beneath the water, was situated in the neighbourhood of Weybridge, between Walton Bridge and Shepperton, and where the remains of a defensive work have been discovered called "Cowey-Stakes;" a range of stakes composed of oaken piles shod with brass not *lead*, as mentioned by the Venerable Bede; but no weapons, we believe, have been ever found near the spot; though in the formation of the Weybridge lock, several feet beneath the bed of the river, a species of canoe was met with, formed of the excavated trunk of a large tree, affording an interesting specimen of a *native bark*, and which is preserved at lower Halliford; indeed it seems more likely that Cowey Stakes was a defensive work against the native hostile chiefs, than formed as an obstruction to the Roman army, exclusive of the circumstance, that that particular part of the river has been always recorded as deep and rapid, and not readily fordable; in addition, it would exceed in distance the

Drawn by Hablot Browne from a Sketch by R. Garland. Engraved by J. Woods.

CITY OF LONDON SCHOOL.

limits ascribed by Cæsar that his passage was effected; which was eighty miles from the sea, or the port *Ritupis*, formerly near Sandwich, in Kent, and that part of the Thames which formed the boundary of the kingdom of Cassivelaunus. Others with more apparent justice have fixed on *Kingston* as the probable spot, and which during the greatest part of the Saxon era was designated *Moreford*, or the *Great Ford;* nor is it to be traced by traditionary or recorded observation that any other neighbouring portion of the river was ever known as a regular and established ford the same as Kingston. The intelligent and able author of the "Gleanings," Mr. Jesse, has given an interesting and lucid dissertation, identifying Kingston as the ford in question, and his observations are pertinent, and well worthy perusal. Teddington, Twickenham, and Fulham, have also had their advocates. Mr. Maitland determining to ascertain with accuracy and precision the decided spot, states, "I discovered that the greatest marshes on the Surrey side reached from Wandsworth in the west to Woolwich in the east; then sounding the river at several neap-tides from the first of these places to London Bridge, I discovered a ford on the 18th of September, 1732, about 90 feet west of the south-west angle of Chelsea College garden, whose channel in a right line from north-east to south-west, was no more than four feet seven inches deep. Therefore considering this is the lowermost ford in the river Thames, I take it to be not only the place where the Britons passed, but likewise that which Julius Cæsar forced, when he routed the Britons." For a writer who generally displays much literary acumen and judgment, and whose works deservedly rank high in public estimation, it is not a little absurd to adduce so futile a reason, because near Chelsea reach the water in 1732 was of a certain shallowness, that during the flow of nearly 1800 years, the river had preserved an equal and uniform depth, or that any criterion in the eighteenth century could be formed of the current or bed of the stream half a century before the birth of Christ; when it is notorious that not only are channels frequently completely altered, and sands shifted, but also the accumulation from the sediment and deposits in rivers are immense; as recently exemplified in the excavations made for St. Catherine's Docks and the Tunnel, where distinct layers of deposits were observable at considerable depths; and more especially in those of the London Docks and foundations of warehouses on the banks of the river at Rotherhithe, where from fifteen to twenty feet beneath the level of the bed of the river, hazel-trees and nuts have been found, as well as a bed of withies. Others suppose that the passage was effected at London, at one of the two old fords, Mill-ford Lane, opposite St. Clement's church, where a corn-*mill* originally stood at the *ford*, or York Stairs, belonging to York House, the seat of the archbishops, which occupied the site of the present Buckingham Street, in the Strand, and streets adjacent; and now graced with the elegant and celebrated water gate of Inigo Jones.

In reference to these latter places having been assigned as the original passage of the river, an insurmountable objection, in our opinion, is opposed to the probability, in the fact, that Cæsar as an experienced general invading an hostile territory, and fording the Thames to attack the natives in a new division of the kingdom, uncertain of their resources or means of defence, would not have rashly ventured to pass his army across any portion of the river, subject to the rapid influx and reflux of the tide; as in case of retreat and the flood setting in, destruction would have inevitably awaited his troops both by land and water. Dion Cassius also expressly asserts, that "these temporary fordable passages were of a nature so dangerous as well as intricate, that they were only useful in a slight degree to the natives, who by dint of practice became acquainted with the depths and shallows; and when the emperor

Claudius in his subsequent invasion of the country, endeavoured to pursue the Britons by such a route, his soldiers were brought into the greatest peril by the attempt." Indeed of late years it is not unfrequently observed, that during a period of drought, or very low tides from the effect of wind, that a passage across the Thames at London might have been accomplished, but no one would infer from this accidental occurrence that a regular and acknowledged ford had previously existed; while on the other hand all these difficulties are obviated at Kingston; in addition to which it may in conclusion be stated, that in lately forming the coffer-dams for the new bridge from thence to Hampton, swords, spear-heads, rings, and other Roman *vestigia*, principally implements of war, were found some depth beneath the bed of the river on the Middlesex side, where the conflict must be supposed to have raged the severest; then again in digging brick-earth in a field in Surrey, near the Kingston ford, a number of *male* skeletons were discovered with Roman remains, and no marks of boundaries, inscriptions or other monumental relics which could indicate the place having been dedicated to civil sepulture. About half a mile from the ford on the Middlesex bank is a British barrow, and near it can be traced an encampment, where no doubt the bodies of the Britons were buried after the battle, the Romans soon afterwards occupying the spot; evidently denoting that a mortal struggle must have taken place at this passage between the natives and invaders; at the same time it corresponds with the distance from the sea alluded to by Cæsar, and is the first known ford where the stream is uninfluenced by the tides.

The different assumed facts to which *London* owes its derivation are too numerous and inconclusive to allow us to occupy much of our reader's attention, and we shall therefore merely allude to those which wear the semblance of any probability. Though the first application of the word *Londinium* and then *Lundinium*, to the infant city is from Roman authority, we do not recognize any constituent Latin words in the component appellation; and think it must have been a latinized designation of the name applied by the natives, and which Mr. Maitland maintains originated from two Gaelic terms, *Lon* a plain, and *don* an eminence, or hill; from the plain which formerly extended on the northern side of the river and the hill adjoining it on the north, which by the Anglo-Saxons was called *Corn-hill*, which in former times was allotted for the sale of grain. Camden derives it from *Llawn-dinas* or *din*, a city of ships; other authorities *Caer-Lud*, or *Lud-din*, Lud's city, king Lud having been elder brother to Cassivelaun, and *renewed* the city walls, a derivation so full of anachronisms as not to need serious refutation. *Llin-din*, or the city of the lake, an appearance the Thames presented from the flooding of the low lands on the Surrey shore; after the Saxon conquest it was termed *London-Byrig*, *Lunden-Ceaster*, *Lundenne*, and *Lundain*, *Lunden-Wyc*, *Lunden-Berb*, or *Lunden-Burg*, and since the Norman possession *Londonia*, *Lundonia*, *Londine*, and *Londres*.

Previous to the defeat and death of the heroic and patriotic Boadicea in the year 61, it is authenticly recorded that the queen in her revengeful march against the enemy had compelled the Roman general Suetonius to evacuate Londinium, which was reduced to ashes by her followers; the inhabitants who were attached to the Romans, sharing a similar fate to those of Camalodunum and Verulam. After this destruction of the city, the Romans on regaining their ascendancy assisted in its reconstruction, and the inhabitants having acquired the mode of making bricks, erecting houses and temples, draining and embanking, cutting roads and forming causeways, were under the judicious government of Agricola enabled to attain in those arts some degree of perfection; we can therefore readily imagine that a new city speedily arose on the same favourite site, similarly devoted to that commercial enterprise, which had been before so eminently conducive in rendering it flourishing and ensuring its aggrandizement. We have already alluded to the rapid rise of cities, the elements of which are based on traffic, commerce being the main-spring of social intercourse, more especially if we assume that the high prerogative of man, the distinguishing characteristic of his proud pre-eminence over other animals consists, as it is stated to do by the learned author of the "Wealth of Nations," in the capability of interchanging commodities: "Man," says Dr. Adam Smith, "is an animal that makes bargains—no other animal does this; one dog does not change a bone with another." The early trade of London as alluded to by Strabo consisted of imports of salt, earthenware, works in brass, and polished bone, horse-collars, ornaments, and toys in glass, amber, and other articles of the same kind. The exports comprised cattle, especially horses, skins, corn, and dogs, those bred in England having been highly esteemed on the continent for their excellent qualifications for the chase; qualities which it is estimated by the same authority were inherent in them, and not the effect of tutorage of their foreign masters; to these must be added the dealing in ***human flesh***, slaves constituting a considerable item among the exportations; and for the promotion of this revolting traffic, feuds were often provoked and warfare waged by the petty sovereigns of the inland districts of the island. We however as Britons have nobly redeemed the disgrace which attached in this respect to the character of the aborigines, having been mainly instrumental in abolishing the slave trade throughout the ***old world***, and conferring the god-like prerogative on this our native land, that the foot of every stranger the instant it touches British ground is free, from that moment man becomes liberated from bondage in mind and limb; though unhappily the picture is sadly reversed in the ***new world***, in that ***boasted*** land of liberty, "the lustre of whose ***stars*** it is vaunted was never dimmed," where there are nearly ***one-sixth of the population*** still labouring in an abject state of slavery. It is also thought that the *gagates*, or jet stone, which may have been our native *coal*, formed part of the exports, as Solinus mentions it as one of the productions of Britain.

London, which had now become entirely a *Præfectura* under Roman government, though not subjected to the inconvenient restrictions of a garrison town, remaining a free city, where Roman and Briton mingled happily together, was not confined to the ancient limits between Fleet river and Walbrook, but extended from the eastern side of Tower Hill to the western declivity of Ludgate Hill, the width being bounded on the north by the causeway, which ran parallel with Cheapside, winding at each extremity towards the Thames, the town being intersected by a high street, or *Prætorian way*, known as *Watling Street*, or *Fosseway*. For the capability of being enabled exactly to define the northern extremity, and many other important and interesting discoveries connected with the primitive history of the city, posterity is mainly indebted to the researches and discoveries of Sir Christopher Wren, who on rebuilding the church of St. Mary-le-Bow, after the fire of London in 1666, found, on opening the ground, a foundation firm enough for the new-intended fabric, which on further inspection proved to be the walls and pavement of a temple or church of Roman construction, entirely buried beneath the level of the present street, on which he resolved to build the new church; and with the intention of bringing the steeple in range with the houses, he excavated the ground in advance to the depth of eighteen feet, when to his surprise he came to a Roman causeway of rough stone close and well rammed with Roman brick and rubbish at the bottom, and all firmly cemented, being four feet in thickness, and on which he based the tower: from this fact, and, "divers other reasons," a similar road having been ascertained to have passed by the end of Bread Street, Cheapside, no doubt exists that this highway ran along the north boundary of the town;

[illegible] nature
[illegible] its foundations [illegible]
[illegible]
[illegible] *Londinium* [illegible]
[illegible] to be in ancient [illegible]
[illegible] a free city, where
[illegible] together, was not confined
[illegible] river and Walbrook, but
[illegible] of Tower Hill to the western
[illegible] the width being bounded on the
[illegible] which ran parallel with Cheapside,
[illegible] the Thames, the town being
[illegible] or *Praetorian way*, known as
[illegible] For the probability of being
[illegible] western extremity, and many
[illegible] connected with the
[illegible] is mainly indebted
[illegible] of Sir Christopher Wren.
[illegible] of St. Mary-le-Bow [illegible]
[illegible] ground, on clearing the ground, a
[illegible] firm [illegible] dilapidated fabric, which
[illegible] proved [illegible] the walls and pavement
[illegible] church [illegible] construction, [illegible]
[illegible] the [illegible] street, on which he
[illegible] with the intention of
[illegible] range with the houses, he excavated
the [illegible] to the depth of eighteen feet, when to
his surprise [illegible] came to a Roman causeway of rough stone
[illegible] Roman brick and rubbish at the
[illegible] firmly [illegible] four feet in thickness.
[illegible] this fact, [illegible]
[illegible] to have
[illegible] Cheapside, [illegible] extension
[illegible] north boundary of the town:

and that the western confines did not exceed the top of Ludgate Hill, was decided by digging up at the same period near Lud-Gate, a sepulchral stone, where Ludgate church is now situated; the monumental remain was dedicated by a wife to the memory of a Roman soldier of the second legion, styled Augusta; it being expressly forbidden by the Roman law to bury within the precincts of cities, an edict always scrupulously adhered to. The soldiers were usually buried *in vallo*, or in the trenches, which here bordered the river Fleet, the Prætorian camp having been on the western side of the causeway, and most probably extending to the hill of Ludgate.

Under the wise jurisdiction of the Roman Præfects, especially the government of Agricola, who was eminent for his public and private virtues, London continued to advance in importance, and we find by Herodian, in his life of the emperor Severus, who reigned from 190 to 211, that it was called " a great and wealthy city," and there is convincing evidence that its traffic and intercourse with the interior must have been materially extended, as in the *Iter Britannicum* attributed to the emperor Antoninus, out of the fifteen roads which are laid down as having traversed our island, seven of them are concentrated in London, either leading to or emanating in all probability from the Stone in Cannon Street, at the side of St. Swithin's Church, called now the London Stone, but by the Romans *Milliarium*, or standard mile stone, from whence the distances to their stations were measured; and though by some authorities it has beed considered a druidical remain, and set apart for religious and civil uses, yet its locality to the causeways and the distances computed from it coinciding exactly with history, seems to identify it for the purport alluded to; at all times however it has been preserved with great care, having been deeply embedded in the earth and bound with iron, and seems in early ages to have been looked upon as the *palladium* of the city, and is now cased like a relic within free stone with a hole left in the middle which discovers the original. According to Hollinshed, a certain degree of superstitious respect also was paid to it; for when the notorious *Jack Cade*, the Kentish rebel, in 1450, who feigned himself lord Mortimer, came through Southwark to London, he marched to London Stone, which striking with his sword, said "Now is Mortimer lord of this citie," as if it had been a customary ceremory in taking possession perhaps of the government of the city; or may have originated from the stone, which stood then in the principal thoroughfare, as Cheapside now is, having been the spot from whence proclamations and public notices were delivered to the citizens.

The principal military roads were Watling Fosseway, which led from port *Ritupis*, near Sandwich, now engulphed by the sea, through Kent, and Surrey, by the Kent road to *Stan* or *Stein*, or *Stoney* Street, across Clink Street, by the present Winchester wharf, where the bishops of Winchester in later years had the stairs to their palaces, connecting by the *trajectus*, or ferry, the Surrey and Middlesex shores, and entering the city by the *Dwr* or *Dourgate*, or *Watergate*, now Dowgate, and called by Stow, Downgate, from "the sodaine, descending, or downe going of that way," which now forms a continuation from Walbrook at the end of Cannon Street; taking a south-east and north-west direction, and passing to the site of the late New-Gate. The *Ermine Street* causeway traversed a south-westerly and northerly course, accompanying the Watling Street from Southwark, likewise entering by Dowgate, passing through by Cripplegate taking its way by Highbury Barn to Stroud Green, The *Vicinal Way* conducting from the city by Aldgate to Bethnel Green, and then to the *trajectus* at Old Ford, across the river Lea to *Duroleiton*, the modern Leyton, or Laytonstone, in Essex.

Though much controversy has been created respecting the period of the city having been enclosed with walls, yet little doubt can exist that in the year 296, during the reign of Dioclesian and Maximinian it remained unfortified, as the city narrowly escaped being pillaged by a party of pirate Franks, who after the defeat in that year of the army of the tyrant and usurper Alectus having evaded the Roman forces, determined to ransack London, and escape to sea with their booty; but fortunately a Roman squadron, detached from the main fleet in a fog, opportunely arrived in the Thames, and liberated the city to the great joy and satisfaction of the inhabitants; had therefore London been protected by walls, it could not have been subjected to these surprises. Some authorities are in favour of the opinion that either Constantine the Great or his mother Helena had founded the walls, which is corroborated according to Mr. Pennant, by the circumstance of a number of coins of Helena having been discovered beneath the foundation, supposed to have been placed there in her honour by her son. Mr. Maitland and others support the conjecture, and we are inclined to think with more truth, that Theodosius, governor of Britain in 368, caused them to be erected, a fact strengthened by the coincidence, that the Roman forces had been so gradually diminished in numbers during the reigns of Constantius, Julian, and Valentinian, that they had not been enabled to contend successfully against the Picts, Scots, Franks, and Saxons, who by turns invaded Britian, and reduced the country to the greatest distress, until the arrival of the Romans in triumph, "then in the utmost misery and affliction, occasioned by the great ravages committed by those insatiate freebooters." Had the city been environed with walls by Helena or Constantine they would have been in a good state of defence, after their recent erection, not more than thirty-seven years having transpired from the death of Constantine to the arrival of Theodosius, so that the inhabitants and garrison might have temporarily defied the occasional assaults of the predatory bands. As to the discovery of the coins of Helena, we are of opinion, that the occurrence may be readily reconciled, when it is taken into consideration that *Chlorus Constantius*, the father of Constantine, husband of Helena, had been resident in Britain till his death, which occurred at York, little more than half a century previously, having obtained the title of Cæsar, which he merited from his victories in Britain and Gaul; therefore it was more than likely that coins in memory of his wife and the mother of the *Great Constantine* should have been deposited beneath the foundations, commemorative of the various benefits conferred, and which were fresh in the recollection of the citizens.

It is generally supposed that the name *Augusta*, which for a short period superceded the ancient appellation of Londinum, until the occupation by the Saxons, and which has been since often poetically alluded to, was applied to the city, not in honour of the empress Helena, but was assigned to it by Theodosius, as the capital of the Roman British dominions; having been at first a name of distinction conferred on seventy cities in the Roman provinces, in honour of Augustus Cæsar, but was afterwards adopted in the later years of the empire to designate any city of importance or grandeur. We are told by the historian of these times, Ammianus Marcellinus, that Theodosius, by repairing some cities and castles, and fortifying and erecting others, left every thing on so good a footing, that peace was preserved in Britain till the Romans quitted our shores, in the reign of Honorius, when their own territories being invaded by Alaric, the Goth, the emperor required the combination of all his forces, and London had to regret the final departure of the beneficent founders of her fame and greatness. Chronologers are undecided respecting the date when this event took place, some fixing it in the years 402, 422, and 437, but the greater number, among whom is M. Playfair, in 426; as, however, king Alaric, who it is assumed was the cause of the withdrawal of the last Roman legion, died in 410, and the emperor Honorius in 423, the earlier period merits the greatest credence.

The walls of the city commenced from a fort built by the Romans on the site of the present Tower, which Mr. Bagford is of opinion still remains that portion of the fortress called the "white tower." Early authorities have erroneously attributed its erection to Julius Cæsar, and it is alluded to occasionally in history as Cæsar's Tower, an application however often indiscriminately applied to a commanding part of many of the castles of antiquity; but the more authentic supposition is in favour of the White Tower having been constructed by William the Conqueror. The walls were built at first in a northernly direction towards the present *Aldgate*, passing by *Postern Row*, and across George Street, Tower Hill, adjoining which street are the most perfect remains now extant of this ancient bulwark of our forefathers; the walls appear to have been about twenty-two feet in height and nine feet in thickness, composed of Roman brick or tiles, and rag-stone, the mortar, as is usual in Roman works, cementing itself as hard as the stone itself; the walls then skirted the Minories by *Hounds-ditch*, traversing *Bishopsgate Street*, forming a direct line with the northern side of *London Wall* to *Cripplegate*, turning southward from the churchyard of St. Giles, where exists the only specimen of the round towers by which the walls were defended; these towers consisted of fifteen in number, including the principal eastern tower near the Thames, and calculated to have been forty feet in height; the wall then passed *Alders-gate* along the back of *Bull and Mouth Street* to *Newgate*, thence to *Ludgate*, edging the declivity which sloped towards the Fleet river to the spot afterwards occupied by the castle of *Mountfitchet*, built by a Norman noble of that name in the time of William I. and stood near Printing-house Square; from that point the wall extended to Thames Street, from whence with the towers it ran parallel with the river until united with the eastern fort or tower; the portion of the wall fortifying the banks of the Thames is alluded to by Fitz-Stephen, who writing in the reign of Henry II. states, "the wall was high and great, well towered on the north side, with due distances between the towers; on the south side also the city was walled and towered, but the fish-abounding river Thames with its ebbing and flowing, has long since subverted them." The circuit of the walls inland comprised two miles and 208 feet, and including the river frontage three miles and 165 feet.

The city was originally entered from the country by three gates; the eastern portion by the *Ald-gate*, supposed to have been named by the Saxons *ald*, or old, from the dilapidated state in which they found it; from the north by the *Alders-gate*, or according to other highly respectable antiquarian authorities, by *New-gate*, or *Cripplegate;* the derivation of the former is uncertain, but stated to have been the "Older-gate;" that of Newgate, not from the gate having been of later origin, but from its having been renewed; and it would appear probable from the Watling Street causeway pointing in that direction to have been one of the earlier egresses of the city; and it is on record, that in the year 1218, the gate was appropriated to its present use as a gaol for felons taken in the city of London or county of Middlesex. At *Cripplegate* the lame and *cripples* were wont to station themselves craving charity, traditionary miracles having been there wrought, "so that the lame from thence did goe upright, praising God; occurrences which are stated to have taken place in the year 1010, when the coffin of King Edmund the Martyr passed through it from *Bedrisworth*, or St. Edmund's Bury, in order to preserve the sanctified remains from the indignities of the piratical Danes. The gate is therefore of considerable antiquity, and is supposed to have been erected over the Ermine Street cause-way. The western division of the city was attained by the *Lud-gate*, a corruption of *Flud*-gate, from the Saxon *flod*, *vloet*, *fleote*, or *flete*, implying a small navigable watercourse, as the Fleet rivulet was in former ages.

[illegible]

[illegible] "the wall was high [illegible]
[illegible] with due distances [illegible]
[illegible] the city was walled [illegible]
[illegible] river Thames with its [illegible]
[illegible] subverted them." The [illegible]
[illegible] two miles and 29[illegible]
[illegible] miles and 10[illegible]
[illegible] the country by these [illegible]
[illegible] supposed to have [illegible]
[illegible]
[illegible] from the north by the *Alders-* [illegible]
[illegible] highly respectable and [illegible]
[illegible]-gate, [illegible] *Cripple[illegible]*; [illegible]
[illegible] to have been the [illegible]
[illegible] the gate having been [illegible]
[illegible] been removed; and it would [illegible]
[illegible] Street causeway pointing [illegible]
[illegible] the earlier egresses of the [illegible]
[illegible] the year 1218, the gate was [illegible]
[illegible] gaol for felons taken in [illegible]
[illegible] Middlesex. At *Cripplegate* the [illegible]
[illegible] themselves crawling [illegible]
[illegible] been [illegible] "so that the [illegible]
[illegible] upright, praising God; [illegible]
[illegible] taken place in the year 10[illegible], [illegible]
[illegible] the Martyr passed through it [illegible]
[illegible]'s bury, in order to preserve [illegible]
[illegible] indignities of [illegible]
[illegible] of considerable antiquity, and is [illegible]
[illegible] over the Ermine Street cause- [illegible]
The [illegible] of the city was attained by the [illegible]
[illegible]-gate, from the Saxon *[illegible]*, [illegible]
[illegible] navigable watercourse, as the [illegible]
[illegible] ages.

In process of time, the suburbs becoming more extended, other gates were erected for the convenience of the citizens, as the Postern-gate, by the Tower, which was built soon after the conquest "in a beautiful manner, with stones brought from Kent and Normandy," and close to which was a famous spring, "much admired by the citizens, and well preserved," and the spot is now marked by some posts, and the pump still supplies the parishioners with wholesome water. The original gate fell down in the year 1440, in the reign of Henry VI., and according to Stow, "was never re-edified, but a homely cottage with a narrow passage, made of timber, lath, and loame, hath been in place thereof set up;" the ruin of the said postern having began in the year 1190, when William Longchamp, bishop of Ely, and chancellor of England, caused part of the city wall, "to wit, from the said gate towards the river Thames, to be broken down for the enlarging of the Tower, which tower he compassed about with a wall, and now forms the outer wall of the Tower, and caused also a broad and deep ditch to be made without the same, intending to have had the river Thames to flow about it; by means of this ditch the foundation of the gate being loosened, at length fell down." *Bishops-gate*, "but of what antiquity or by whom erected, or on what occasion named, is unknown," though generally conjectured to have been built by Bishop William, the Norman, in the reign of William the Conqueror, but not so early as the year 675, when Erkenwald was bishop of London, the foundation of the wall having been discovered to have been four feet deeper than the foundation of the gate. *Moor-gate*, situated near the north end of Coleman Street, was built in the year 1415, for the easier access of the citizens to their gardens and the adjacent fields for recreation, at which time, from its vicinity to the moors and marshes, it received its appellation. *Bridge-gate* was so named, from its situation on the old London Bridge. Dowgate, or *Dour*, or water-gate, we have before alluded to, as being erected where the *trajectu* or Roman ferry was situated, and the entrance of the Watling Street causeway from the Surrey shore. The other gates mentioned in history, as Wolf-gate, Eb-gate, Puddledock-gate, Oyster-gate, Butolphs-gate, Billings-gate, and the water-gates by the Tower and Custom-house, were not places of thoroughfare through the city's walls, but only wharves, or certain localities for the landing of goods, and were designated from the names of the owners, neighbouring places, or articles landed, and were most probably erected long after the Conquest and the breaking down of the wall; but as the principal wharf, or original landing place, retained the name of Dow-gate, from the gate which once stood there, the owners and builders of the wharves and quays also dignified them with the epithet of gates. Some of the city's gates were very handsome and costly structures, especially in later times, when the citizens emulated each other in benefactions and bequests for their embellishment. Ludgate, which was taken down and rebuilt in the reign of Elizabeth, was not even at that time re-constructed at a less expense than £1500. When in the last stage of decay the gates were pulled down; the old materials brought considerable prices. Aldgate was sold for £157 10s.; Ludgate for £148; and Cripplegate for £91.

The Barbican, an Arabic word for watch tower, according to Camden, called also Specula, or *Burhkenning*, as mentioned by Stow, was customarily attached to fortified towns, and at London stood near the walls to the east of Aldersgate, and though all vestige has been for centuries removed, and the dangers which it was erected to avert have long ceased to exist, yet the name is still preserved. The Romans kept here cohorts of soldiers, watching during the day the approach of any hostile force, and by night keeping lights on its summit to direct the course of the weary traveller, or market people coming to the city with provisions; the same was the intention of a lantern at the top of the steeple of Bow church previous to the fire of London.

Towards the latter period of the Roman occupation of London, the fort or tower in all probability formed the mint, as it did the treasury, in which the public money was deposited; a silver ingot and some gold coins of the Emperors Honorius and Arcadius having been discovered in 1777 in digging the foundation of a new office for the board of ordnance. Though we have no certain date afforded us by which we can arrive at any distinct account of the extent or increase of the commerce of the city, previous to the secession of the Romans, yet some idea may be formed of the augmented resources of the port from extended agriculture and facility of inland communication, by the exports which are recorded to have taken place in the year 359, amounting to no less than 800 cargoes of grain. We find likewise that the Romans had not only instructed the London youth and citizens in military tactics and means of artificial defence, but imparted to them the results of their more enlightened knowledge and education, initiating them in those arts and sciences most conducive to their future comfort and prosperity. Thus in the reign of Constantine, the Britons had acquired so much celebrity in the art of building, that the emperor ordered the dilapidated towns of Gaul and fortresses on the Rhine to be repaired by British architects and artificers.

According to Bagford the Romans established in London a field of Mars in imitation of that at Rome; in alluding to which he says, " on the further side of Whitchapel Street, near Bishopsgate Street, was another station of the Romans, in that part which formerly bore the name of 'the old artillery ground,' and was then the field of Mars, in which place the Romans trained up and exercised their young soldiers, and likewise the youth of the neighbouring Britons, in the skill and exercise f arms, that they might be more expert in the use of them upon all emergent occasions, and it must needs have been a very large place as the same is excellently described, and likewise observed to have been a Roman camp by a judicious author in the reign of Queen Elizabeth."

Of the sports and pastimes of this early period little authentic information has reached us, which is the more to be lamented, as in order to form a correct estimation of the character of any particular people, it becomes essential the investigation of the manner in which they have passed their leisure hours. It is remarked with much discrimination, that war, policy, and other contingent circumstances may effectually place men at different times, in different lights and shades, but when we follow them into their retirements, where disguise is necessary, we are more likely to see them in true colours, and may better judge of their natural dispositions. Unfortunately all the information that remains respecting our ancestors is derived from foreign writers, only partially acquainted with them as a people, and totally ignorant of their domestic amusements. We learn however from the imperfect hints of ancient historians, that our forefathers were ever tenacious of their native liberty, and inured to great bodily fatigue, being expert in hunting, for which the native dogs have been ever celebrated, in running, leaping, swimming, wrestling and hurling; to which no doubt were added those pastimes most in vogue with their conquerors; as we know that the Romans generally philosophized on most of their actions and institutions connected with the weal of the mass of the people, and seem ever to have held in view the necessity of creating not only a love of exercise in a martial point of view, but likewise as a source of amusement, and appear to have been more fully aware and more to have appreciated the knowledge than we are prone to do in the nineteenth century, that the withdrawal of the people from public games and places of amusements is the sure and gradual means of conducing to a greater degree of demoralization. The mind of the lower classes of society unoccupied during those hours it is freed from professional calling, without any decided point of attraction or means of pastime, is thrown upon its own resources with too often few mental ualifications. The man wanting relaxation from the toils of the day, and in many instances with little means of securing much domestic comfort, is induced to resort to houses where he must drink exciting liquors in order to procure society, instead of being enabled to meet companion ship in the fields, or in assemblages where sports or spectacles are carried on;—a relaxation to his nervous system, as advantageous, in a moral, as it would be, in a physical consideration, and the beneficial results would be more particularly applicable in this our densely populated city, as well as the larger towns in our manufacturing districts, where the principal portion of the inhabitants pass great part of their lives in a close and sedentary occupation, and absolutely require every facility to be afforded them of procuring fresh air and salutary recreation.

In reference to our early field sports, one fact is identified with our ancestors, which we glean from Cæsar's history, that they did not reckon hares as animals of chace, nor did they eat their flesh, although the island abounded with them; an abstinence which arose "from a principle of religion;" a principle, preventing them from being worried to death by dogs, which as a tame, inoffensive animal, was a cruelty reserved for more enlightened ages. During also the establishment of the Romans in Britain, there do not appear to have been any restrictive laws enacted for the preservation of game; but it was an established maxim in the jurisprudence of that people to invest the right of such things as had no masters with those who were the first possessors; wild beasts, birds, and fishes, became the property of those who first could take them—an honest feeling! which it would much have redounded to the honour of this country had it been handed down inviolate to the present generation, like the laws of the Persians of old and would have prevented many instances of disgraceful litigation, demoralization, persecution, and bloodshed.

The protecting genius of the kingdom seems for a time to have winged its flight from our shores on the removal of the Roman *eagles;* for shortly after the final departure of the Romans, the natives left to their own resources and means of defence, soon finding themselves incompetent to resist the desperate incursions of the Picts and Scots, were induced to solicit the assistance of the Saxons: a fierce, untamed, but courageous people, who with their leaders Hengist and Horsa, landed on the Isle of Thanet, in the years 448-49; but the Britons found out too late the fallacy of trusting their independence to a foreign power, and to their chagrin discovered that they had, in relieving themselves from the terror of one enemy, laid themselves open to the assaults of another; as the Saxons soon took occasion to violate the compact which authorized their appearance in arms in Britain. During however eight to nine years after their arrival, the Britons continued to retain possession of London, as in the year 457, having been defeated at Crayford in Kent, they fled precipitately, according to the Saxon chronicles, to their capital "*Lunden-Byrig.*" Vortigern and Vortimer were the royal leaders under whom the Britons continued the war; but Hengist unable to obtain any decisive advantage in the field, had resource to treachery and stratagem to complete his conquest; and having made Vortigern prisoner, received as the king's ransom the provinces of Essex, Middlesex, and Sussex; London becoming the chief city of the Saxon kingdom of Essex; and though during the fruitless and sanguinary struggles of the Britons to free themselves from the Saxon yoke, London, from the mercantile importance it maintained, was more than any other part of the island subjected to the evils attendant on intestine warfare, yet in the early part of the seventh century it had recovered its ascendency, being alluded to by Bede as the "emporium of many nations," and became placed under the government of a *Portgrave*, or *Portreve*, which implies the consideration the port was held

Drawn by Hablot Browne from a Sketch by R. Garland. Engraved by J. Woods.

m to require the specific superintendence of a magistrate or governor.

After the establishment of the Saxon heptarchy, Ethelbert, king of Kent, to whom the other sovereigns were feudatory, established his seat of empire at Canterbury, thus constituting the metropolis of England; London loosing the protective and prespective power of the court, an influence which is reckoned mainly contributive in promoting the opulence and importance of a city; but London could not be deprived of its local advantages as a trading port, and therefore retained its commercial superiority. Unfortunately the *hiatus* which occurs in the early civil history of the heptarchy precludes any definitive information being collected respecting its mercantile relations, from the period of the reign of Eadbald, who succeeded Ethelbert in 616, to the year 764. We merely learn that in 658 the city was ravaged by a plague; in 764 and 798 it suffered severely from fire, especially in the latter year, numbers of the inhabitants perishing in the flames; and in 801 before sufficient time had elapsed for its revival, a third conflagration nearly completed the work of destruction. To this devastation the very construction of the city rendered it liable, the Romans having built the streets after the model of those in their own country, which were extremely narrow; and the houses being principally composed of wood covered with straw thatch, which had superseded the British roofings of reeds, were subject to frequent and rapid ignition. Latterly during the Roman occupation the roofs of the principal structures were protected were *scindulæ*, or shingles, and some with *tegulæ*, or tiles, and a few with *glatta*, or slates. The holes which originally formed the escape for the smoke, were by the Romans transformed into cupola chimnies; and as the valuable formation of glass for windows had not been then introduced, the windows, or *Uynt-dor*, passage for the wind, serviceable also for the admission of light, were furnished with wooden lattices or sheets of linen.

In filling up the chasm which occurs in the domestic history of London, we are indebted to the ecclesiastical annals of the country for throwing some light on the obscurity of the city during this lapse of years; and we find that in 600 the monk Augustine having been appointed archbishop of England by Pope Gregory, ordained Mellitus, bishop of the East Saxons, who having been successful in the conversion of the people, Ethelbert about the year 610 erected for him a church in London, on the site occupied by the present St. Paul's, and dedicated it to that saint, who in his migrations is supposed to have visited the British Islands. Sebert, who at this period was king of the East Saxons, and had adopted the Christian religion, witnessing the rapid advance of the new tenets among his subjects, erected another place of worship on the Isle of Thorney, where a Roman Temple stood Sacred to Apollo, which formed the origin of St. Peter's Cathedral at Westminster.

London now began to acquire an additional degree of consequence, as it was enabled to dispute the right of *ecclesiastical*, as it did of *civil* authority with Canterbury and York, though it did not attain the grandeur of either of these two cities for nearly three centuries afterwards. The Londoners on the accession of the three sons of Sebert, expelled Bishop Mellitus and returned to Paganism; the see of London remaining without a bishop till the year 653, when King Segbert espousing the Christian doctrines, Cedda, or Chad, was advanced to the bishopric. In 666 *Wulpher*, who had sole ecclesiastical control in the kingdom of Essex, committed the *first* act of *simony* in England by selling the bishopric of London to Wina, who had been *expelled* from Winchester: this bishop was succeeded by Erkenwald, who had received his education under Mellitus, and was distinguished for his sanctity, having been at the same time the instigator of several religious foundations, and a benefactor to the city; on his death the possession of his body became an object of dispute on the part of the canons of

St. Paul's and the monks of Chertsey, or according to Rapin's History, of Barking: but the inhabitants of London siding with the canons, possessed themselves of the mortal remains of the revered bishop, and had them honourably interred in his own cathedral, the revenues of which he had enriched, besides having extended its buildings.

A transient gleam of brightness again illumined the prospects of the Londoners under the reign of Egbert, who having in 823 consolidated the seven divisions of the state into one kingdom, the southern portion of which was designated England, he in 833 caused a ***Witena-Gemot***, or ***council of wise men***, a ***Parliament*** in fact, to be convened at London to deliberate on the most effectual means of protecting the island from the invasion of the Danes, and it is therefore justly inferred, that from this date London became the metropolis of the kingdom, though Pennant favours the idea that Alfred first constituted it the capital. All the Saxon efforts to repulse the Danes proved fruitless, and in 839 they effected a landing in Kent, pursuing their victorious route to London which they pillaged, massacreing great portion of the citizens. This and other successful piratical expeditions induced them to attempt the ultimate subjugation of the island, and in 851 the city was again reduced beneath the Danish yoke; and finding it a convenient garrison for making inroads into the neighbouring states, they kept up a constant and irritating system of annoyance and spoliation. At length ALFRED, with whose chivalrous name and exploits is emblazoned on the page of British history all that is noble and heroic; in whose reign dawned that liberty of privilege, that right of justice, which as Englishmen we hold as vital to the existence of a free-born citizen, as the air we breathe, and from whence emanated that excellent system of municipal goverment, which, with various modifications and improvements, exists at the present day. Alfred feeling that the partial establishment of the Danes in the country continued the exciting cause of misery and disquietude to his people, and that the hostile settlers were regardless of their most solemn oaths and treaties, resolved to free his kingdom from the marauders, and having repaired his decayed fortresses, suddenly laid siege to London, which he forced to capitulate in 884. After improving the buildings and strengthening the city's walls, he appointed his son-in-law Ethered, governor, with the title of the Earl of Mercia. This nobleman seems to have held the city in fee, being vested with more than ordinary authority as governor, and had no doubt some tenure of power delegated to him, but which is not clearly defined by historians; for on his death, his widow Ethelfleda formally delivered up the custody of the city, with that of Oxford, to her brother, King Edward the Elder. During the last-named year Alfred caused several large vessels to be constructed on an improved system both as to sailing and stowage, which he allowed the merchants of London to hire, assisting them also with the loan of money, to undertake lengthened voyages; some of these traded to the east, most probably to the Levant, and amongst other commodities brought home precious stones, with which the regal crown was embellished. In 893 Alfred had the mortification of witnessing an extensive demolition of his capital by another accidental fire. The wise and prudent regulations however of the monarch had already made considerable advancement in the mode of building the houses, not only by improving the style of their construction, but their durability and partial safety against fire, having erected his palaces with stone and brick instead of wood. The opulent citizens and resident nobility by degrees emulated each other in copying this novel and "wonderous style" of architecture, though it did not come into general adoption for some ages afterwards; but the dwellings from this date became less subject to the destructive element which had so frequently laid waste the city.

The restless and ambitious spirit of the Danes, and the rich booty our island afforded, still led them onward with the hope of its final conquest. Their hordes therefore again appeared off the coast, and effecting a landing near Tilbury, in Essex, under the command of ***Hæsten***, or Hastings, erected a strong fort at ***Beamfleote***, now called South-Benfleet, near the Isle of Canvey, from whence they were eventually routed and their castle taken by Ethered. So rapidly had proceeded the renovation of the city, and the revival of the spirit of its citizens, that they were in a condition, for the first time since the departure of the Romans, not only to defend their walls against aggression, but to sally forth and meet the invaders; and under the command of Ethered, were by their brave and intrepid conduct mainly instrumental in the success of the engagement. Thus in the earliest records of London it is authenticated, that though the inhabitants had become addicted to commercial pursuits, they were not incapacitated by their peaceful occupations from signalizing themselves in the field, when their country needed their services, and rendering themselves as conspicuous in deeds of arms as they had done in their ability and diligence in traffic. Indeed the heroic acts which distinguished the citizens at various periods of our history are so numerous, that our limits prevent their constant specification, and therefore it is to be inferred, that on all occasions where their presence was required, they ever opposed a dauntless front to danger, and were as remarkable for their individual courage as they were for their loyalty. Fitz-Stephen in eulogizing the citizens says, "they were always glorious in manhood, and notable beyond all other citizens in urbanity of manners, attire, table, and talk; the matrons being the very modest Sabine ladies of Italy."

London, which had claimed the especial regard of Alfred, experienced all the benefit which would naturally accrue to a city from the direction of a mind embracing in its comprehensive grasp the requisites to constitute its possessor a great and enlightened statesman: but as neither his authority nor example could be omnipotent, without it had the effect of stimulating the spiritless nobility to similar acts of political wisdom and patriotic virtue, we find that as he had ***no model***, it was some years before he had ***an imitator***. It is uncertain the exact character of the civil government of thecity at this era, but we collect from the "Saxon Chronicle," that "the king moved by the importance of the place, and the desire of strengthening his frontier against the Danes, restored London to its ancient splendour, and observing that through the confusion of the times, many both Saxons and Danes lived in a loose and disorderly manner, without owning any government, he offered them now a comfortable establishment if they would submit and become his subjects. The proposition was better received than he expected; for multitudes grown weary of a dissolute kind of life, joyfully accepted such an offer." In continuation, we do not think it inconsistent to assume, that as Alfred in his regulations of the commonwealth divided the counties of his kingdom into ***hundreds***, and ***tythings***, he may have first separated the city into ***wards*** and ***precincts***, and as the king constituted the office of ***Scyre-Gerefa***, or Shire-reive, the present sheriff of counties, the nature of the office would require a similar institution in London, though no record extant establishes either of the facts in reference to the metropolis.

During the succeeding reign of Edward the Elder, the welfare of the city which had been based on such admirable foundations by the king's father, continued to reap the advantage of his salutary laws; and on Athelstan, or ***Adelstan***, ascending the throne, London attained a brilliant era of prosperity, which was not equalled by any other city in the Kingdom; as illustrative of which it may be instanced, that in 939, when it received the distinguished privilege of coining, a greater number of mints were allotted to it, than even Canterbury. But the maritime commerce does not seem to have extended in proportion to its internal improvement, as in 925, Atheistan

[illegible] t of
[illegible]
[illegible] *del.*
[illegible] tain the
[illegible] ra, but
[illegible] moved
[illegible]
[illegible]
[illegible]
[illegible]
[illegible] ed
[illegible] ey would submit
[illegible] been received
[illegible]
[illegible]
[illegible] Alfred in his
[illegible] counties of his king-
[illegible] have first separated
[illegible] the king constituted
[illegible] or Shire-reeve, the present sheriff
[illegible] of these offices would require a similar
[illegible] London, the [illegible] record extant establishes
[illegible] reference to the metropolis.
[illegible] during the reign of Edward the Elder, the
[illegible] had been based on such admirable
[illegible] continued to reap the advantage
[illegible] Athelstan, or *Adelstan*, according
[illegible] ed a brilliant era of prosperity, which
[illegible] other city in the Kingdom; as illus-
[illegible] be instanced, that in 938, when
[illegible] privilege of coining, a greater
[illegible] allotted to it, than even Canterbury.
[illegible] does not seem to have extended
[illegible] improvement, as in 925, Athelstan

enacted "that every merchant who made three voyages to the Mediterranean on his own account, should be raised to the honour and enjoy the privileges of a gentleman. The monarch resided in the centre of the city, and seems to have been endeared to the people, his palace being situated on the spot where *Addle Street* now runs, commencing from No. 58, Aldermanbury, to Wood Street, Cheapside, and is mentioned in ancient records as King Addle Street, and the church of St. Alban, in Wood Street, is traditionally related to have been founded by him. In 945, during the reign of Edmund I., another parliament was held in London for the discussion of ecclesiastical affairs. Little worthy of note occurred during the sovereignties of Edred and Edwy; but after Edgar had been proclaimed king, 959, the fame of the king's abilities and wise administration caused a considerable number of foreigners to resort to his capital, but this more intimate intercourse with distant nations appears to have been injurious to the morals of the inhabitants, drunkenness having become so habitual, that Edgar in order to check the vice, instituted a law that within every drinking cup of certain dimensions there should be pins fixed at particular distances, and if any person was convicted of "*drinking beyond the mark*," he should be mulcted.

In 961 the cathedral of St. Paul fell a sacrifice to the flames, while a malignant fever proved fatal to a great number of the citizens. According to the narrative of several early historians St. Paul's was rebuilt during the same disastrous year, which would at once lead to the conclusion, that the public buildings of London had, even in the tenth century, attained little architectural importance, and must have been on a small scale, and composed of wood.

It may be noted among the earlier references to agricultural subjects, that land in this reign was not valued at more than *one shilling* per acre; and among other politic measures adopted by Edgar, was the enactment, that the *Winchester measure* should become the standard of merage. He also ordained that one and the same money should be current throughout his kingdom, and that the king's coin was alone to be received; though the practice of having private mints was not wholly abolished until some time after the Norman conquest.

The zenith of London, as the Saxon capital had now passed its meridian and the state of agitation in which it was kept from the reign of Ethelred II., who succeeded Edward the Martyr in 979, until the Danes had gained sole possession of the kingdom, rendered the chance of any improvement almost impracticable; though its commercial interests obtained all the attention and protection that the turbulency of the times could be expected to permit. At the commencement of the feeble and pusillanimous sovereignty of Ethelred, the devoted city was again nearly consumed by fire. and had scarcely recovered from its desolation, when a powerful Danish armament threatened a general invasion; and in 982 seige was laid to London, but successfully repulsed by the gallant citizens. At this date, owing in all probability to the partial dread of fire, the greater number of the dwellings were outside the city to the west of Ludgate, the houses within the walls being irregularly built, and few contiguous to each other.

In 992 a numerous fleet was fitted out at London in order to prevent the landing of another army of Danes and Norwegians, in which the Londerers performed a conspicuous part, and the enemy were dispersed. Two years afterwards Anlaf and Sweyn, or *Swegen*, kings of Norway and Denmark, appeared before the city with a fleet of *ninety-four* ships with the dire intent of burning and sacking it: but to the valour of her own undaunted citizens, to their unshaken loyalty, did London at this momentous crisis owe its salvation, and the Danes were obliged to raise the siege. It appears that if Ethelred had possessed a *spark* of British courage, it would have caught *flame* from the heroic conduct of his faithful citizens, and he might have driven back the invaders discomfited to their inhospitable shores, but he had recourse to the despicable expedient of purchasing a respite by paying a large sum, amounting to 36,540*l*. in silver, equivalent to 400,000. of the present value of money, and whence arose the onerous tax of ***Danegelt***, of which London bore a large proportion. The expedient, however, proved only an alternative of temporary efficacy; as it was based on pusillanimity and inertness, arising from a wish to avoid an imminent peril without any personal effort or risk of danger, which could have been alone obviated by nervous, instant action, and chivalric conduct. In 1013, London being the only city left in possession of the irresolute Ethelred, he retired to Normandy; the city, deserted by its king, was ultimately induced to open its gates to the Danes; and in the same year, Sweyn was proclaimed in London king of England, but dying in the spring of the succeeding year, and his son, ***Cnut***, or Canute, not obtaining the affections of the people, Ethelred was recalled, and for a short period resumed the reins of government; ending his inglorious career in the early part of 1016, his remains being deposited in the chancel of the old cathedral church of St. Paul's. During his sovereignty we find the first reference made to the exaction of any toll in the port of London on the importation of foreign merchandize; it appearing by the Saxon Chronicles, that Ethelred when at Wantage fixed certain regulations of customs on ships and goods to be paid at the principal quay of ***Belinsgate***, ***Blynesgate***, or Billingsgate. In one of the clauses allusion is made to the "***Emperor's men*** coming with their ships," who were accounted worthy of good laws, though not allowed to forestall the markets from the burghers of London; referring, it would seem, to persons usually residing in London. Now, as the German merchants of the ***Steel-yard*** were very early established here as a trading company, it is probable that by the ***Emperor's men*** were designated that society, none other than that of the Steel-yard having ever existed in the Metropolis.

Edmund Ironside, who succeeded his father, was unanimously elected to the throne, and was the first king crowned in London; the coronations having been latterly performed at Kingston-on-Thames. The courage and ability of the youthful monarch ought to have insured him the confidence and love of his subjects, but the defection of the nobility an powerful opposition of the clergy, rendered his cause extremely desperate, though it was the occasion of exhibiting another striking instance in our city's history of the loyalty of its inhabitants. At this juncture, when the aristocratical and clerical influence, an influence which seems ever to have been co-existent in history, and too frequently combined in the cause of oppression, or protection and perpetuity of abuse, having transferred its preponderating power in favour of the pretentions of the "Royal Dane," he was proclaimed by this lordly faction king of England. But amidst the gathering storm of rebellion, the citizens of London stood dauntless, their honour still unimpeached, which they stamped on their annals in crimson characters of blood. Canute, apprized of the disaffection in the land and his proclamation at Southampton, hastened to the Thames with a large fleet, and appeared before London with two hundred ships. Finding the city impregnable to his attacks on the east, as it was enabled to draw succours from the westward, and being prevented passing through the BRIDGE, owing to its *fortifications*, he resolved on the Herculean task of cutting a trench through the marshes of Surrey, in order to circumvent the bridge and bring his ships to bear on the western division of the city, thus completing its blockade, his troops having invested the walls by land. In this historical event we observe the first recurrence to the existence of a *bridge* across the

Thames, and though no precise data are afforded to determine the period of its erection; yet, as King Anlaf, in the year 993, is stated to have sailed up the river as far as Staines, ravaging the counties on each bank, and in 1016 the progress of Canute's navy was checked by a bridge, it must have been constructed within the intervening twenty-three years, and during the reign of Ethelred, which is partially corroborated by the tenor of the custom-regulations enacted by this king, wherein it is recited, that tolls shall be levied on vessels coming to *Belinsgate* or "*ad pontem.*" According to the traditionary account of Bartholomew Linsted, *alias* Fowle, the last prior of *St. Mary of the Ferry, or St. Mary Overie's* convent in Southwark, he asserts that "a ferrie was kept in a place where now the bridge is builded; at length the ferry-man and his wife deceasing, left the same ferrie to their only daughter, a maiden, named Marie, which with the goods left by her parents, as also with the profits arising of the said ferrie, builded a house of sisters, in a place where now standeth the east part of St. Marie Overie's church, above the Queere, where she was buried, unto the which house she gave the oversight and profits of the ferrie; but afterwards the said house of sisters being converted into a college of priests, they builded the bridge of timber, as all the other the great bridges of this land were, and from time to time kept the same in good reparations; till at length, considering the great charges of repairing the same, there was by ayd of the citizens of London and others, a bridge builded with arches of stone." Many learned authorities doubt the truth of this narrative, as no record or tradition, except the one cited, is discoverable of any convent having existed in Southwark before that of Bermondsey, founded by Alwin Childe in 1082; St. Mary Overie having been established in the reign of Henry the First. Stow is the only early authority supporting the Prior's history, though in Doomsday-book a reference is made in Southwark to a *Monasterium*, which it is urged by Bishop Tanner in contradistinction to Dugdale, that if it denoted anything more than an ordinary church, may be thought to mean this religious house. The Prior's account also is incorrect as to the repairs of the bridge, as it is on record, that the expenses were defrayed by a public charge. Nor is it likely that a small sacred order could have afforded the heavy outlay of its erection; but more probably received a consideration and allowance for the loss of the profits arising from the ferry, which formed its chief support. More probability being attached to the suggestion, that the bold enterprize of Anlaf might have instigated the citizens and government in building a bridge, not only in a political point of view in preventing the future invasion of the upper districts of the Thames, but as a source of convenience for the more ready egress and ingress into the city from Surrey.

The circuitous extent of the cut or trench through which the Danish vessels were towed is not correctly ascertained, but its commencement is generally acknowledged to have been at *Dockhead*, by Rotherithe or *Redriff;* fascines of hazel, willows, and other small wood, fastened down with stakes, having been discovered in digging the dock in 1694. But it is difficult to subscribe to the opinion formed by Maitland:—"That after diligent search of several days, he found the *vestigia* of the canal to have traversed Rotherhithe fields, across the Deptford-road, to Newington Butts; thence to the Lambeth-road on the north of Kennington, running west and by south through the Spring Garden at Vauxhall to its influx into the Thames, at the lower end of Chelsea-reach." No doubt a water-course may have, at some former time, existed in this direction; but it is almost incredible that Canute would have attempted so needless a labour in excavating such a lengthened canal, of sufficient depth and breadth to admit his transports, or that he would have had time to execute the design in an enemy's country, even if contemplated. The supposition is, therefore, more feasible, that from Dockhead the cut formed a small semicircle by Margaret's-hill into the Thames by St. Saviour's-dock. The citizens, though now entirely surrounded by the enemy, sustained the fury of their assault, and defended themselves with so much bravery, that Canute withdrew his army, leaving the fleet to preserve the blockade; but his troops on land being defeated by Edmund, he was obliged to recall his ships to cover the retreat of his own army in case of necessity. During Edmund's absence from England, in order to recruit his army from West Saxony, Canute again attacked the city, but in vain, until a peace was concluded: and Mercia being ceded to Canute, of which London was the capital, the city submitted to the Danish dominion. On the assassination of Edmund, Canute arrived at the plenitude of his power, and the citizens felt the weight of the sovereign's resentment for their attachment to the ancient monarchy. The *Danegelt* was increased from one shilling to seven shillings for every hide of land, equal to about 100 acres, out of which about a seventh part of the assessment on the whole kingdom was imposed on the citizens, an instance not only of the disposition of the Danish sovereign, but the increased opulence of the city to liquidate so enormous a tax. Canute eventually relaxed his severity towards the Londoners, and endeavoured to reconcile the people generally to his government by his justice and impartiality, and London became indebted to him for the extension of its foreign commerce, the source from whence has sprung all its splendour. Canute scrupulously maintained the codes previously enacted for the protection and furtherance of the mercantile interests, and directed peculiar attention towards the cultivation of a commercial intercourse, by which the prosperity and security of the people might be guaranteed. William of Malmsbury has preserved an interesting document, instancing the attention

Canute paid to the mercantile advancement of his subjects during the performance of a pilgrimage to Rome. Addressing the authorities left in charge of his kingdom, the king writes:—"I have conversed with the pope, the emperor, and all the princes whom I found at Rome, respecting the grievances imposed on my subjects, whether English or Danes, on visiting their several states, and have *insisted* that in future they shall be treated more favourably, and exempted from the tolls and exactions of various kinds with which they have been hitherto harrassed. The emperor, king Rodolphus, and the other sovereigns, have accordingly listened to my remonstrances, and have assured me that henceforth no subject of mine, whether *merchant* or *pilgrim*, passing through their territories, shall meet with any obstruction, or be made liable to the payment of any impost whatever."

Canute, dying in 1036, did not reap the fruits of his wise and politic measures, though at this era the traffic of London, and indeed England generally, attained the height of its prosperity during its first *Millennium*; yet how prodigious has been its augmentation during the succeeding epoch of only eight centuries; what a contrast does the year 1036-37 afford with 1836-37; in what strong antithesis is placed the social interests of the subject, and the organized state of society in Britain. Mr. Hunter has so truly depicted the feelings naturally arising in forming any comparative analogy between the periods, that we cannot refrain from quoting his words:—"We now," he continues, "laugh to scorn the idea of invasion; the tongue in parliamentary debate, and the pen in political pamphlets, are the only weapons of our warfare. Every breath of wind carries out or brings home exhaustless mines of treasure; the slave becomes free from his master the moment his foot alights on these hallowed shores; unnumbered mansions and palaces swell the cities and embellish the plains, and golden harvests wave on the lately barren wastes." If we pursue the contrast

[illegible]

[illegible]

further, we note that about this period, not any city, except London and Westminster, contained 10,000 inhabitants, being one seventy-fifth part of the population of the present day, or as 20,000 to 1,500,000; and that the amount of 10,000 people is only now equivalent to the number of retailers of spirits and beer within the metropolis; and while the houses within the city's walls and western precincts were then thinly scattered, the eye at a single survey being enabled to estimate their extent and number, that now there are upwards of 10,000 courts, alleys, streets, lanes, squares, places, and rows; and from the opposite points of their respective situations, no individual would pass through them in the space of a whole year. It may be added, that in the early part of the 11th century, agriculture was at so low an ebb that land sold at equal to four shillings per acre of our present money, which was likewise the value of four sheep.

On the demise of Canute a *Witena-gemote* was held, (the term Parliament, according to Sir Robert Cotton, not occurring until the sixth year of the reign of John,) to which was summoned as usual the nobles; and for the first time, in 1036, London sent its representatives to the State Council under the name of *Lidromen*, a Saxon designation, the translation of which is disputed, being rendered *nautæ* or *mariners*, but evidently indicating the *magistrates* or *principal merchants* of the city. At this assembly was discussed the succession to the throne, Harold, surnamed *Harefoot*, son of Canute, being elected, during whose short reign and that of his brother, Hardicanute, few occurrences took place relative to the city. Edward the Confessor, in whom was resumed the Saxon dynasty, was recalled from Normandy and declared King of England, in the City of London, by the general voice of the nation. Two years after his accession, in 1043, a dreadful famine prevailed throughout the country, and wheat sold at the then exorbitant rate of five shillings per quarter. The bigotry of this king, and his neglect of *temporal* for *spiritual* affairs, caused him to slight the international interests, and little improvement or advance was made in the mercantile prospects of London. Though Edward is accused of disregarding the existing state of his kingdom, and paying comparatively trifling attention to current circumstances, he was not unmindful of his own future state in building and endowing churches. He re-edified, with architectural magnificence, the monastic pile of St. Peter, Westminster, and endowed it munificently, granting to it all the rights and privileges which papal decrees could enforce. While this royal foundation was erecting, Ingilricus and his brother, Edwardus or Gerardus, founded, in 1056, a large and beautiful college in St. Martin's-lane, Aldersgate, and endowed it for a dean, and secular canons or priests by the name of *St. Martain's le Grand.*

Among the principal laws, however, which Edward did enact is a statute, wherein he acknowledges the pre-eminence of London over all his cities, confirms to it all its ancient customs and usuages, so as not to be violated by his successors, and particularly grants to the citizens the privilege of holding and keeping "*the hustings,*" a court or council, every Monday. As additionally illustrative of the condition of society in the middle of the 11th century, and the state of London and Westminster, may be recounted the history of Godwin, the powerful Earl of Kent, and father-in-law of the kings, who by base insinuations made to Edward, principally by the Normans at court, had been cited to appear before the Great Council assembled at London, to investigate the truth of the allegations. Godwin, aware that his ruin was pre-determined, refused to attend, unless his personal safety was guaranteed by pledges, which being denied, he was banished the country, and his estates confiscated. Confident in his own innocence, the earl had recourse to arms to enforce the restitution of his rights: and having induced many of the citizens to espouse his cause, he raised a considerable army, and fitted out a fleet, with which he sailed up to London Bridge, and meeting with no opposition from the Londoners, passed through the arches on the Southwark shore, with the intent of attacking the *Royal Navy*, consisting of fifty sail, *lying off Westminster*—a fact, implying that the ships of war could not have been very formidable, as they were enabled to pass and repass with so much facility the wooden arches of the bridge. The warlike array, however, of the Earl's army, which had taken a position on the southern banks of the river, induced some of the influential nobility to interfere as conciliators, and the effusion of native blood was spared. Godwin being reinstated in the possession of his titles and estates, and the Norman courtiers dismissed the kingdom.

During the reign of Edward, we find that the *rights* and *privileges* of the citizens received their first *statutary recognition*, having previously depended on usage and tradition; but it is to be lamented that we cannot recapitulate the nature and extent of these liberties, which would be illustrative of the immunities which had incited them to commercial operations, forming the fundamental principles of that greatness which the city has now attained. There is, however, so much romance, blended with the few accounts extant "of London being after the manner of *Old Great Troy*," that no certainty prevails, except that London possessed from time immemorial the noble right of conferring *freedom* on such slaves and vassals as should reside for a *year and a day* within the city, unclaimed by their lords; and hence London received the distinguished appellation of "The Free Chamber of the King." Exclusive of the high and noble character of this prerogative, it was of inestimable value to the mass of the population, as it was the first ray of liberty dawning on a people still nearly benighted in the gloom of the darker ages; the state of vassalage, being only a slight amelioration from that of slavery. It was, therefore, the means of pointing out to them that there were other sources from whence the blessing of freedom could spring, than the caprices of their feudatory lords; and so scrupulously did the citizens appreciate the privilege which for some time they exclusively enjoyed, that cases are on record, of individuals having been degraded from the rank of citizens, solely from the circumstance of their having descended to hold in *villinage* lands without the limits of the city.

On the death of Edward the Confessor, in January, 1066, Harold, the son of Earl Godwin, was placed on the throne; the citizens, in conjunction with some of the nobles and a few of the clergy, having been foremost in repelling the claims to the succession of William, Duke of Normandy, a descendant of Canute. Harold, however, in opposing the advance of the Duke's troops into England, was killed the same year, in the battle fought near Hastings. On the approach of the Normans to London, the citizens sallied forth, but were repulsed in Southwark, and compelled to retreat within their walls. This "courageous onslaught," however, induced William, after destroying Southwark by fire, to march his army into the Western counties, fearful in winter of attacking the stronghold of the metropolis. Disaffection and treachery among the nobles, and intrigues of the clergy, made his eventual conquest more easily attainable; and William, on his re-appearance near the walls, was met by the magistrates and citizens, who tendered the city's keys, and acknowledged him sovereign, when he assumed the name of *Conqueror*. The submission of London was effected entirely by internal faction, and not the absence of means and power to have withstood the siege; the peaceful acquiescence to his rule having been principally effected by treaty and compact. But the king seems to have been fully aware of the necessity of holding in check the gallant spirit of the inhabitants, as one of his first acts was to augment and strengthen the fortress of the Tower, and the additions he then made have now become an interesting architectural relic of his reign.

Whatever feelings of displeasure or animosity William might have harboured against the Londoners for the hostile disposition they had evinced, he was wise enough to perceive that the opulence and commercial importance of the city would act as the mainspring to the successful issue of his future political designs, and the reconciliation of the citizens was the sure method of establishing his dominion on a firmer basis; he, therefore, granted to them a *written* CHARTER, which is now preserved with sacred veneration among the archives at Guildhall. As it is the first document of the kind the citizens are recorded ever to have possessed, it merits a more particular description. The charter consists of four lines and a quarter, well and legibly written on a slip of parchment, six inches long and about one inch broad, in the Saxon character; and not in French, which was then beginning to supersede the Saxon, the national language.

"WILLIAM *the* KING *friendly salutes* William *the Bishop and* Godfrey *the Portreve, and all the Burgesses within* London, *both* French *and* English, *and I declare that I grant you to be all Law-worthy, as you were in the days of King* EDWARD; *and I grant that every child shall be his father's heir, after his father's days, and I will not suffer any person to do you wrong. God keep you.*"

To which is attached a seal of white wax, impressed with the *Conqueror* on horseback, and on the reverse, sitting in a chair of state; the only words remaining of the superscription being M. WILL. In elucidation of this charter it may be necessary to remark, that being *law-worthy*, implied that the individual, in all cases of disputed right or alleged crime, should be entitled to a legal trial, and not like men under vassalage, liable in their persons or possessions to arbitrary rule, insuring at the same time the secure transmission of property on the decease of a relative to the nearest of kin; whereas, holding lands and goods at the will of feudal lords, the owners were never certain that any part of the fruits of their industry would be inherited by their relatives and friends. The importance of the grant was still further enhanced by being given at a time when the feudal system was acquiring a firmer and wider range, by the settlement of the Norman Barons in England under the military tenure.

We have now arrived at one of the most eventful periods of the history, not only of our island but also of London, when the sceptre of the Saxon no longer controlled the destinies of the British, and when new characteristics were on the eve of influencing the manners and customs of the people. During the Saxon rule, the turbulency and disorganized state of society had induced the Londoners, in their hours of relaxation from business, to apply their attention to those pastimes requiring exertions of bodily strength, which naturally communicated to the mind a predilection for military pursuits, especially as it was likewise the sole occupation of the aristocracy. Emulation was soon created in the youthful breast to excel in some of the usual pastimes of the day, as hunting, hawking, leaping, running, wrestling, slinging, casting of darts and stones, the use of the bow, the club, and the buckler; and which, in accordance with the public taste, far exceeded the utility or necessity of mental accomplishments; study, beyond that of the ledger, was deemed superfluous, and literature thought more congenial to the gloom and retirement of the cloister. But the infatuation of gaming, especially with dice, had unhappily become too prevalent among all classes; a vice which the Anglo-Saxons inherited from their ancestors, as Tacitus assures us, the Germans would not only risk their whole fortunes on the turn of the die, but even stake their personal liberty, the winner having the option of selling the loser as a slave. Chess formed another favourite source of

[illegible]

amusement, and also backgammon, which is stated to have been invented about the tenth century. It is related that Bishop Œtheric, having obtained admission to Canute about midnight upon urgent business, found the king and his courties at play, some at chess, others with dice. At the termination of the Saxon era, little alteration occurred in the people's pastimes; the Normans only diverting more of the popular attention towards jousts and tournaments; and we then find, that the sons of the citizens and yeomen practised various attacks and evolutions on horseback, and also on foot, as running at the *quintain*, &c., the youth being armed with shields and pointed lances, resembling the *ludus Trojæ*, or "Troy game," described by Virgil, and doubtless the origin of tournaments.

The most destructive fire which had befallen London occurred in 1077, and in the succeeding year William caused the present large square tower to be erected, called now the *White Tower*, under the direction of the celebrated military architect, Gundulph, Bishop of Rochester, which remains as a noble specimen of the prelate's innovation in the art of castle building. A similar plan was adopted by the bishop in the construction of Rochester Castle. Fitzstephen designates this tower as the *Arx Palatina*, or Palatine Tower, the commander having the title of Palatine conferred on him, being at the same time endowed with regal powers. Within the tower is a chapel, which, according to *Stow*, was coeval with the structure, but even in his time was used as a repository for records.

During the reign of William *Rufus*, London bore a large proportion of the heavy taxes imposed by the king, in order to rebuild of wood London Bridge, which had been in great measure destroyed by a serious flood occurring in 1091; also for the erection of Westminster Hall, and the enlargement of the Tower, the king having caused the addition of the castellated building on the south-side facing the Thames, afterwards called St. Thomas's Tower, beneath which is *Traitor's Gate.*

On the accession of Henry I., in the year 1100, to the exclusion from the throne of his elder brother Robert, who was in Normandy, the king deemed it politic to obtain the favour and co-operation of the citizens by granting them the confirmation of their prescriptive rights, with additional municipal advantages. Indeed, throughout the history of our city it is observable, that its preponderating importance in the state secured to it privileges, which, in the usual course of occurrences, no metropolis could have hoped to have attained; and the city seems, in a more especial degree, to have profited by the intrigue, perfidy, schemes, or extravagance of the sovereigns, compelling them to require the influence or money of the citizens. It was, however, in this reign, that the first detailed and circumstantial account is found of the immunities enjoyed by the city, contained in a charter of ratification of the usages ascertained and established, and which henceforward were not to be dictated or regulated by the caprice and humour of favouritism. The charter was granted in the first year of Henry's sovereignty; and besides radicating all former customs, added to the city the jurisdiction of Middlesex in fee-farm, without homage or other condition than a quit rent of £300, with power of appointing a sheriff, and also a justiciary from among their own body for holding the pleas of the Crown. This sum, however, considering the prosperous condition of the country, must have been equivalent to £12,000 of our present currency, provisions having since increased at least forty-fold; for it appears that Henry, who was more in want of money, than sustenance for his army and retainers, ordered that his tenants in future, instead of finding *bread* for a meal for a *hundred men*, should pay in lieu *one shilling*; for a stalled or fat ox, *one shilling*; for a night's feed of oats for *twenty horses*, *fourpence;* and for a ram or other sheep, *fourpence;* a pint of wine selling at the London taverns for *one penny*, with bread included! The citizens became now also exempted from *Scot* and *Lot* and *Daneguild;* and were not obliged to plead to any charge *without their walls;* the rule which is at present observed by the king's courts, of holding sittings in each term in Guildhall, being merely the practical result of this privilege. They were, from the same date, freed from having any of the king's household, or of the "*king's livery*," or *soldiers* quartered upon them, with exemption from all toll, passage, and lastage, "in all parts and sea-ports of the kingdom." The stability of their liberties thus guaranteed and shielded from the arbitrary will of the king, the citizens were desirous of securing their municipal usages, by causing them to assume the appearance of legal authority, and converting them into written statutes. Hence "their arts and mysteries," which had been kept up merely by prescription, became strengthened by established *fraternities*, and *gildes* of trade and professions; the king, however, reserving to his right the nomination of the Portreve, or chief officer of the city. Without disputing the subject, though not yielding to the assertion, that Secular Gilds did not originate with our Saxon progenitors, thinking it more probable that the "**Gildam**" were adopted from Germany and not France, it is worthy of remark, that with the exception of the *Gilda Teutonicorum*, or Steel Yard Gild, and the "*Sadlers*' Gild," the *Tellarij*, or Woollen-Cloth Weavers' Gild, is the most ancient in the corporation, as it appears on record, that they rendered to the crown a rent or *ferme* for their *gilde* in this reign; the "*Baker's company*" claims also an early rank in antiquity, circumstances which, in reference to the two latter, are of themselves a natural sequence, food and clothing being the essentials of humanity.

The religious and charitable spirit of the age began to be conspicuously exemplified about this period, by the erection and endowment of various religious fraternities, churches, and hospitals, which we shall more fully detail, in narrating the past and present state of the different wards.

On the death of Henry, the contentions for the crown between the Empress Matilda or Maud, the daughter of the late king, and Stephen, his nephew, fermented by the treachery and perjury of the bishops, not only involved the Londoners, as partizans, in heavy losses and amercements, but caused serious infringements of their charter; while the agitation of the times proved adverse to the advancement of commerce. But it afforded the citizens a fresh instance of displaying their firmness and consistency of conduct, as well as their national importance: for when the fortune of Matilda, during a brief space, was ascendant, and the citizens were summoned to Winchester, to give their concurrence in recognizing Matilda Queen of England, they refused to accede, though the council and nobles and prelates had tacitly yielded to the proposal before their arrival; denying their consent on the ground of having, in the first instance, sworn allegiance to Stephen, and eventually they were instrumental in restoring the crown to the king.

The fire which occurred during this reign was the most grievous with which the metropolis had been visited, destroying London Bridge, and great portion of the city, together with part of St. Paul's Cathedral. Another memorable circumstance happened in 1140, a total eclipse of the sun, which occasioned the good people of London much consternation, dreading that "chaos was come again;" having then acquired little general knowledge of the law or motion of the heavenly bodies.

It is difficult, amid the romance of this age, to penetrate the veil of fiction and legend which conceals the historical facts. Fitzstephen, who too frequently indulges in hyperbole, desirous of communicating grandeur of effect to the description of his

C Marshall J C Varrall

favourite city, states in allusion to the population in the reign of Stephen, that at a great review of the King's troops, London sent into the field 60,000 foot, and 20,000 horse soldiers, all *its own citizens;* whereas, part of these 80,000 men consisted of the marshal retainers of the various nobles assembled from different portions of the country, and part of the Royal forces of the King; and therefore little idea is conveyed of the existing population. But Peter de Blois, who was Archdeacon of London, resident in the metropolis, estimates the number of inhabitants at 40,000, an amount more correspondent with probability; though still considerable, recollecting that it was composed of the people dwelling *within* the walls. This is the earliest date afforded of judging of the extent of the internal power of the city, and presents an interesting and important basis on which we can construct a comparative analogy of the relative capabilities and resources of the people during the succeeding reigns which intervened, before the first authorized census was taken in 1631, and which was ordered by Government in anticipation of a dearth; the leading queries requiring a return of "the number of mouths esteemed to be in the city of London and Liberty, and what proportion of corn would suffice to feed that number by the month." The result we have annexed in a tabular form.

In reviewing the population of the twelfth and seventeenth centuries, for the purpose of ascertaining the extent of commerce from the proportionate differences in the total amounts between the two periods, however impressed we may be with the certainty, that more diligence and perseverance were practised by the merchants and dealers of olden times, their lives more closely dedicated to commercial pursuits than in later years, and that individual exertion was forced to its extreme bounds, which would lead to the inference that more business was in a proportionate degree transacted in the earlier than the later mercantile history of the city; yet we must not omit to make allowance for the facilities which have from time to time been afforded to commerce by the means of machinery; as even the most simple invention, which first proved a substitute for manual labour, conferred on the people so vast an advantage over their predecessors, that the premises become very uncertain for attempting to work out any comparative problem. The commerce of Venice, of Amsterdam, and of Antwerp, more than rivalled London, nor was it till the reign of Elizabeth, that the British flag was wafted over every sea, and that British merchants and British produce were found at the marts of the most distant climes. In the ensuing reign the foundation of the colonies in America gave a powerful impulse to trade, which was still farther promoted by the free and liberal institutions established at the Revolution; and England and its metropolis began to occupy a foremost rank among the European powers as a commercial and manufacturing nation. It was not, however, until towards the close of the eighteenth century, that the mighty revolution was effected in commerce, which was to place London on the pinnacle of its mercantile glory, nullifying all previous calculations of gradationary aggrandizement. This wonderful epoch in trade was effected by the invention of *Hargreaves*, in 1767, of the *spinning jenny*, for the manufacture of cotton, of the *spinning frame* by Wyatt, for which Arkwright took out a patent in 1769; by the invention of the *mule*, by Crompton, succeeded by the *power loom* of Dr. Cartwright, and other improvements, the whole being stimulated by the application of steam power to machinery; added to which, the supply of the raw material by the invention of Whitney's machine for separating and cleansing the cotton from the pod, enabling the Americans to meet the rapidly increasing demand, all co-operated in returning the enormous products exhibited by the following figures; the success of the different inventions strikingly exemplifying how essential each individually was for the completion of the grand result, so true is it, "*Omnes artes quæ ad humanitatem pertinent, habent quoddam commune vinculum, et quasi cognatione quadam inter se continentur.*" From these ever memorable periods manufactures and commerce, wealth and population, have increased in a ratio far exceeding all human anticipations, and have been the means of rendering the British capital the largest exporting and consuming city in the world, and, with the exception of *Pekin* and *Nankin*, the most populous. The annexed short summary will exhibit the magnitude of our exporting capabilities at the different periods referred to. The earliest historical allusion to cotton manufacture in England is in the year 1641, and the first authentic account of the imports of cotton wool previous to the improvement in the manufacture, is from the year 1697.

Years.	Raw Cotton Imported.	Official value of Exports of Cotton manufactures, Cotton-Twist, and Yarn.
	lbs.	£
1697	1,976,359	5,915
1701	1,985,868	23,253
1751	2,976,610	45,986
1764 {Three years previous to *Hargreaves'* invention.	3,870,392	——
1772 {Three years after *Arkwright's* patent.	4,764,589	——
1780	6,766,613	355,060
1790	31,447,605	1,662,369
1800	56,010,732	5,854,057
1810	132,488,935	18,951,994
1820	151,672,655	22,531,079
1830	263,961,452	41,050,969
1836	406,959,057	58,520,876

Recurring again to the subject of population, much exaggeration and absurd theory have existed, at various times, respecting the number of the inhabitants of the city; and even so late as the year 1683, *Sir William Petty*, F. R. S., and who was considered on some points an authority, gavely asserts, in an essay he wrote on "*Political Arithmetic* concerning the Growth of the City of London, with the Measures, Periods, Causes and Consequences thereof," "That as in the year 1840 the population of London would grow to 10,718,880, it must stop before that period, and be at its greatest height in 1800, when it would be *eight times* greater than now;" the estimated population being then 669,930, which would give a product of 5,359,440, and the mode of calculation adopted by the author is seriously stated to have been "necessary to *justify the Scriptures* and all other good histories concerning the number of people in ancient times;" yet though we are now in the 19th instead of the 17 century, how little is still known of the laws which govern and influence the animal economy of man. The above extract also fully illustrates the dangerous consequences of erroneous data, and proves how essential it is to endeavour to wean the public mind from the hitherto controlling influence of mere assertions, opinions, and vague generalities, and from giving too willing credence to abstract reasoning. It is, however, with pleasure we perceive a growing avidity to seize hold of facts, especially when conveyed through the valuable medium of statistical knowledge, which enables the inquiring mind, from comparative results, to gain by direct and certain means sterling information, qualifying society more readily to balance, duly regulate and scrutinize the complications emanating from the machinery necessarily attendant on the relative position and workings of so dense a mass of population. But at present our statistical knowledge of trade is more incidental to our fiscal regulations, more confined to the object of taxation, as applicable to the revenue, than prosecuted with the view to the advancement of civilization, and developing the combined resources of the nation; and when we reflect that this important science comprehends the materials

on which alone we can with safety found our deductions respecting the soil, climate, population, and the internal and external connexions of the country; the state of its physical, technical, intellectual, and moral culture, its constitution and government, we must join in expressing our surprise, with others of our contemporaries, that in this age so many are still found who exclusively indulge their appetite for works of fiction and imagery, and "starve their reasoning faculties by abstaining from the rich nourishment" afforded by statistical information.

We have been induced to make this short digression, and dwell with more attention on the subject, being deeply impressed with its importance; as in evidencing the augmentation of the inhabitants of a city or country, we are affording incontestable proof of the growth and vigour of its constitution, of the waxing strength of its sinews and muscles of war, its power to resist any invasion of its rights, and to promote and consolidate its commercial and political prospects.

Cities of London, Westminster, and Suburbs.	1631.		1801.		1811.		1821.		1831.	
	Population.	Houses	Population.	Houses	Population.	Houses	Population.	Houses	Population.	Houses
London, within the walls,	73,126	12,000	74,594	9,985	55,484	8,158	56,174	7,826	55,778	8,002
London, without the walls,	57,142	—	53,027	6,523	63.629	7,949	67,714	7,634	66,634	7,546
Total of London -	130,267	—	127,621	16,508	119,113	16,107	123,888	15,764	122,412	15,548
Southwark, - - -	—	—	67,448	10,933	72,119	11,802	85,905	1 ,477	91,501	13,430
Inns of Court, - -	—	—	1,907	1,230	1,796	1,406	1,546	1,406	1,271	1,187
Westminster, - -	—	—	153,272	17,462	162,085	17,555	182,085	18,502	201,842	20,616
Out Parishes, - -	—	—	514,597	75,017	654,433	94,962	832,270	116,532	1,054,915	145,885
Total of Metropolis,	—	—	864,845	121,150	1,009,548	141,732	1,225,694	164,681	1,471,941	196,66

The numerical results of the above tables afford, on comparison, some remarkable details. We have omitted the population of the city between the years 1135 and 1154. which we have shown was estimated at 40,000, though necessary to be kept in view. From these dates to 1631, a space of five centuries, an apparent diminution took place in the city of London, and during the present century the decrease has continued, and thus paradoxically, as the prosperity advanced, the population has fallen off; but the fact is, that exclusive of the late improvements in the city, as the widening streets, enlarging buildings and wharfs, the habit of only resorting to the counting-houses during hours of business, and returning at night to the suburban or country-houses, has so much increased, that the cause of the fluctuation is readily accounted for within the walls, while the population has become more condensed without the older precincts of the wards; the population of the whole metropolitan district having augmented, between 1801 and 1831, from 864,845 to 1,471,941, or more than 70 per cent.; but having within the walls decreased more than 25 per cent.; and from a comparison of the houses in London at the two periods, we find that there were 773 persons in 100 houses in 1801, and 787 in 1831.

During the reign of Stephen's successor, Henry the Second, a more enlightened and liberal political view was taken of civil society, which became the fruitful source of benefit and advantage to the various towns and cities, and more especially to London, being the means of communicating a fresh stimulus to its home and foreign traffic. This desirable improvement in the social state of the country was instigated by the arbitrary and imperious conduct of the barons, whose feudal sway not only impeded the progress of commercial intercourse and adventure, but threatened at times the freedom and independence of the throne itself. The antiquarian, Selden, informs us, that Henry after his accession demolished 1115 castles, which had been erected during the civil wars of Stephen and Matilda. This reduction of the strongholds of feudalism was succeeded by the adoption of a new system of creating a revenue and levying a military force, free from the despotic will of the nobles, by granting charters and sundry privileges to the principal towns, in consideration of their paying certain sums of money or an annual fine or tallage to the crown, which, while it restrained the power of the barons and feudal lords and weakened the general system of their tenure, was highly instrumental in fostering and encouraging trade.

Irrefutable evidence is adduced during Henry's reign, that some radical reform was demanded in the moral state of society, the civic authorities retaining little or no influence in controlling the unruly spirits of the age. Midnight brawls, robberies, and murders, being of frequent occurrence in the streets of London, and the committal of these depredations and crimes, not confined to the lower and more depraved classes, but the sons of wealthy citizens, and even citizens themselves, being found among these predatory gangs. *John Senex*, a rich, and, previously considered, a reputable merchant, was convicted of burglary, and "offered for his pardon the prodigious sum of 500 pounds weight of silver, which was rejected, and he was hanged according to his deserts."

Another striking instance is exhibited in the Royal charter granted to the city, which, after confirming the immunities bestowed by Henry the First, renders the citizens free from certain fines, such as *Jeresgive* and *Scotale*, the former being a bribe given to the king's or other officers for connivance and being favourable in their respective judicial duties; and the latter exactions made by the king's officers who kept alehouses, invited the people to drink, and fraudulently extorted money from them under pretence of preventing their informing against them for some imaginary crimes; and "these villainous practices were countenanced by some great men, the citizens requiring a special clause in their charter to liberate them from their continuance."

The growing opulence of the merchants, the advancement of the arts, and improvement in public and private buildings, now induced the citizens to contemplate the plan of substituting a stone in place of the wooden bridge across the Thames, the latter requiring constant repair and incurring heavy expense. In briefly alluding, however, to the improvement in the *private buildings* of this period, it does not appear that the comforts in the domiciles of the worthy citizens had arrived at any luxurious extent; for in the following reign of Richard the First, houses of stone or brick were very limited in number, being still composed of timber covered with reeds or straw. But their insecurity from depredation and liability to destruction by fire, led to the issue of an order in 1191, for settling any dispute arising from the enclosure of ground and erecting *new houses*, the party-walls of which were to be made of stone and *at least sixteen feet in height* and three in thickness, which would imply that much space was not allowed in the altitude of "these more commodious" residences. These dimensions were to be regulated by jurats, consisting of twelve aldermen, "chosen in full hustenge, who decided and appeased all the contentions in question."

The stone bridge was commenced in the twenty-second year of the reign of king Henry the Second, in the year 1176, and the site chosen rather to the westward of the original bridge which abutted Botolph's Wharf. The event was looked forward to with so much interest, that the king, clergy, and laity, subscribed funds for its completion, and a tax was imposed on wool towards defraying the expenses, which occasioned the vulgar belief that "the bridge was built on woolpacks." The great architect of the day, *Peter, of Cole-church*, was employed to superintend the construction; this clergyman, who had attained much skill in architecture, was minister of St. Mary, *Cole-church.* The church, previous to the fire of London, in 1666, forming the western corner of the Old Jewry, having received its latter appellation from its

founder, who was named *Cole;* the parish being now united to that of St. Mildred, Poultry. The Reverend Architect did not live to complete his great undertaking, for among the records in the Tower, is a letter, dated in the third year of the reign of King John, recommending "The learned and worthy clerk, *Isenbert*, as a proper person to finish the bridge;" he having superintended the erection of the bridges of Xainctes and Rochelle; though the bridge at Rouen, built by King John's grandmother, the Empress Matilda, which remained in use 500 years, seems to have formed the model of that of London. But the citizens appear not to have paid much attention to the Royal recommendation, as no historical notice is made of Isenbert's labours, the superintendence of the work having been entrusted to *Serle Mercer*, *William Almaine*, and *Benedict Botewrite*, merchants, "who finished the first stone bridge in London in the year 1209."*

* In addition to the remarks we have already made in reference to the first construction of this bridge in the reign of Ethelred, we would here allude to a passage found in the works of *Snorre*, detailing an occurrence that seems generally to have escaped historical notice, or to have been confounded with the expeditions of Canute, and which recounts a successful attack against the wooden bridge of London, previous to its assault by Canute at the time the Danes were in possession of the city. The enterprise is stated to have been undertaken by Olaf, chieftain of a band of Northern adventurers, at the instigation of Ethelred. The bridge was partially destroyed, by the piles of some of the middle arches having been broken or torn away, and the besieged obliged to retreat, some into the city, and others taking refuge in the *South-works, or fortifications, vulgo dictum Sudverkium.* Snorre supports his narrative by citing contemporary war-songs, descriptive of the exploit, adding, that Olaf, who was afterwads king of Norway, became converted to Christianity, and being massacred by his Pagan subjects, was eventually canonized, and a church in Southwark near the bridge named after him St. Olavus, in memorial of his success. Torfæus repeats this legend, and proceeds to prove that Olaf never co-operated with Canute.

Previous to the demise of Peter of Colechurch, "a chapel of beautiful arched structure," dedicated to St. Thomas, had been erected at his own expense on the east side of the ninth pier from the north end, and endowed by him for two priests, four clerks, &c., and where, according to Stowe, the architect himself was afterwards buried. The chapel, which communicated with the water by a circular flight of steps round one of the pillars of the bridge, remained nearly in its original form until the total demolition of the houses. The century had however not elapsed, before the bridge had become so ruinous from various accidents, such as destruction of the starlings, and five of the arches "being borne down by the ice and floods," that according to the tenour of a brief granted in 1280, by King Edward the First, "unless it be speedily repaired it must inevitably fall down, and the great numbers of inhabitants dwelling thereon are in great danger of being destroyed;" proving, at the same time, that from its earliest date, houses were erected on it; and which, by King John's letter of recommendation, it was purposed that Isenbert should cause to be erected; the rents to be appropriated to the repairs. On the north side was constructed a draw-bridge, defended by a Tower, which proved the means of repulsing *Fawconbridge* in his assault on the city in 1471, and checked also the ill-devised insurrection of *Sir Thomas Wiat* in the reign of Queen Mary, besides that, this division of the bridge facilitated the progress of masted vessels up the river, especially those laden with provisions bound to Queenhithe. On the top of the Tower were wont to be affixed the heads or parts of the bodies of different partizans who were hostile to the reigning Government, or who had had recourse to arms to enforce redress for their real or imaginary grievances. As late as 1598, Hentzer, the German traveller,

counted more than *thirty heads*. On the bridge was situated one of the early gates of the city, though it is not specified by Fitzstephen. The houses at different periods suffered much damage by fire, and in the general conflagration in 1666 were, with the exception of a few of the original buildings on the Southwark side, entirely destroyed; they were, however, soon rebuilt and constructed four-stories high. These houses overhung the arches, many of which they even nearly concealed, or left little visible to the passing eye beyond rude piers. The street thus formed, was about twenty-feet in width, and dangerous to foot-passengers from the number of carriages, as no direct foot-path was formed, while several arches of timber crossed the street from the tops of the houses, to prevent the probability of their falling into the eddying tide beneath, whose constant roar of water, varied at times with the shrieks of the numerous beings whose lives were sacrificed in passing through the ill-constructed arches, must have required considerable nerve and long usage, especially in the fair occupants of the houses, to have rendered their minds free from all dread and apprehension. Latterly most of the houses were tenanted by pin and needle makers, and "œconomical ladies were wont to drive from the St. James's end of the town to make cheap purchases." *Fuller*, in his "*Worthies*," tells us, that Spanish needles were made first in London in Cheapside, by a negro, who died without communicating the art; but *Elias Krowse*, a German, in the reign of Elizabeth, was more liberal, and first taught the method to the English. Fuller facetiously gives the derivation of the name NEEDLE, *equasi* NE IDLE.

In the reign of Elizabeth, mills and water-works were erected under the arches of the south end; the former for grinding corn, and to rectify the price of manufacturing flour in times of dearth, and the exorbitant rates demanded at such times for meal, by "*Badgers*, or *Mealmen*;" and in the year 1582, Peter Morice, a Dutchman, contrived a water engine, to supply the citizens with Thames water, the wheels being moved by the common tide-stream. The machinery was improved by Saracold and Hadley, and ultimately occupied four of the arches; with sufficient power, it was calculated, to raise 46,896 hogsheads of water per day, to the height of 120 feet.

The civic authorities, owing to the numerous lives that were lost, from the narrowness of the arches and the immense size of the starlings, which occupied one-fourth of the water-way, and occasioned a fall, at low water, of *five feet*, creating a number of temporary cataracts, besides that the annual repairs had for several years amounted to £2,000, came to the resolution in 1746, to pull down the houses; for which purpose an Act of Parliament was passed in 1756, for carrying the plan into immediate execution; and the two centre arches of the old bridge were thrown into one, in which state the bridge remained till its total demolition, in 1831. Reverting to the period when the houses were erected after the fire of London, the bridge, according to the eulogists of the day, was the admiration of all beholders, being the most stately erection in the world.

> "Let the whole earth now all the wonders count;
> This bridge of wonders, is the paramount."

Its praises and fame were sung and recounted by poets and historians; yet had these panegyrists witnessed the present bridge, we know not what language they would have found to have celebrated with its due meed of praise, the magnificence, elegance, and beauty of this *chef d'œuvre* of *pontifical* architecture; and in order to place in juxta-position the dimensions and public convenience of the two bridges, we have annexed the following tabular account; adding the similar particulars of the five other splendid structures crossing the majestic

Thames, enabling a comparative view at once to be taken of their respective proportions.

Bridges.	Length.	Width.	Height.	No. of Arches.	Span of centre	Materials.	Commenced.	Opened.	Architects.	Waterway.
	feet.	feet.	feet.	—	feet					feet.
Old Bridge.	930	20	40	19	70	Stone & rubble.	1176.	1209.	Peter, of Colechurch.	Above Starlings, 540.
Altered by Mr. Dance & Sir R Taylor.	—	48	—	20	—	—	—	—		Below, 273.
New Ditto.	920	56	55	5	150	Granite	15 Mar. 1821.	Aug. 1, 1831.	Sir J. Rennie.	690.
Westminster.	1066	43	58	15	76	Portland stone.	Jan 1739	1750.	Labelye, a Swiss.	8[illegible]0.
Blackfriars	1000	42	62	9	100	Ditto.	June, 1760.	1770.	R. Mylne.	793.
Vauxhall.	809	36	—	9	7[illegible]	Iron & granite.	May, 1811.	July, 1816.	Jas. Walker	—
Waterloo.	1326	42	51	9	120	Cornish granite.	Oct. 1811.	March, 1817.	Sir J. Rennie.	1080.
Southwark.	700	42	53	3	240	Iron.	Sept. 1814.	1819.	Ditto.	660.

Before concluding the history of our once famed bridge, we must relate the heroic conduct of ***Edmund Osborne***, and which has formed the subject of more than one legendary theme. About the year 1536, Sir William Hewet, afterwards Lord Mayor, inhabited a house on the bridge, carrying on the trade of a clothworker. The nursery-maid was standing at an open window overlooking the river, with Sir William's only daughter in her arms, when the child sprung from her arms and fell into the "whirling pool" beneath. The merchant's apprentice, the youthful Osborne, witnessed the melancholy catastrophe, and with knightly bravery plunged into the "mighty rush" of waters, rescuing the sinking infant from a premature grave. As the fair maiden grew to womanhood, her hand and dowry were sought for by courtiers and nobles, and among others, by the Earl of Shrewsbury; but Sir William, ever grateful to his apprentice for preserving the being in whom his fondest hopes were concentrated, decided in favour of Osborne, saying, "*Osborne saved her, and Osborne shall possess her;*"

a decision by no means adverse to the pretty maiden's wishes. Osborne, inheriting the wealth of his father-in-law, became Sheriff in 1575, and Lord Mayor in 1582, and founder of the noble and ducal house of Leeds.

We must again recur to the time of Henry the Second, as it supplies us with some other interesting facts worthy of comment. We find that the *Weavers'* Company had a confirmation of their guild from the king, "with all the freedom and customs they had in his grandfather's days," Henry the First; and Stowe quotes a charter purporting, that "if any cloth were to be found made with Spanish wool, mixed with English wool, the chief magistrate of the city should have it burnt;" which implies that the early woollen clothes used in England, were composed entirely of Spanish wool. About the middle of this reign, the importation of wine from Bordeaux first took place; and so great was the spirit of commercial enterprize, that several fraternities were incorporated without the Royal letters patent, being styled *Adulterine Guilds*, and were ultimately, in 1180, amerced to the king, for their "presumptuous proceedings." These guilds are designated, either from the name of their alderman, or their trade, and, in some instances, from their patron saint or locality; and, as it is to be surmised that only a portion of these companies subjected themselves to penalty by an infringement of the law, it bears out *Glanville's* remarks, that at this period guilds were common institutions. Madox furnishes us with a curious account of the current value of commodities: an ox selling at 4*s*; a working horse at the same rate; a sow, 1*s*.; a sheep with fine wool 10*d*., and ditto, coarse, 6*d*.; 33 cows, and 2 bulls, were purchased at £8. 7*s*.; 500 sheep, £22. 10*s*.; 15 brood mares, £2. 12*s*. 6*d*.; and 22 hogs, £1. 2*s*.; and according to Bishop Fleetwood, 4 hens were valued at 2*d*., and a ram at 8*d*.

The *knight-errant* spirit of Richard the First, led him into gross inconsistencies, and regardless of his nation's welfare, he, in too many instances, bartered the property of the crown in order to enable him to indulge his romantic prepossession of wresting the Holy Land from the dominion of ths Infidels. London, however, through its wealth was enabled to profit by the occasion, and to purchase of the king some valuable immunities; among others the right of the removal of the *wears* in the river Thames, whereby the navigation became much improved, and as an additional encouragement to the citizens, the king resigned all his right to the annual duties arising therefrom. From this year, 1197, the city claims its jurisdiction and conservancy of the river Thames, which it has preserved to the present day, extending up the river as far as Staines, and as low down as the small Port of Leigh, in Essex, near Canvey Island; a right which, according to modern notions of reform, " would be more honoured in the breach than in the observance;" as it is doubtful whether the *ownership* of the river ought now to be confined to any local authority to which it might have been granted, particularly when that authority constituted in fact the whole metropolis; and it is an important question, whether the jurisdiction and conservancy of the river Thames, to the preservation of the navigation of which the empire owes so much of its greatness, and which is of the utmost importance, not only to the contiguous inhabitants, but those in all other parts of the dominions, is properly within the province of any local municipality, and why the administration should not be under the direct control of the general Executive Government of the country.

The gracious favour with which Richard regarded the citizens was most probably actuated by their loyalty during his absence abroad, and the ready liberality with which they contributed towards his ransom, when detained a prisoner in Austria, on his return from his chivalrous expedition into Palestine. One of the last acts of his reign, exhibiting the confidence he reposed in their integrity and wisdom, was in 1198, when he committed to the sheriffs of London and Middlesex, the execution of a plan for affixing a standard of weights and measures for the regulation of the *whole kingdom*. In the above year, wheat, owing to the failure of the crops, advanced as high as 18*s*. 4*d*. per quarter.

At this period so great was the increasing political importance which the citizens had acquired in the State, that when John, earl of Moreton, Richard's brother, and afterwards himself king, had assembled the bishops and nobles, in order to devise the means of resisting the tyrannical conduct of Longchamp, bishop of Ely, chancellor of the kingdom, and one of the regents during the absence of Richard abroad, he convoked a *commission of the citizens*, and by the unanimous resolve of the meeting, Longchamp was degraded; the bishop having incurred the displeasure of the citizens by the arbitrary encroachments on their limits, in forming an embattled wall and fosse around the Tower, which latter he connected, as at present, with the river, having destroyed the mill belonging to the hospital of St. Catherine, standing on the spot now called the Irongate, and appropriated the ground from the White Tower to the Postern-gate, besides other small parcels of land.

The chief magistrate of the city, who officiated as *butler* at Richard's coronation, in the year 1189, was then first allowed to assume the title of *bailiff*, and though the honour of presenting wine to his Majesty at this regal ceremony was also claimed by the chief magistrate of Winchester, both referring to previous custom, yet the office was confirmed to London on a *free gift* of 200 marks, and has been claimed

in perpetuity by prescription, the Mayor receiving as perquisite the golden cup containing the wine, and likewise a golden ewer of the same precious metal. *Fitz-Alwyn*, who had been nominated bailiff, was vested by the King, two years afterwards, that is in 1191, with the rank of *Mayor*, the title with its functions being borrowed from the Norman *Maire*, though it was not till the reign of John, A.D. 1213, that the charter was granted permitting the citizens to elect their chief magistrate from their own corporate body, and allowing them to remove him from the office at the expiration of twelve months.

Before animadverting on the progressive improvement of the city during the 13th century, we must endeavour partially to familiarize ourselves with its local character and that of the environs, as well as the state of society at the close of the twelfth century. We are afforded the means of correctly ascertaining these interesting points by consulting the works of *Fitzstephen*, who lived at that period in the service of Archbishop Becket, and having written his patron's biography, has introduced a short but graphic description of London, the native place of the Archbishop, which being professedly the earliest account extant, merits our marked attention. It appears that the city was connected by an irregular line of houses along the *strand* of the river with the village of Charing, proceeding thence to the King's Palace at Westminster, a distance reckoned at about two miles. In this line of communication were situated the houses of different noblemen and wealthy citizens, who had spacious and beautiful gardens, some running to the borders of the Thames, planted with trees and flowers. The northern suburbs were composed of corn-fields, pastures, and delightful meadows, intersected with pleasant streams, "on which," in the words of our author,* "stands many a mill, whose clack is so grateful to the ear. Beyond them an immense fores extends itself, beautified with woods and groves, and full of lairs and coverts of beasts and game, stags, bucks, boars and *wild bulls*. The fields are by no means of a hungry gravelly soil or barren sands, but may vie with the fertile plains of Asia, as capable of producing the most luxuriant crops, and filling the barns of the hinds and the farmers 'with Ceres' golden sheaf.' Around the city, and towards the north, arise certain excellent springs at a small distance, whose waters are sweet, salubrious, and clear, the rivulets murmuring 'o'er the shining stones.' Amongst these, Holy-well, Clerkenwell, or *Fons Clericorum*, and St. Clement's well, are most esteemed and best frequented both by scholars from the schools and the youths and maidens of the city."

It is not our province to attempt any lengthened disquisition on the rise or fall of the drama, nor to trace the gradations in this country, from the early and rude efforts of the followers of *Thespis*, to the classic transition effected by the disciples of *Æschylus* and *Aristophanes;* but still it is pertinent to our history, in exemplifying the manners of the period we are more especially alluding to, that we should cursorily describe the scenic representations which gratified the public taste, as theatrical performances are generally indicative of the "ruling passion" of the day, depicting, in forcible colouring, the intellectual or vitiated propensities of the people. Fitzstephen mentions that the theatrical exhibitions then in vogue were called "*Miracles*," consisting of sacred dramas, descriptive of the miracles wrought by the holy confessors, and the sufferings by which the faith of

* This description is collated from the *five* MS. copies known as authentic.

WESTMINSTER HOSPITAL

AND

ABBEY CH[illegible]

martyrs was manifested; the stages were fitted up in the churches, the ecclesiastics and their scholars the actors, and the *capæ chorales* and other pontificals serving as dresses. These pieces afterwards acquired the name of "*Mysteries*," the most *mysterious* subjects of Scripture being chosen for the composition; and Dugdale states, "for the performance of these plays they had theatres for the several scenes very large and high, placed upon wheels, and drawn to all the eminent parts of the city for the better advantage of the spectators."

By availing ourselves of a convenient figure in rhetoric, which enables the logician to take "a part for the whole," we shall be enabled to avoid prolixity, and yet give the reader a general idea of the prevailing characteristics of these scriptural plays, by the detached portion we have selected from the ancient and celebrated *Mystery* of "*Corpus Christi*, or *Ludus Coventriæ*." The prologue to this curious drama was recited by three actors, called *vexillators*, and comprised the argument of the several *pageants* or *acts* that composed the piece, and which amounted to no less than *forty*, each of these acts referring to some particular subject from Holy Writ, beginning with the *creation* of the universe, and concluding with the *last judgment*. In the first pageant, or act, the Deity is represented seated on his throne alone on the stage, delivering a speech of forty lines, beginning—

> " 'Ego sum de Alpha et Emega, principium et finis
> My name is knowyn God and Kynge,
> My worke for to make now wyl I wende,
> In myself restyth my reyneynge,
> It hath no gynnyg ne non ende."

The angels then enter singing, from the Church service, "To thee all angels cry aloud," &c. Lucifer next makes his appearance, and demands whether the hymn was chanted in honour of God or of him? The good angels readily reply in honour of God; the evil angels incline to worship Lucifer, and he presumes to seat himself on the throne of the Deity, who commands him to depart from heaven to hell, which dreadful sentence he is compelled to obey, and with his wicked associates descends to the lower regions. These representations at times continued for three days, and sometimes longer. A play performed at Skinner's Wells, near Smithfield, was *endured* for *eight* days, displaying most of the historical events of the Old and New Testaments, and was well attended *throughout* by great part of the nobility and gentry. The dulness and length of these performances required some interlude, some pantomimic entertainment, in order to render them palatable to the plebeian taste, and to keep the spectators in good humour. The principal personage, whose mimic powers were called in to eliven the audience, was *Beelzebub*, assisted by a merry troop of *subordinate devils*, "who with variety of noises, strange postures, gestures, and grimaces," excited the laughter of the populace. When these mysteries ceased to be played, the subjects of the drama were not taken from historical facts, but consisted of moral reasonings in praise of virtue and condemnation of vice, on which account they were called "*Moralities*," and these performances, requiring some degree of imagery and inventive genius, conduced ultimately to the composition of dramas more replete with incident, connected with history or passing events; thus holding up "a mirror to the age," from whence emanated the present comedies and tragedies. The dialogues of the Moralities were carried on by allegorical characters, such as Charity, Faith, Prudence, Good Doctrine, Discretion, &c., but the province of amusing the auditory was transferred from the *Devil* of the "Mystery" to *Vice* or *Iniquity* of the "Morality," who generally personified some one of the evil passions co-existent with human nature. A slight allusion to

"Vice," from an ancient play, will illustrate the peculiar dress and bearing of the character.—"*Vice* came in like Hokos-pokos in a juggler's jerkin, with false skirts like the knave of clubs;" and again, "Here is never a fiend to carry the *Vice* away, besides he has never a *wooden dagger; I'd not give a rush for a Vice that has not a wooden dagger to snap at every one he meets.*" Even when the legitimate drama was introduced, we may discern that the feeling of the public still favoured the appearance of the facetious descendants of "Vice" and "Iniquity," in the clowns and jesters, whose ribaldries too often disgraced the stage. Even our immortal "Bard of Avon," the great master and painter of the human passions, was obliged to be subservient to the false taste of the age in which he wrote, and to introduce this motley personage amidst his highest wrought and most noble characters.

All these representations, however, differed materially from the *secular plays* and *farces*, which were acted by strolling companies, composed of minstrels, jugglers, tumblers, dancers, bourdours, or jesters. These pastimes are of higher antiquity than the ecclesiastical plays, and were patronized not only by the lower classes, but likewise the nobility, the court of kings and the castles of barons being the constant resort of these performers, where they were well received, and munificently rewarded; and the sums lavished on these itinerants induced the monks and other ecclesiastics to adopt the *profession* of *actors*, in order to reap a share of the public bounty, jealous that so fertile a source of profit should be monopolized by this portion of the laity. The secular *shewmen*, however, *retained* their *popularity*, notwithstanding the exertions of their *clerical rivals*, who diligently endeavoured to bring them into disrepute, by *writing* and *preaching* against the immorality of their exhibitions.

Extravagance in living was too prevalent an evil in this era, and we are informed by Fitzstephen, that an Archbishop of Canterbury paid for a single dish of eels *five pounds*, a sum equivalent to nearly eighty pounds compared with the present amount of our currency and provisions. In reference to the average value of commodities between the thirteenth and nineteenth centuries, 10*l.* per annum would have gone as far in housekeeping as 150*l.* at present. Wheat was 3s. per quarter, and French wines, which were then freely imported, chiefly from Anjou, Auxerre, and Gascony, obtained from 20*s.* to 20*s.* 6*d.* per ton; the money, however, expended thus in luxuries, did not lead to much dissipation of time, or perverting the course of nature by carousing throughout the night, and incapacitating the reveller from performing the social duties required during the day, as has been too much the case in more modern times; the hour of dining, even at court and the families of the highest aristocracy, was *nine* in the *morning*, and of supping *five* in the *afternoon*, a division of time which was reckoned not only conducive to health, but favourable to business. The hours thus set apart for family arrangements have been preserved in the gingling verse of the day—

Lever à cinq, diner à neuf,	To rise at five and dine at nine,
Souper a cinq, coucher à neuf,	To sup at five and bed at nine,
Fait vivre ans nonante et neuf.	Lengthens life at ninety and nine.

Among the distinguishing characteristics of superiority possessed by the citizens, was the honourable appellation they enjoyed of *Barones;* "whilst the inhabitants of other cities are styled citizens, they are dignified with the name of Barons." Spelman, in his Glossary, renders *Barones* synonimous with *cives* or *homines*, citizens or men; and though it has been assumed that the *Barones* were composed of the wealthiest and most illustrious citizens, yet when it appears that the inhabitants of the *Cinque Ports* without *discrimination* were distinguished as *Barones*, we may rather imply that the term, *par excellence*, was a designation of MAN in the full development of those high prerogatives bestowed upon him, as the noblest type of the creation.

"Let us come now," as our historian says, "to the sports and pastimes, seeing it is fit that a city should not only be commodious and serious, but also merry and sportful." In the holidays during summer, the young men were wont to exercise themselves in leaping, dancing, archery, cross-bow shooting, wrestling, hurling, running at the Quintain and practising their shields; the city damsels playing on their *citherns*, or, as rendered by Stow, "on their timbrels," and dancing, until the evening closed upon their merriment, and which was often continued by the light of the moon.* In winter, every holiday before dinner, the bears prepared for brawn were set to fight, or else bulls or bears baited. When the great lake or fen which watered the walls of the city on the north side, now *Moorfields*, was frozen over, the young men amused themselves on the ice, "some striding as *wide* as they can, do slide swiftly, others, more expert, place leg-bones of animals beneath their feet, and with a pole shod with iron push themselves forward with a velocity equal to the flight of a bird, or bolt from a cross-bow." The citizens also delighted in hawks and hounds, having the liberty of hunting in Middlesex,

* Stow, who wrote between three and four centuries later than the period now referred to, states, that it was then customary for the maidens, after evening prayers, to dance in the presence of their masters and mistresses while one of their companions played the measure upon a timbrel; and in order to stimulate them to pursue this exercise with alacrity, the best dancers were rewarded with garlands, the prizes being exposed to public view "hanged athwart the street" during the performance.

Hertfordshire, all Chilton, and in Kent to the waters of Grey.

Though the reign of John was attended with severe amercements and oppression of the citizens, yet on the aggregate the city was ultimately benefited by the temporary privations it endured through the extravagance, evil disposition, and mercenary character of the King. At first, John appears to have been instigated either by a kindly feeling, proceeding from grateful remembrances of the attachment and loyalty of the Londoners during his regency, or by a sense of political fear which induced him to conciliate their good opinion, knowing the importance of their support, being at the time aware of the usurpation of which he had been guilty in suppressing the rightful claim to the crown of his nephew Arthur. That the government of John was generally defective, and his character vacillating and tyrannical, no doubt can exist, yet, fortunately for the city and the kingdom at large, he persevered, on ascending the throne, in the system he had adopted during the absence of his brother, King Richard, in the Holy Land, of constituting demesne towns, *free burghs*, which was a main incentive to the diffusion of commerce throughout our island; and instead of the King's collectors continuing vested with the power of levying tolls and customs from towns, they were merged into the payment of one annual sum; termed the fee-farm rent of each burgh, the amount being levied by the corporate body by local assessment; while the privilege was conferred on the towns-people of electing their own chief officer, a right hitherto held by the crown. Hence arose the present annual magistracy of corporations; on which Speed as well as Camden justly remark, that John was either "the first or chiefest who appointed those noble forms of civil government in London, and most cities and corporate towns of England, endowing them also with their greatest fran-

chises." He granted during the first year of his reign, in 1199, *three* charters to the city, one confirming their former privileges of "being quit from toll or lastage, and every other custom," and for which the treasury received 3,000 marks, evidencing that the Royal favour was not dispensed out of pure grace, but meted in proportion to the known opulence of the citizens; another, permitting the jurisdiction of the city to be extended over the River Medway, with power to inflict a penalty on the erection of weirs in either that river or the Thames; the third was indicative of that regard towards the citizens before alluded to, as it granted them the fee-farm of the Shrievalties of London and Middlesex, of which they had been deprived by Matilda, with permission to elect their own Sheriffs, and for which the sum of 300*l.* was paid. In a fourth charter, given at the request of the Mayor and citizens, the guild of *Weavers* was "from thenceforth not to be permitted to be held in the City of London, nor to be at all maintained;" the citizens paying to the King twenty marks per annum instead of the eighteen marks usually received from the Weaver's Company. This extra-judicial proceeding on the part of the corporation was most probably prompted by jealousy, as by charter of Henry II. the weavers had been allowed to exercise their privileges in the city in almost an unlimited manner, and without any right of the citizens to intermeddle or control them.

Altercations with the See of Rome, fomented by the rebellious spirit of the Church at home, induced the Pope to lay the whole kingdom under an interdict, which was only removed by the abject submission of the King and payment of a large sum of money; towards which the Londoners contributed 2,000 marks, and received in lieu their fifth and last charter from the King, dated the 19th day of May, in the sixteenth year of his reign; beginning, "Know ye, that we have granted to our *Barons* of our City of London, that they may choose themselves every year a Mayor, to be presented to us or our justice, and at the end of the year to amove him and substitute another, or return the same, confirming all previous liberties, saving to us our chamberlainship." At this time, the King held his Parliament at his palace at St. Bride's, where Bridewell Prison, Bridge-street, Blackfriars, now stands. In 1204, we find an incident strongly corroborative of the importance and extent of the commerce of London, from the circumstance that *Guy de Von* appears to have been indebted to the crown the sum of 1,066*l.* 8*s.* 4*d.* for arrears of rent for the *Cambium*, or *Exchange of London*, which he had leased for a term of years. Another fact may be adduced illustrative of the profitable character of the office of Chamberlain; the appointment, as has been shown, belonging to the King, by William de St. Michael having obtained the situation for a fine of 100*l.*, and an annual rent of 100 marks.

At length the imbecility, misrule, and wanton rapacity of John alienated the affections and allegiance of the citizens, and knowing the perfidy and implacable temperament of their Sovereign, they directed their attention to the more effectual fortification of their city, before displaying any overt act of resistance, and with this view protected their walls by digging a deep ditch two hundred feet in width.

It is often remarked through life, "that great events from minor causes spring," though frequently the fact is at the moment overlooked, that a combination of circumstances remote at first in their origin, have been for some lengthened time gradually converging to a certain point, and require only some ultimate exciting occurrence to produce the catastrophe, while the final issue is attributed to some recent or comparatively trifling incident. We have been led to this observation by one of the later acts of oppression, on the part of the King, in persecuting the gallant knight, ***Robert Fitzwalter***, Castellain and Standard-bearer of the City, Lord of Baynard's Castle, an ancient and princely fabric, which " banked the River Thames" near St. Paul's Wharf; Addle-hill, Thames-street, skirting the western portion of the building. The daughter of Fitzwalter was famed for her personal charms, which had acquired for her the envied celebrity of Matilda the " Fair." This maiden's beauty had captivated the monarch, who proffered his affections, but not on honourable terms. His suit being in consequence indignantly refused, John intimated his determination to have recourse to violence. This tyrannical threat aroused her noble father's resentment, who appealed to his brother Barons to protect his virtuous child from the polluting grasp of their Sovereign. With chivalrous alacrity they rallied their forces round the injured parent, and the city banner floated in proud defiance from the castle-walls. John, unable to collect a force sufficient to contend against the formidable opposition Fitzwalter offered, affected to have relinquished all designs against the honour of his family, and by well-feigned assurances of respect for the rights of the Barons, prevailed upon them to disperse their forces. As soon as he found himself master of the field, he violated his plighted faith and promises, seized Fitzwalter's castle by surprize, which he destroyed, and forced him to fly the country. Matilda, who was prevented accompanying her father, fell into the power of the King, and heroically resisted all his seductive entreaties, until John, with remorseless vengeance, is recorded to have caused the destruction of that beauty by poison which he had failed when living to possess. This incident may be reckoned one of the collaterally stimulating causes which afterwards conduced to the general resistance of the Barons, and compelled the King at ***Runnymede*** to accede, ***unconditionally***, to their demands for a ***Charter***, which would not only reinstate the nobles and people in their former rights, but bestow upon them important additional immunities, as set forth in that glorious and ever-memorable declaration of the rights of Englishmen, MAGNA CHARTA and CHARTA DE FORESTA; in the former of which it is stipulated "that the City of London should have all its ancient privileges and free customs."

London was now "a noble city," according to William of Malmesbury, "renowned for the opulence of her citizens, and crowded with the merchants who resort thither with their commodities," the trade in corn, as in the time of the Romans, forming one of the principal articles of commerce, which was entirely monopolized by the London merchants, "who had their granaries always filled, whence all parts of the kingdom were supplied."

John is said to have been the first monarch who coined the money called *sterling* or *Easterling** penny, which obtained this name from the circumstance of his sending for artists from the German states to rectify and regulate the silver coinage, gold coin not being then appropriated as a circulating medium of exchange. The penny was of silver, and the twentieth part of an ounce, and was enacted as well during the reign of John's successor, Henry III., to be round without any clipping, and "to weigh thirty-two wheat-corns taken out of the midst of the ear." The King's Exchange for the receipt of "bullion to be coined" was situated

* The Germans derived the name of *Easterlings* from there having been a commercial confederacy, first formed on the *Eastern* shores of the Baltic, in the eighth century; and Pennant styles the *Easterlings*, "our masters in the art of commerce."

WINDSOR CASTLE.

near the middle of the street now called *Old Change*, by St. Paul's.

The long reign of Henry III. exhibits a disgraceful catalogue of heavy pecuniary penalties extorted from the inhabitants of London under the most frivolous and unjustifiable pretexts, levies which were made to meet the emergencies of the lavish and extravagant expenditure of the Crown. So onerous eventually became the nature of these exactions, so impressed were the citizens with the conviction that honour and justice, conscience and religion, were alike sacrificed at the shrine of expediency, and that their dear-bought liberties and charters were merely nominal, finding them no restriction against any innovation instigated by the momentary caprices of royalty, that many of the principal merchants absented themselves from business and retired into the country, resolved no longer to submit to such spoliatory and ruinous government. This determination alarmed the King, as the resources he obtained from the city were his only salvation in the hour of need; he summoned, therefore, the chief officers of London, and promised, in the presence of the nobility, not again to oppress the citizens; promises which were as readily broken as he had been free to make them; and about six years afterwards, in 1256, the nation being visited by a dreadful famine, in consequence of a wet harvest, wheat, according to the *Chronicon Preciosum*, having risen to 24*s.* per quarter, the City of London was so drained of money by the continual demands of the King, in addition to those of the Pope, that many of the *eminent* citizens found great difficulty in procuring provisions for their families, and the poorer classes were constrained to devour dogs and carrion, and even the wash given to swine. The spirit and energy of the Londoners, however, remained unsubdued, and though, through the prodigality of the Court, the riches of the country were materially exhausted, yet the little wealth still remaining in the kingdom was deposited in the coffers of the metropolitan merchants. The King, therefore, when his necessities became so urgent that he was compelled to pawn the Crown jewels, was forced to have recourse to the citizens for the loan. Enraged that they should still possess the means of raising the sum required, and that they should accept a pledge which it was ignominious in him to offer, he passionately exclaimed, "Were the treasures of Augustus Cæsar exposed to sale, the City would buy them. These fellows, who call themselves Barons, are wallowing in wealth and every species of luxury, whilst we labour under the want of common necessaries." But in honest candour it must be acknowledged, that when the citizens had to negotiate with princes, who were not embarrassed through their ***personal prodigality and folly***, but impoverished by enterprises undertaken for the national fame or aggrandisement, they required not securities and pledges to administer most liberally to the State exigencies. The assertions may be illustrated by the gift of the citizens of 20,000 marks to the hero of Cressy to prosecute his valiant warfare in France, and the celebrated ***Whittington***, who at an entertainment given at Guildhall to Henry V. as conqueror at Agincourt, cast into a fire of spices bonds which he held from that monarch for loans of money to the amount of 60,000*l.* Yet we are prone to confess, that though liberality at times conspicuously distinguished the civic character, yet generally it may be perceived that there was much reserve on the part of the citizens in all their pecuniary transactions with the Court; and even until the reign of Elizabeth, the British Sovereigns were wont to have recourse to foreign merchants, chiefly those in Flanders, in order to raise the sums of money required by way of loan; and though the London merchants often became security, as the money in few instances would have been otherwise granted, yet they were never induced except in the case of the Crown jewels previously mentioned, to advance the cash themselves, a line of conduct suggested by common worldly policy and mercantile forethought, especially after the experience, so dearly obtained, that grants and charters were no safeguard to property against the arbitrary will of the Sovereign; and that the King might deny to his own subjects the justice which he would be fearful of refusing to those of a foreign State. The first important loan effected in England, wholly on the personal security of the Sovereign, was negotiated by Sir Thomas Gresham for Queen Elizabeth, a fact which may be assumed as a certain index that the administration of public affairs approximated nearer a system of order and equity than England had known since the reign of our British *Lycurgus*, Alfred. The maiden Queen paid regularly the interest of the loan, and eventually the principal, exemplifying the precept, which in earlier ages as at present would have held its maxim, that it is only required to keep in view the straightforward and simple rules dictated by honesty in order to insure, throughout the kingdom, assistance to meet the pressing emergencies of the public service.

An ostentatious show of opulence, and an overweening rivalry in the sumptuousness aud costliness of their living, seem from the earliest data to have characterized the London merchants; a display, not confined, which would perhaps have been more creditable, to the reception either of their Sovereigns, foreign potentates, or ambassadors, and other illustrious foreigners, but exhibited at their own corporation feasts. In 1363, *Henry Picard*, who had previously served the office of Mayor, gave a splendid entertainment at his house in

Cheapside to *King Edward III.*, *King John of France*, *King David of Scotland*, and the *King of Cyprus*. After these illustrious guests had departed, the worthy host kept his hall open for all comers that were willing to play at *dice* and *hazard*, and in like manner the lady Margaret, his wife, kept her chamber to the same intent, showing that the vicious habits of gambling were participated in by *both sexes* even in these early days. *Eels*, most lusciously dressed, before *turtle* was introduced, appear to have been the *acme* of *Corporation goût*, and considered the "one thing needful" to complete the gourmanic list of civic epicurism. At length, the extravagance of feasting became so intolerable, that the citizens, in 1554, were induced to pass a by-law to restrain this *prevailing passion;* "so huge and great," says this curious document, "had become the charges of the mayoralty and shrievalty, that almost all good citizens flee and refuse to serve in this honourable city, only because of the great excess and chargeable fare and diet used in the time of the said offices;" to remedy which it was ordered, that no mayor, sheriff, alderman, or commoner, should have at dinner or supper more courses than one, and not more dishes at one course than *six*, whether hot or cold; but as a special mark of *delicate sympathy* for the privation thus imposed, it is declared, that one or two of the same six dishes may come to the board hot, if they will, after the first *three* or *five* are served; and by way of *bonus*, that neither brawn, nor collops with eggs, nor sallads, pottage, butter, cheese, eggs, herrings, sprats, shrimps, nor any shell-fish, nor any kind of unbaked fruit, are to be accounted for as any of the said list of diminished fare! The only exception made to these "short commons" was "at their necessary meetings," when full indulgence to the appetite was permitted.

DU[illegible]E [illegible]

Notwithstanding the various oppressive measures adopted by Henry III. towards the citizens, he was unable to check the improvement of the city, which emanated from sources more pure and permanent than those of courtly favour. In 1218, the forest of Middlesex was disforested, and the citizens availed themselves of the opportunity of purchasing lands and erecting houses, which was the means of considerably enlarging the suburbs. Commerce, however, though it continued to advance its numerous connexions, progressed slowly, owing to the constant irritation and distraction of the merchants from business through the factious conduct of the Court. It appears that ***Queenhithe*** was the principal port of the city, and ***Belin's-gate*** only of secondary importance; for we find that Henry III., in 1225, commanded the constables of the Tower to arrest the ships of the Cinque Ports, and compel them to bring their corn to no other place than ***Queen's Hithe***, and afterwards ordered all fish to be destrained if offered for sale in any other place; all commodities paying certain tolls, chiefly in kind. The impediment, however, which London Bridge presented to the unrestricted progress of vessels coming from sea, ultimately forced the trade to Belin's-gate, or Billingsgate, though Queenhithe, as late as the reign of Edward IV., struggled to maintain its ancient pre-eminence. In 1264, the city purchased from Richard, Earl of Cromwell, brother to Henry, the fee-farm of Queenhithe, with all its rights, customs, and privileges, and in 1268, we have an interesting historical account, the earliest cited, of the customs and tolls received at the port of London, which manifests the superiority of Queen's Hithe.

Among the items are the following:—

	£.	s.	d.
Amount of customs on foreign merchandize for six months	75	6	10
Metage of corn and customs at Belin's-gate	5	18	7
Customs of fish brought to London Bridge-street	7	0	2
Amount of the produce of Queen's Hithe	17	9	2
Stallage dues from the markets of *West-Cheap*, *Grass-Chirche*, *Wool-Chirche-hawe* with the annual scotage of the butchers of London	42	0	0
Amount of tonnages at the King's Weigh House and petty standages	97	13	11
Other sundry dues	119	4	6
	£364	13	2

Making an *annual* average of 729*l.* 6*s.* 4*d.* paid to the Crown from the port of London for customs, tolls, &c. Two years previous to this revenue account, in the year 1266, Henry granted to the Hanseatic merchants the extensive immunities which they enjoyed for three hundred years, and enabled them to realize considerable fortunes. *Werdenhangen*, the historian of the Hans Towns,* states that the Hanseatic ships, on their

* The whole confederacy constituting the German or Hanseatic League was very extensive. The *Easterlings* were the most celebrated branch, and settled in London. The societies abroad were divided into four classes, each having a presiding city, and the grand separations were into east and west. The first had *Cologne* for its capital; the other branches were formed by the union of Lubeck, Wismar, Rostock, Stralsund, Griefswald, Anclam, Stettin, Colberg, Stolpe, Danzig, Elbing, and Königsberg. The term *Hanse*, or *Hansa*, is synonymous with *Gild*, and was so usually understood in the twelfth and thirteenth centuries. King John, in his charter to *Dunwich*, says, "We grant them a *Hanse*," and Henry III. uses the expression,

return from assisting Henry in a successful enterprise against France, were almost all lost in a tempest, whereupon the Hanseatics demanded their value; but they agreed to remit the debt on condition of the King granting, for himself and successors, free liberty to the ***Easterlings*** to ***import*** and ***export*** all merchandize whatever, at no higher duty or custom than one per cent., which was the rate then paid. The merchants also of Lubeck obtained a grant of commercial privileges on the same terms; and we learn from Gerard Malynes, that a society of Englishmen had existed previous to this period, under the name of the "Merchants of Staple," as they exported the staple-wares of the kingdom, comprising the rough materials for manufacture, as ***wool***, ***skins***, ***lead***, and ***tin***; the fabric of woollen cloths and importation of Spanish wool being of more ancient date. From these sources of export alone, England long supplied all its foreign wants, and brought home annually a considerable balance of bullion.

So strong ran the tide of party feeling at this era, and to so great an extent had the influence of the gilds arrived, that in 1226 a dispute having arisen between the ***Goldsmiths*** and ***Tailors***, each Company, with their friends, met on an appointed night, to the number of five hundred, completely armed, and proceeded to decide the difference by force of arms. Many were killed and wounded, nor could the combatants be parted till the sheriff and civil authorities came and apprehended the ringleaders, thirteen of whom were condemned and executed. The various tumults and revolts, which either the direct injustice and tyranny of Henry excited, or the refractory spirit to which they gave birth, rendered, at times, the streets at night unsafe for the peaceable inhabitants; and

"Quod habeant Hansam suam." The citizens of Cologne paid Henry III thirty marks to have seizin of their Guildhall in London, terme "Gilhaudi Teutonicorum."

their houses were not unfrequently plundered by parties assuming the garb of the patroles employed for the public safety, which instigated the citizens to establish an organized body of men called the "city watch," whose first appointment took place about the year 1262.

In 1272, wine gaugers were appointed in London and other principal seaports, and in the metropolis the new gauge duty amounted to 15*l.* 16*s.* 7*d.*, which at 1*d.* per *dolium*, or ton, makes the quantity imported amount to 3,799 tons; indeed the chief article of import at this date seems to have been wine, principally from France and the Rhine, as scarcely any mention is made of entries from Spain, Portugal, or Italy.

The increased population and encroachment of buildings on the springs and rivulets near the city, created a great want of pure and wholesome water. Previous to this period, the western parts of the city and adjacent villages had been supplied from the River of *Wells*, or *Fleet* River, which was formed by the influx of several springs, whose course became impeded by the erection of different mills by the Knights of St. John, the stream afterwards assuming the name of *Turnmill Brook*, passing where Turnmill-street, Holborn, now stands; *Olbourne* was a rivulet rising near Middle-row, and flowed into the Fleet at Holborn Bridge; the eastern parts of the city were watered by the Wallbrook rivulet, which united with the Thames near Dowgate, but being choked up by the numerous bridges and erections on it, dwindled into a common sewer; *Langbourne* rivulet, which took its rise near the east end of Fenchurch-street, ran with a swift current due west, and then turning south, divided into several rills or *shares*, and was called *Southbourne*-lane, or *Sharebourne*-lane, *share* being the old English for *divided stream*, and was afterwards united with Wallbrook. Besides these, there was *Holywell*, rendered *sacred* for the miraculous virtue of its water, now

C. Marshall W. Henshall

filled up with soil, and called Holywell-lane, Shoreditch, Clerkenwell, Skinner's Well, and, more eastward towards the Charter-house, Fogg's Well, Tod's Well, Loder's Well, and Shadwell, which, with another in Smithfield called the *Horse-pool*, all united their streams in forming the river of Wells before mentioned. Without Cripplegate was a large pool, supplied from Crowder's Well, adjoining the north-west side of St. Giles's Churchyard, and at times contained so great depth of water, that people have been drowned who accidentally fell in. In order, therefore, to furnish the inhabitants with a more plentiful supply of water, the corporation of the city obtained a grant from *Gilbert de Sandford*, lord of the manor of Tyebourne, then a village "at a considerable distance," of certain springs in the vicinity of St. Mary-bourne, from whence water was to be conducted into the city in leaden pipes, of six inches in diameter, and was the first attempt of thus conveying water for the use of the inhabitants. The water was distributed into various large reservoirs or cisterns, composed of lead cased with stone, the most capacious of which was erected in an open field, called "*Crown-field*, in West Cheap, so denominated from the "Crown Inn," at that time situated at the east end of this open space, and which is now occupied with the populous and opulent street, *Cheapside*. At the time we are now describing, the middle of the thirteenth century, the principal dwellings in the city ran nearer the Thames, and more to the eastward, the houses being still, for the most part, thatched, and which, in 1246, required a renewal of the ordinance, that all buildings should be covered with tiles and slates, instead of straw, more especially those which stood contiguous to the few principal streets. Even the introduction of the comfort of having a free egress for the smoke by chimneys, was of only partial adoption until the middle of the thirteenth and fourteenth centuries, the citizens being wont to have their wood-fires lighted on the hearth in the middle of the room, the smoke making its escape by the door or window, whichever chance might permit; indeed, before the days of Richard I., chimneys were hardly known in London, and then only existed in the halls of the principal nobility, and in religious houses. While this method of preventing the inmates from being *choked* or *smoke-dried* was considered a vast advancement in the art of civilization and indication of increasing *luxury*, it was left to nearly the close of the year 1700 before all the disagreeable effects of smoky rooms were dispelled by the *Rumford* stove; and we are now advancing towards the middle of the nineteenth century, anticipating the *luxury* and *comfort* of entirely dispensing with chimneys and their draughts, by either having our houses heated by gas, warm air, water, steam, or of superseding their utility by stoves which *consume their own smoke*, or by means of a still more modern invention, of introducing a simple iron vase of classic form into our apartments which generates its heat without coal, feeds on its own cumbustion, ignites nothing extraneous, and is transportable at pleasure from the carriage to the drawing-room.

Reverting from this momentary digression to our original subject of supplying water to the metropolis, it was found that these conduits involving considerable labour and expense, the foreign merchants were called upon to contribute towards the charge, and were accordingly assessed in the sum of 100*l.*; but in consideration of which, and in addition to the payment of forty marks annually, they acquired in return the privilege of *landing*, housing and selling *wood*, and other *bulky commodities*, which before they had been compelled to vend *ex ship*. It was also customary for the Lord Mayor, Aldermen, and principal citizens, to repair on horseback on the 18th of every September, to examine the springs from

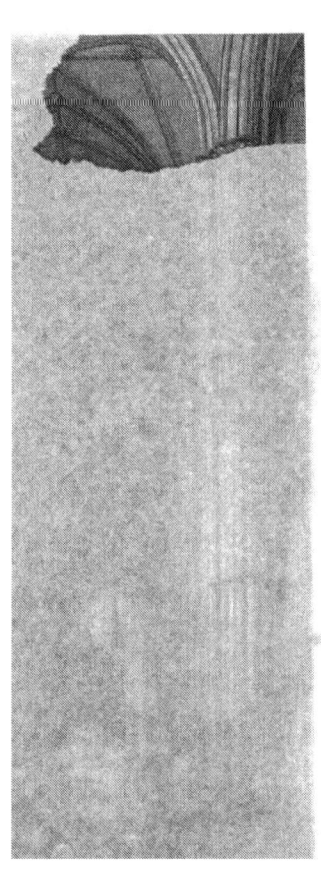

wont to have t[illegible]
middie of the roon[illegible]
or window, whiche[illegible]
the days of Rich[illegible]
[illegible]don, and [illegible]

Drawn by J. Salmon from a Sketch by R. Garland. Engraved by Wood.

whence the conduits were supplied, and "to hunt a hare in the morning, and a fox after dinner, in the fields adjacent to the town of Tyebourne." Ultimately, the numerous conduits which received water from Hackney, Hampstead, Hoxton, Red Lion Fields, &c., became disused, owing to the successful efforts of Peter Morice, in the reign of Elizabeth, in raising water from the Thames, as before alluded to; in addition to the Herculean attempt of Sir Hugh Middleton, in 1608, of bringing water by artificial ducts from a spring at Amwell, between Hertford and Ware, assisted by a branch of the River Lea, to the north side of London, near Islington, where reservoirs were constructed to receive the "maiden stream." The channel of this "*New River*" was narrow, and from the inequality of the ground varied considerably in depth, which in parts was upwards of thirty feet; it formed a winding course of about forty miles, and was crossed by eighty bridges, the whole undertaking being completed in five years. As the magnitude of the metropolis has so prodigiously enlarged, the facilities for furnishing the inhabitants called forth fresh energies, and there are now eight *Water Companies* established, as detailed in the annexed table. Well-founded complaints are, however, made as to the *quality* of the water, which is no doubt capable of considerable improvement, more particularly the supplies derived from the River Thames, which, being the grand reservoir of all the common sewers and filth of London and Westminster, cannot be the purest source for obtaining a wholesome cleanly beverage, which forms so essential a portion of one of the chief necessaries of life, and which ought to be regulated and guarded by such restrictions as would ensure these requisites; and though Committees of the House of Commons have, within these few sessions, reported to this effect, no steps have been taken to ensure the execution of the Parliamentary recommendations.

SUPPLIES OF WATER TO THE METROPOLIS.

Names of Companies.	Number of houses and buildings supplied.	Average rates per house or building.		Total quantity supplied yearly.	Average daily supply per house or building.	Highest elevation to which water is raised.
		s.	d.	Hhds.	Galls.	Feet.
New River . .	73,212	26	6	114,650,000	241	145
Chelsea . . .	13,891	33	3	15,753,000	168	135
Grand Junction .	11,140	48	6	21,702,567	350	151¾
West Middlesex.	16,000	56	10	20,000,000	185	188
East London. .	46,421	22	6	37,810,594	120¼	107
South London .	12,046	15	0	6,979,031	100	80
Lambeth . . .	16,682	17	0	11,998,600	124	185
Southwark . .	7,100	21	3	7,000,000	156	60
	196,492	30	1½	235,893,792	180½	—

There are numerous wells which lend their assistance in supplying a more pure beverage, and the water derived from this source is healthy and palatable. Several wells in London are between 200 and 300 feet deep, and on rising grounds the thickness of the stratum is much greater. At Primrose Hill the ground was bored to the depth of 500 feet without success, and at Lord Spencer's, at Wimbledon, a well was sunk 530 feet. One mile east of the City, the "London clay" is estimated only 77 feet thick; while at a well in St. James's-street it is 235 feet, and at High Beach 700 feet.

Before closing the *memorabilia* of Henry's reign, we must not omit allusion to the origin of a trifling circumstance, the remembrance of which has been transmitted to our own times at the annual ceremony of swearing in the Sheriffs before the Cursitor Barons of the Exchequer, when six horse-shoes, with their nails, are tendered as a quit-rent, the custom having arisen from the possession of a piece of ground in the Strand, within the parish of St. Clement Danes, by

Walter Le Bruin, a farrier, who, in 1235, purchased the same of the Crown for the construction of a forge, on condition of making payment of the said shoes and nails. Though the forge no longer exists, yet the acknowledgment continues to be made, the ground being claimed by the city by a subsequent conveyance.

The reign of Edward I. dawned more auspiciously on the interests of the citizens, and being favoured with the consideration of their Sovereign, they experienced the gratifying contrast of his more equitable government, compared with the oppression they had submitted to under the lengthened dominion of his father. On Edward's immediate return to England as King, his conciliatory interposition was called into requisition by the internal dissension of the citizens on the election of their Mayor; and so uncompromising was each party, that it was found necessary to appoint a *custos* of the city; until the excitement of the moment subsiding, the citizens on cool reflection became convinced of the danger to which intestine broils would have subjected their liberties under the rule of a sovereign less inclined to moderation than Edward; they therefore chose their Mayor at full *Folkmote*,* and arranged their differences. As a special mark of royal favour, the King, in the third year of his reign, employed the Mayor, *Gregory de Rokeslie*, to execute a foreign mission of some considerable importance, in preference to many dignitaries in Church and State, who solicited the appointment. The King's attention was next occupied in ordering the Mayor and Sheriffs to enforce the laws in protecting the public against the frauds and impositions of the venders of provisions, and

* A Folkmote was an assemblage of the whole of the commonalty in St. Paul's Churchyard, to which they were summoned by a great bell in a tower at the east end of the church, and this meeting was deemed the supreme meeting of the city.

the iniquitous practices of engrossing and forestalling, a system ever prejudicial to the fair trader. The bakers and millers seem more particularly to have shared the public odium, two branches of business which we ever find, in ancient and modern history, singled out as objects of popular resentment. Millers were restricted to the rate of one halfpenny for grinding each quarter of corn; and if convicted of extortion or giving short measure, to be punished by being drawn through certain streets in a dung cart, exposed to the derision of the passengers; the baker, for selling short weight, was, on the third offence, to be put in the pillory, the first and second being punished by forfeiture of his bread and imprisonment. Poulterers and fishmongers were also placed under the civic control, prices being affixed to their different commodities, by which we find that, in 1277, a best hen was valued at 3½*d.*; a goose, 3*d.* to 5*d.*; partridge, 3½d.; pheasant, 4d.; two woodcocks, 1½*d.*; swan, 3*s.*; peacock, 1*d.*; best rabbit, with skin, 4*d.*, and 3*d.* without skin; hare, 3½*d.*; lamb, 4*d.* to 6*d.*; best fresh salmon, 3*s.* to 5*s.*; turbot, 8*d.*; lampreys, per 100, 6*d.* to 8*d.*; eels, per 25, 2*d.*; smelts, per 100, 1*d.*, &c. It was also ordered, that no market should be held on London Bridge, or elsewhere, "except as should be appointed by the city authorities; and that no person should go into Southwark to buy cattle, or any wares to be brought into the city, on penalty of forfeiture of the thing purchased." Towards the close of Edward's reign, and commencement of the fourteenth century, provisions were again regulated in price; poultry and game had sustained little variation; lambs, however, from Christmas to Shrovetide, had risen in value to 1*s.* 4*d.*; a quarter of wheat was worth 4*s.*; ditto of ground malt, 3*s.* 4*d.*; ditto of peas, 2*s.* 6*d.*; ditto of oats, 2*s.*; a bull, 7*s.* 6*d.*; a cow, 6*s.*; a fat *mutton*, 1*s.*; a ewe sheep, 8*d.*; and while recording the cost price of the necessaries of life, we may allude to the scale of salaries of some of the chief officers of State, as demonstrative of the low range of emoluments of that period compared with the present. The Chief Justice of the King's Bench received 50 marks, and of the Common Pleas, 100 marks; Chief Baron, 100*l.*; and each of the other judges of the three benches 20*l.*; the Chancellor of the Exchequer 40*l.* ***Exactions of fees*** and ***gratuities*** no doubt formed a considerable additional item of the incomes, but the absolute amount of expenditure required to support the dignity of their office was but small, if we take a general estimate of the necessaries of ordinary living; for it appears that, in 1307, when the Archbishop of St. Andrew's, Scotland, was a prisoner at Winchester, that he was allowed 1*s.* per day, for the maintenance of himself and servants, divided in the following proportions:—for the Archbishop's own daily expence, 6*d.*; one man-servant to attend him, 3*d.*; one boy ditto, 1½*d.*; a chaplain to say daily mass to him, 1½*d.*: and the Queen of Robert Bruce who was a prisoner in England, in 1314, was allowed only 20*s.* per week for herself and household.

From the year 1283, London, as well as other principal cities and towns in England, have to date the origin of that noble system of legislative representation which was mainly instrumental in inflicting a mortal blow at the feudal tenures, liberating the people from local oppression and thraldom, and imparting freedom and security to commerce; and though through successive reigns only slow and partial improvements and advancements were made towards the liberty of the franchise of the subject, in the selection of members most eligible to represent the particular interests of the divisional portions of the kingdom; yet ***reform did*** succeed ***reform,*** until the glorious measure of "***Parliamentary Reform***" was partially consummated by the Bill of 1832, and which, according to the growing popular feeling, only awaits the climax of the "vote by ballot," shortening the "duration of Parliaments," and "extending the right of suffrage," to make the present law attain a temporary degree of *perfection*. It is proved by Rymer, in his "Fœdera," that, in 1283, Edward summoned to his Parliament at Shrewsbury two knights for each county, and two representatives for the twenty-one principal cities and towns in England, including LONDON, being the first instance in which writs were issued by the Crown to cities and towns; but no regularity appears to have been preserved in the sending these writs for 300 years after this time; many places being occasionally omitted at some elections and sent to at subsequent ones, while others were added without the direction of the King or his Council, but according to Dr. Brady, at the discretion of the Sheriffs.

During the remainder of the sovereignty of Edward, and succeeding reign of Edward II., a striking instance is afforded that in proportion as feudalism declined, commerce was extended, by the number of charters of privileges granted to foreign merchants; besides that, the increased use of gold and silver among the citizens was strongly indicative of their growing opulence and splendour of living; and which, as early as the twenty-eighth year of the reign of Edward I., instigated the passing of an Act of Parliament, ordering all vessels of gold and silver to be assayed by the Company of Goldsmiths of London.

In 1304 we meet with the first recurrence to the office of *Recorder* of London, when *Geoffrey de Hartilepole* was invested with the appointment, and allowed to wear his gown as an alderman. The succeeding year is stigmatized in the annals of the country by the perpetration of one of those State crimes which nations sanction under the disgraceful palliative of political expediency. Happy would it have been for England's fame "if the recording angel could have dropped a tear upon the deed, and blotted it out for ever;" but that stain of blood made too indelible an impression ever to be effaced. It was in 1305 that the hero and patriot, Sir WILLIAM WALLACE, was taken prisoner in nobly defending his country's rights, and, contrary to the law of nations, hanged and quartered in Smithfield, and his head affixed on a pole on London Bridge.

In 1306, an ordinance was issued for the prohibition of burning coal, which was occasioned by a complaint made by the nobility and gentry to the King, alleging that the air was infected with a noisome smell, and a thick cloud from the coals used in the suburbs by brewers, dyers, and other manufacturers requiring large fires, to the great endangering the health of the inhabitants. Upon which representation his Majesty issued his proclamation, forbidding coals to be burnt in London and suburbs under severe penalties, and in the early days of the celebrated *Whittington*, the use of coal was still considered so great a public nuisance, that the burning of it was made a capital offence, and in Sir Everard Home's "Dissertations," it is cited from a record in the Tower, that a person was once actually executed for infringing the law. It is, however, remarkable that, in 1419, when Whittington had been "thrice Lord Mayor of London town," though during the intermediate period, no repeal of this rigorous statute appears to have occurred, yet the import of coal formed a considerable branch of the commerce of the Thames. As early as 1421, it was a trade of great importance, and a duty of 2*d.* per chaldron had been imposed upon it for some time. The only reasonable mode of accounting for the trade making so extensive progress, when such severe penal enactments were unrepealed, is by assuming that the Crown so far abrogated the statute by exercising a dispensing power, by no means unusual with the court practices of those days, of granting to some favoured individual a license to make his fortune by violating the laws; and many circumstances combine in inducing the supposition, that Sir Richard Whittington was the party on whom this privilege had been conferred; a presumption which, if correct, will readily elucidate part of the traditionary history of Whittington having made his fortune "by a king;" as he was in business at the commencement of the trade, through it realized his property, and from the first opening of the coal trade in England, and for centuries afterwards, it had the reputation of making fortunes, only exceeded by the mines of Golconda and Peru. As to the "cat," we must have recourse to the ingenius suggestion of *Foote*, who, in his comedy of the "Nabob," makes "*Sir Matthew Mite*" offer to the Society of Antiquarians a solution of the popular legend. "The commerce," says Sir Matthew, "which this worthy merchant carried on was chiefly confined to our coasts; for this purpose he constructed a vessel, which, from its agility and lightness, he aptly christened a 'cat.' Nay, to this day, gentlemen, all our coals from Newcastle are imported in nothing but *cats*; from hence it appears, that it was not the whiskered, four-footed mouse-killing *cat*, but the coasting, sailing, coal-carrying *Cat*,—that, gentlemen, was Whittington's *Cat*." If to these chances Sir Richard owed his prosperity, it had only to become a by-word, that by a "cat and a king" he had made his fortune, and popular invention would soon supply all the other features of the legend.

We have reserved until now more particular allusion to an event, which occurred during the first Edward's reign, the division of the city into *twenty-four* WARDS, of which we have the first historical record in 1285. Some few of the wards at this time were hereditary, but the others elected an

Alderman, who presided at the judicial council of the city. The deliberations, however, of the Aldermen, in all public concerns, were mainly influenced by the advice of the more immediate delegates of the citizens, the *Council-men*, a body of members who consisted of forty-four, selected, at first, from certain *Gilds*, *Mysteries*, or *Crafts*; thus the Mayor, Aldermen, and Councilmen, acted for the city in the capacity of the King, Lords, and Commons. The number of common-councilmen proved too limited to represent the numerous and divided interests of the citizens, and neglecting the trust confided in them, acted more as a "packed jury," seeking to secure to themselves individual advancement, rather than acting as the guardians of the citizens, for whose special protection they were appointed. Petitions were therefore presented to the Mayor, in 1384, in the seventh year of Richard II., praying the number to be augmented, as "divers things were passed more by clamour than reason." It was in consequence determined by the authorities, that each Alderman should cause to be chosen by the citizens *four* Common-Councilmen for each ward; this privilege, in the ninth year of the same reign, was further increased, the wards, according to their extent, choosing from *four* to *eight* members, and which varied in progress of time, as the limits of the city were enlarged from *six* to *twelve*; at present the numbers range from *four* to *seventeen*, comprising a total of 240 Common-Councilmen, including the different deputies of each ward, forty Common-Councilmen forming a Court. It was not, however, till the reign of Edward II., that we discover, as observed by Mr. Norton,* the first authentic mention of the mercantile nature of the civic constitution of London, and of the mercantile qualification requisite in the candidates for admission to the freedom of the city. By one of a number of

* Commentaries on London.

articles of regulation, ordained by the citizens for their internal government, which articles were confirmed by Edward II., and incorporated into a charter, it was provided that no person, whether an inhabitant of the city or otherwise, should be admitted into the civic freedom unless he was a member of one of the *Gilds*, or unless with the full consent of the whole community convened; only that apprentices might still be admitted according to the established regulations. Before this period, no mention occurs of any mercantile qualification to entitle the householder to his admission to the corporation.

The Saxon appellation of ***Ealderman***, ***Alderman***, or ***Elderman***, is synonymous with the Latin designation of ***Senex***, whence is derived ***Senators***. The epithet, among our early progenitors, was one of high distinction, and corresponding with that of ***Earl***. Madox states, that "Alderman was a name for a chief governor of a secular gild, and in time it became also a name for a chief officer in a gildated town or borough," and quotes, in illustration, the circumstance of the prior of Holy Trinity, Aldgate, becoming an Alderman of London, in consequence of the grant to that priory of the "English Knighten Gild," and to which Stow assigns the origin of Portsoken Ward.* In the seventeenth of Richard II., 1394, it was enacted by Parliament, that the Aldermen of

* There is no trace when the name of Alderman was first applied to the president of the London wards or gilds; the probability is, it was introduced after the Conquest. The denomination was common in the Saxon times to various judicial dignities and offices, but there is no record of it as applied to the heads of *particular districts* in London during that period; and there is reason to believe that the appellation was not used in that sense until the reign of Henry II., when they are first mentioned as presiding over gilds, some of which were *territorial*, and others *mercantile*. In the reign of Henry III., *Aldermanries* had become a common term for a civic district comprised within a leet jurisdiction, as well in London as in other cities.

of the city should not from thenceforth be elected annually but continue in their several offices during life or good behaviour; and amongst the qualifications enumerated in earlier days to render the candidate eligible to the dignity, he was to be of ***comely person, wise, grave, wealthy, faithful,*** and ***generous;*** not of ***mean and servile condition,*** so as to disparage the place and state of the city.

The term ***Ward*** is also of Saxon derivation, denoting a ***district,*** which has given rise to the opinion, that certain ***portions*** or ***quarters*** of London, like other cities and towns, were originally held of the Saxon monarchs and noblemen in ***demesne,*** to whom they appertained as so many ***sokes*** or ***liberties;*** and corroborative of this supposition, we read in "*Liber Albus,*" that the earlier designations of certain wards emanated from the name of the proprietors or their residences, as ***Castle Baynard, Farringdon,*** and ***Basinghall.*** We have before observed that some ***wards*** were hereditary, while others were transferable, the purchaser becoming ***ex-officio*** an ***Alderman*** No vestige remains by which we can ascertain in what manner the original subdivision of the city was apportioned; but in the year 1393, the Ward of Farringdon having greatly increased, was separated and distinguished as Farringdon within the walls, and Farringdon without, making the total number of wards twenty-five; and in 1550, the citizens, having purchased of Edward VI. the borough of Southwark, it was constituted the twenty-sixth ward; but the power granted them by charter not proving sufficiently authoritative to entitle them to exclude the jurisdiction of the magistrates of the county of Surrey, and their partial interference in its government, it was considered merely a ***nominal*** ward; serving to dignify the senior Alderman, called "the Father of the City," who generally, by his age, is rendered unable to sustain the fatigue of ward business, and the situation therefore, reckoned an honourable sinecure.

The original names of the wards were as follow; to which we have affixed the amounts raised by an assessment made in 1339 by Edward III., in order to carry on his expensive wars for the conquest of France, which, being the first general assessment of the city recorded, shows the proportion the several wards were charged with, and those which were then esteemed the most opulent:—

Ward	£.	s.	d.
1. Ward Fori, or Foris . .	114	13	4
2. Lodgate and Newgate .	730	16	8
3. Castle Baynard	63	6	8
4. Aldersgate .	57	10	0
5. Bred Strete .	461	16	8
6. Queenhythe .	435	13	4
7. Vintry . .	634	16	8
8. Dougate .	660	10	0
9. Wallbroke .	911	0	0
10. Coleman Strete .	1,051	16	8
11 Bassishaw .	79	13	4
12. Cripplegate .	462	10	0
13. Candlewye Strete. .	133	6	8
14. Langeford .	352	6	8
15. Cordewan Strete. .	2,195	3	4
16. Cornhill .	315	0	0
17. Lime Strete .	110	0	0
18. Bishopsgate .	559	6	8
19. Aldgate. .	30	0	0
20. Tower Ward.	365	0	0
21. Billingsgate .	763	0	0
22. Bridge Ward	765	6	8
23. Lodingeber .	1,105	10	0
24. Portsoky .	27	10	0

Deeming the most eligible plan for communication an accurate but succinct account of the various public buildings and different objects of interest throughout the city, will be to describe them in detailing the origin and description of the separate wards, we purpose now pursuing the general history of the commerce and government of London, and in conclusion reverting to the wards from the period of their earliest authentic formation

We find, with few exceptions, that the internal condition of the city generally exhibited the character and disposition of the reigning sovereigns; the charters proving ineffectual in protecting the citizens from tallage, subsidies, or gifts, either to promote the political schemes, or alleviate the pressing emergencies of the crown, the civic character may be said, in great measure, to have fluctuated with the habits and humours of the Court; the dwelling of many of the nobility within the precincts of the city, vested the aristocracy with a certain degree of influence, and the possession of the Tower, as a regal fort and residence, created a constant and close connexion between the principal grades of society. The distracted reign, therefore, of Edward II. was little conducive to the peaceable government and disposition of the Londoners. The justice of the civic authorities seems to have been tainted by the vitiated example of the nobles, for we find them assuming an arbitrary jurisdiction over the commonalty; the Mayor and Aldermen retaining their authority during pleasure, and if they resigned, it was only for a limited space, and in favour of individuals of their own appointment; they levied taxes on the inhabitants, and disposed of the revenue as suited their purpose; taking upon themselves the expulsion of those Councilmen who stood forward in honest rectitude to protect the interests of their constituents. This tyrannical conduct led to remonstrances, cabals, and invectives, and from 1311 to 1322 the citizens existed in a perpetual state of excitement, until the King, under the specious pretext of arranging amicably the differences, took the government of the city into his own hands from which it was only redeemed on payment of 2,000*l.*; thus again evincing the uncertain tenure of the *city's rights*.

The prodigal favours and riches lavished on the two *Spencers** by Edward, alienated entirely the wavering affections of Queen Isabella, who siding with the discontented Barons, led to the rebellion, in which the Londoners ultimately joined, espousing openly the cause of the Queen, and assisting, with forces and money, to liberate the kingdom from the thraldom of favouritism, and to establish Edward III. on the throne of his deposed father.

In addition to the political commotions impeding the regular progress of commercial transactions during Edward the Second's sovereignty, provisions had advanced to so

* The Spencers, father and son, were banished at the dictation of the Barons, but soon restored to favour by the King; and as instancing the wealth the father had amassed, it is curious to note the principal items set forth in his petition to Edward against the Barons, praying indemnity for his losses, exemplifying, at the same time, the dangerous extent to which the favouritism of the Monarch might be carried in those days, and the monopolizing influence which became vested in the hands of a designing and insidious courtier, to the detriment of the public service. This misapplication of the revenue, and perverted channels into which the public money, set apart for benificent purposes, has been, from time to time, directed by the Crown and its ministers, gradually conduced in exciting the popular clamour against the *Pension List*, and has tardily induced the Government of the day to investigate the merits and claims of the individuals enjoying the Royal bounty. The elder Spencer's real estate consisted of sixty-three manors; his personals of two crops of corn, one on the ground, the other in granary; in cash, jewels, silver, and golden utensils, 10,000*l.*; armour for 200 men, warlike engines, and his houses, 30,000*l.*; the furnitures of his chapel and wardrobe, 5,000*l.*; 28,000 sheep, 1,000 oxen and horses, 1,200 cows, with their calves for two years; 40 mares, with their foals for two years; 560 cart-horses, 2,000 hogs. 400 kids, 40 tuns of wine, 600 barons, 80 carcases of beef, 600 muttons in larder, 10 tuns of cyder, and 36 sacks of wool, with a library of books.

Drawn by J. Salmon from a Sketch by R. Garland — Engraved by J. Woods

ST KATHERINES HOSPITAL
REGENTS PARK

exorbitant a height, that the Government erroneously deemed itself bound again to interfere between buyer and seller, and place a restriction on the maximum range of prices. Thus an ox, grass-fed, was not to be sold for more than 16*s*., and if grain-fed, 24*s*.; a "best cow," 12*s*.; best shorn mutton, 1*s*. 4*d*., &c. We are at the same time enabled to form an accurate estimate of the relative value between the exchangeable medium, ***silver***, and other commodities, by an account handed down of the domestic disbursements of the Earl of Lancaster for the year 1313. It would appear that the total expenditure of this nobleman's household amounted to 7,309*l*., it being specially notified, in reference to the purchase of different silver articles, that ***silver*** was then worth 1*s*. 8*d*. per ounce, ***making twelve ounces of silver equivalent to a pound sterling***. As illustrative also of the low price of the luxuries of life, one item sets forth 369 pipes of red wine, and two of white costing only 104*l*. 17*s*. 6*d*. The impolicy, however, of thus fixing an arbitrary price on the principal commodities of existence, instead of allowing the natural operation of ***supply*** and ***demand*** to regulate their marketable value, became so apparent by holders refraining from sending their articles for sale, that the order was soon rescinded. In the year 1316, the high price of wheat was mainly attributed to the quantity used for malt in London; and a Parliamentary edict was issued, prohibiting the use of wheat for this purpose, and also regulating the price of ale, the strongest malt liquor being sold at ***three halfpence per gallon***, and the small ***one penny***. Corn, however, continued to advance till it reached the starvation point of 53*s*. 1*d*. per quarter, and, according to some authorities, even 80*s*.; the greatest famine visiting the land that had ever been experienced; "parents eat their own children or those of others they could come at, as did the malefactors one another in prison; and here followed so terrible a mortality that the living scarce sufficed to bury the dead.* The country, however, the succeeding year, being blessed with an abundant and early harvest, wheat sustained a rapid decline, and sold at 10*d.* instead of 10s. per bushel, a reduction in the value almost incredible, except we consider the diminished ratio of consumption from the effects of the previous mortality. In 1318, the Parliament being summoned to assemble at York, the King's writ was issued to the Sheriffs of London to elect *two* members to represent their fellow-citizens in the "Great Council of the nation." Instead, however, of *two*, they returned *three* representatives; and by an Act passed in this Parliament, apportioning the number of soldiers to be furnished by each city against the Scots, London was ordered to provide 200 men, being *five times* the number of any other city, instancing, at this date, the comparative extent of its population and opulence.

The reign of Edward III. not only shines forth conspicuously in the annals of chivalry, holding forth the early promise of the brilliant career of the fine arts, but as the age when the commerce of the city widely expanded the sphere of its operation, occupying a more prominent position in the horizon of the mercantile world, while the charters of the citizens were established on a more solid basis, and the trading fraternities re-constituted and identified with the State. The King, gratified at the able assistance afforded the Queen mother, which was the means of placing him on the throne; had only two months swayed the sceptre, when he bestowed upon the citizens extensive immunities, comprised in a grant which may be termed the *Golden Charter* of the city. He not only confirmed all the ancient rights of the city, but annulled every innovation which had been made upon them from the earliest times. In order, likewise, to

* Stow. Thos. Walsingham's *Hist. Angl.* Speed's *Chron.*

prevent, if possible, their future infraction or suspension, arising from any real or pretended misconduct of individuals temporarily vested with civic authority, it was expressly declared, "that the liberties of the said city shall not be taken into the hands of Us or our Heirs, for any personal trespass or judgment of any minister of the said city. Neither shall a Custos in the said city for that occasion be deputed; but the same minister shall be punished according to the quality of his offence;" in addition to which the following advantageous privileges were conferred:—The Mayor to be one of the judges to sit on the trial of prisoners confined in Newgate; the citizens to enjoy the right of *infang-theft*, that is the privilege of trying a thief or robber, apprehended within the jurisdiction of the city; and of *outfang-theft*, which is the liberty of reclaiming a citizen taken in any other place, in order to bring him to his trial within the city; a right to the goods and chattels of all felons convicted within the jurisdiction of the city: the privilege of devising in mortmain, which is an alienation of the lands and tenements to any guild, corporation or fraternity and their successors without the King's leave, according to ancient custom—The Sheriffs of London and Middlesex to be amerced no otherwise than their brethren south of the river Trent: all foreign merchants to dispose of their merchandizes within forty days, thereby to prevent enhancing the prices of their several commodities: the King's Marshal, Steward, nor Clerk of the Household, to execise any authority in the city: the office of Escheator given in perpetuity to the Mayor. For the greater convenience of the citizens resorting to country fairs, to have the valuable privileges of holding a court of "*Pie-Poudre*," in such places, for settlement of all disputes that happen in each of the said fairs; or, in the words of the grant—"that as the citizens were wont to have among themselves keepers to hold the pleas touching the citizens of the said city assembling at the said fairs, We will and grant that the same citizens may have such-like keepers to hold such pleas of their covenants as of ancient times they had, except the pleas of land, and of the Crown:" that none of the King's purveyors presume to rate any sort of goods belonging to the citizens, nor to deal in any sort of merchandize within the city, and that no market be kept wit[illegible]*even miles* of the city of London." In addition, the[illegible]ns obtained a grant of the "*Village of Southwark* for ever, by paying the farms thereof due and accustomed," having represented to the King, that the village was the "resort and lurking place of various felons, thieves, and other malefactors, disturbers of the peace," who infested the streets of London, rendering them at night unsafe to be traversed by the inhabitants, and on the perpetration of any crime they fled to Southwark, over which district the jurisdiction of the city authorities did not extend. This great addition to their local power failed at first in producing the anticipated benefits in restraining the evil practices of the dissolute, several serious riots occurring, and "people were assassinated, robbed, wounded, and killed in the streets;" the King, therefore, in the sixth year of his reign, was compelled to issue an edict "prohibiting any one from wearing a *coat of plate or weapon* in the city of London or town of Westminster, or the suburbs thereof, on pain of forfeiting all his possessions." The Mayor and magistrates, however, by adopting more energetic conduct, succeeded in partially checking these disgraceful occurrences. A quarrel happened betweeen the Fishmongers' and Skinners' Companies, which they attempted to settle in the streets *vi et armis*, the rioters resisting at first the power of the magistrates, who however succeeded in securing the leaders of the conflicting parties, carried them directly to Guildhall, where pleading guilty, they were beheaded in Westcheap, or Cheapside. This promptitude and decision of conduct had the effect of quelling, for a time, the riotous spirit of the age, and elicited the marked approbation of the act, the King issuing a patent in its justification and commendation.

Though the commencement of Edward's reign was thus marked by judicious laws to promote the best interests of the citizens, yet during the lengthened period th[illegible] swayed the sceptre, the civil and commercial state of [illegible]ndoners was subjected to much vicissitude; and it is to be regretted that the romantic love of chivalry imbued the King with too predominating a feeling for heroic adventure and martial fame, goaded on by an inordinate desire of territorial aggrandizement and the acquirement of wealth by the uncertain tenure of foreign possession, which he allowed too much to divert his attention from the peaceful arts at home of commerce, manufactures, and agriculture, which he ought first to have cultivated as the legitimate source of his riches. But glory was the shrine at which "he bowed the knee," and we find him one year sacrificing to his ambition the success of that commerce, which the previous year he had laboured to establish. No doubt sound and advantageous benefits resulted to the mercantile interest from several of his acts, but still many were thwarted or partially obviated from vacillations, the natural offspring of a character influenced by the impulses of any ruling passion. Thus in 1338 the admirals north and south of the Thames were empowered to compel the service of all *merchant-vessels* for an expedition against France, which created in the port of London a complete stagnation of trad . Besides which, he possessed himself of all the tin in the hands of the English as well as the foreign merchants, and ordered his wool-collectors to seize the wools belonging both to laity and clergy to make up a required deficiency of 17,500 sacks, in order to transmit to Antwerp, where the article found ready sale, the proceeds of which enabled him to fulfil his engagements with his allies. The foreign traffic had, however, been gradually becoming more extensive, the customs of the port amounting in 1331 to 8,000*l.* per annum, which, considering the low rates of duties, shows a considerable increase from the year 1268. Great jealousy continued to prevail on the part of the citizens against the merchants from Flanders, Lombardy, and other parts of the Continent, and oppressions of various kinds were resorted to with the view of crushing their commercial efforts, until the interposition of the Crown became necessary, and a law was passed, honourable to the Parliament, framed on the liberal principle of affording protection alike to the rights of the foreign as well as the native merchant. One of the main commercial objects the King seems ever to have held in view was, the re-establishment of the *woollen-manufacture;* and though his favourite project of conquering France frequently interrupted the execution of his design, yet he always lent an attentive ear to the appeals for justice made by the foreign cloth-weavers, a body of whom had settled in London under the authority of an Act of Parliament, passed in the eleventh year of his sovereignty. The meetings of the Flemish weavers were appointed to be held in the churchyard of St. Lawrence *Poultney* (the latter appellation being derived from the name of *John Poultney*, who founded a college adjoining the church dedicated to St. Lawrence); the Brabant weavers assembling in the churchyard of St. Mary *Somerset*, in Upper Thames-street, opposite Broken-wharf, and from the contiguity of the church to a small *hythe* or *haven*, called *Summer's het* or hythe, assumed the corrupted name of *Somerset*. In these places the woollen and linen cloths were exposed for sale at stated times, as was afterwards the custom in Cloth-fair, West

Smithfield. In 1353 an Order in Council was issued for levying a tax of threepence on every sack of wool and every three hundred of wool-fells, and on other commodities carried either by land or water to the staple* at Westminster. The establishment of this wool-mart had occasioned so great a resort, that Westminster had increased to a considerable town, having before "had no other dependence but the Royal residence and adjacent Abbey." This duty was raised for repairing the highway leading from the gate of London, called *Temple-bar*, to the gate of the Abbey at Westminster, the road, according to the Act, having "by the frequent passing of carts and horses, become so deep and miry, and the pavement so broken and worn as to be dangerous both to men and carriages, and as the proprietors of the houses near and leading to that staple have, by means of the thoroughfare,

* It appears by a record preserved in the seventh volume of the "Fœdera," that in the year 1375 the staple for the port of London had been removed from Westminter to that part of Holborn where *Staple-inn* now stands. It recounts that King Edward the Third having formerly made a grant to the dean and canons of the Chapel Royal of St. Stephen's, in his Palace of Westminster (the place in which the House of Commons now sits), of 66*l.* 13*s.* 4*d.* out of the rents of the Staple at Westminster, and the houses wherein the staple had been held remaining, for the most part empty, in consequence of the said removal; King Richard the Second, in 1380, made provision for the deficiency out of the Exchequer, to the said dean and canons. The jurisdiction of the Mayor and two constables of the staple of Westminster extended from Temple-bar to Tothill-fields, and their proceedings were governed by a *law-merchant*. The principal matters under their cognizance were the five staple commodities of England, *wool* and *wool-fels*, *leather*, *lead*, and *tin*.

Some remains of the place where the staple at Westminster was kept, and particularly an old stone gate fronting the Thames, were in being till the year 1741, when they were pulled down to make room for the abutment o. the new bridge over the Thames; and the place retained the name of the *wool-staple* till then, as appears by the Act of Parliament for the erection of the bridge.

greatly raised their rents, the way before their houses should be paved at their charge, and where no houses are, should be paved anew out of the said duties." Thus we find that the Strand still remained merely a road separating the City from Westminster, with houses interspersed, belonging chiefly to the nobility, whose different names and titles have since designated the several streets erected on the sites of the original mansions; and here it may be remarked, that the numerous additions made to the City beyond its ancient walls, commonly called its *liberties*, appear to have been taken in gradually, since no law is extant by which they are set out or to be ascertained, nor have any of its historiographers been able to discover the precise period when these improvements were made. This toll, with one of a similar nature granted seven years previously to the master of the hospital of St. Giles-in-the-fields and to John of Holborn, are the earliest on record collected in England for the repairs of a public road. The latter was levied for the purpose of repairing the highway, *via regia*, conducting from the said hospital near where the elegant structure of St. Giles now stands, to the bar of the *Old Temple* of London, namely, *Holborn-bars*, near which was erected the Old Temple or house of the Knights Templars, extending through another certain highway called *Perpoole-lane*, from the manor-house of that name, now Portpool-lane, including part of Gray's-inn-lane, and likewise the highway called Charing, probably now St. Martin's-lane, leading to the then village of Charing and its Cross,* erected by Edward

* A portion of this cross remained till the civil wars in the reign of Charles the First, when it was destroyed by the Puritans as a monument of Popish superstition. After the restoration of Charles the Second, the equestrian statue of his ill-advised and unfortunate father, that had been taken down by order of Oliver Cromwell, but concealed by the Royalists during the Protectorate, was erected on the site of the ancient structure. The statue is by Le Sueur, and a remarkable fine specimen of his art.

[illegible] should [illegible]
[illegible]
[illegible]
[illegible] the City [illegible]
[illegible]
[illegible]
[illegible] on the sides of the [illegible]
[illegible] remarked, that the [illegible]
[illegible] the City beyond [illegible]
[illegible]
[illegible] which [illegible]
[illegible] Topographers [illegible]
[illegible]
[illegible] great [illegible]
[illegible] to the [illegible] of St.
[illegible] to [illegible]
[illegible]
[illegible] the highway
[illegible] which [illegible]
[illegible] of S[illegible] stands [illegible]
[illegible] which was
[illegible] of the [illegible]
[illegible] highway called *Poppe*[illegible]
[illegible] of that [illegible] Pope [illegible]
[illegible] and likewise the highway
[illegible] St. M[illegible] to
[illegible] Cross, [illegible]

[illegible]

the First in memory of the death of his beloved Queen Eleanor.

A re-organization of the various trading communities was also effected at this era.* Among the most material alterations may be enumerated their change of name from *guilds* to *crafts* and *mysteries*, and the substituting for the old title of alderman that of *master* and *warden*. A still more important advantage for promoting the interest of the companies, was their being at this time first generally chartered, or having their privileges confirmed by letters patent, which they had only enjoyed through sufferance and the payment of their *fermes*. Exclusive of this right, however, the incorporations of Edward the Third were only partial, and comprehended but few of the privileges which the companies obtained from succeeding monarchs. They had no grant of a common seal even generally, liberty to buy or accept lands, to sue or be sued, and to possess various other liberties necessary to establish them full incorporations as at present.

The chartering, however, of the guilds by Edward the Third, was not that monarch's only favour to them. Having found

* About this time, in the year 1346, Edward the Third acquainted the public that his Parliament had agreed (18th Edward III., cap. 6), to the coining of three different coins of gold, viz., one piece of the value of six shillings, being the weight of two small florins of Florence, a second of half that value and weight, and a third of a quarter of the first. This gold was of twenty-three carats, three grains and a half fine, and half a grain in alloy. The standard of our silver coins was then eleven ounces and two pennyweights fine, and eighteen pennyweights alloy, called old sterling standard; and an ounce of silver weighed exactly twenty pennyweights, and was coined into twenty silver pence. Another proclamation was issued the same year, stating that three other gold pieces had been coined, viz., one of six shillings and eightpence value, which was named a gold *noble*, or *half-mark*; one of half that value, to be called a *maille-noble*; and a third to be a quarter of the value of the first, and to be called a *ferling* or *farthing-noble*. This is the first instance of a gold coinage in England.

that these fraternities were highly conducive to the extension of British commerce, and having conferred on them the means of giving stability to their mercantile associations, he wisely resolved to raise them in public estimation; and in order to effect this laudable resolution he became himself a brother of one of these societies, judging that his example would be soon followed by the Court. The *linen-armourers*, now "merchant-tailors," were then the great importers of woollen cloth, which we have shown his Majesty was desirous to make the staple manufacture of England, and therefore this company boasts the honour of first having had a Sovereign amongst their numbers. Richard the Second became a brother of the same company, and there were also enrolled as *merchant-tailors*, in Richard's reign, four Royal dukes, ten earls, ten barons, and five bishops; the Skinners as well as the Mercers exhibited, about the same period, an equally splendid list of names, while other companies had a greater proportion of City dignitaries; the *Grocers*,* towards the

* By a petition from the Commons of the City to Parliament, printed amongst the Parliamentary Rolls, we learn that before the thirty-sixth of Edward the Third, certain wholesale merchants had formed themselves into a guild, which had become so great and monopolous, that they threatened to ruin the numerous other fraternities that had now sprung up; and this guild was the *Grocers'*, the origin of whose name we find explained by this document. The petition complains that those merchants called "*grossiers*" or *grossers*, had by cover, and by orders made amongst themselves in their fraternities, *engrossed* all sorts of wares, whereby they suddenly raised the prices, and that they had laid up other merchandizes until times of dearth and scarcity. Ravenhill states, that the word *grosser*, or *grocer*, was a term at first distinguishing merchants in opposition to small traders, "for they usually sold in *gross* quantities by great weights, dealing for the whole of any kind." The grocers had seceded from the more ancient guild of the *Pepperers*, which latter fraternity was incorporated as grocers in 1345. The notification of being licensed to deal in *pepper* is still obliged to be specially inscribed over the doors of modern grocers. The remedy for the monopoly suggested by

close of Edward's reign enumerated sixteen aldermen among their body.

In the forty-ninth of Edward, an enactment received the sanction of the whole assembly of the commonalty of the City, by which the right of election of all City dignitaries and officers, including members of Parliament, was transferred from the *ward representatives to the trading companies*, a few members of which were directed to be selected by the masters or wardens to come to Guildhall for election purposes; it was afterwards opened to all the *liverymen* of companies, in whose right the voting for the City's Parliamentary members remained exclusively vested, till the passing of the "Reform Act," which restored the elective franchise to the freemen of London, and further extended it to the inhabitant householders.

The citizens, as succeeding eras progressively develope their character, seem ever to have maintained a decided principle of action, a sterlingness of behaviour throughout the fitful changes and severe ordeals to which they were subjected through the vacillating conduct of the different Sovereigns, and we constantly trace the same jealousy of their liberties, the same attachment to the constitution of the country, the same hospitality, munificence, and charity as signalize the London citizens and the London merchants of the present day; and with justice it may be added, that increase of wealth has only communicated augmented means of doing good, while the lapse of time has not rendered them less watchful and scrupulous of the privileges conferred on them by their

the petitioners and acceded to was, that "merchants shall deal in or use but one kind or sort of merchandize, and that every merchant hereafter shall choose which kind of wares or merchandize he will deal in, and shall deal in no other."—*Herbert's History of the Twelve Great Livery Companies of London.—Anderson's History of Commerce* charters. Thus, while we find the citizens in the olden time good and devout Catholics, as steadfast in the defence of their religious as their commercial rights, yet they allowed reason to remove the mists of bigotry in which the age was benighted, not yielding a blind belief in the infallibility of the priesthood; for at a provincial Synod held in London, in 1342, it was decreed, that whoever should be prevailed upon by the friars and monks to make their wills at the point of death in prejudice to their families, should be deprived of the benefit of Christian burial. On the other hand they showed themselves ready to defend, at the risk of their lives, the person of their Bishop, towards whom they had reason to imagine personal violence was likely to be offered by the Duke of Lancaster, at the assembly held at St. Paul's, to which *Wickliff* had been cited to answer for the presumed heretical doctrines he was promulgating, in opposition to the tenets of the Church of Rome. This exhibition of religious feeling, in hostility to Edward's princely son, was afterwards the source of serious disquietude to the citizens during the declining years of the King, even to the endangering the loss of their right to appoint a fellow-citizen to the civic chair; though in 1346 the election of the Lord Mayor had been vested in the mayor and aldermen for the time being, and in such of the principal inhabitants of each ward as should be summoned to attend.

As a marked indication of Royal favour, Edward, in the twenty-eighth year of his sovereignty, bestowed upon the mayor the privilege of having gold and silver maces carried before him, a privilege previously appertaining only to Royalty; at the same time that all other towns and cities were, by a Royal precept, expressly commanded not to use maces of any other metal than copper; and from this date, 1354, it is assumed that the addition of *Lord* was first annexed to the title of

Mayor of the City, there being no other record to which the event can be referred.

It was to be expected that during the military career of a warlike Prince like Edward the Third, various displays of the chivalrous spirit of the age would form a prominent feature in the pageants of the day and the amusements of the people. ***Smithfield*** was chiefly the ***arena*** on which many a gallant knight ran a course at the gorgeous tournaments held within the precincts of the City; but in 1329 several ambassadors having arrived from France, the King, anxious to display the gallantry of his subjects, entertained them with a solemn tournament held in ***Cheapside***, between the cross at the end of ***Wood-street*** and that of ***Soper-lane***, or ***Queen-street***; and another of the most splendid character was appointed by Edward, when, enfeebled from age in mind and body, he allowed the destinies of the country to be "too much influenced by the intrigues of his 'lady-love,' ***Alice Perrers*** or ***Pierce***. At this celebrated tilt, Alice appeared under the dignified appellation of the Lady of the Sun, drawn in a triumphal chariot, dressed in sumptuous apparel, attended by a number of ladies of quality, each of whom led a knight by his horse's bridle, accompanied by a number of the principal Lords, most richly accoutred; the magnificent procession setting out from the Tower through ***Cheapside*** to ***Smithfield***, where many courageous feats were performed by the young nobility and gentry for seven days."

In 1357 the citizens had a glorious opportunity of manifesting their loyalty and patriotism in receiving, with all the honours due to the illustrious hero of the age, Edward the ***Black Prince***, on his triumphal entrance into London after the victorious battle of Poictiers, bringing as a trophy of his redoubtable valour, John, King of France, captive in his train. The conquering Prince was met in Southwark by more than five thousand citizens on horse back, most of them richly dressed. The mayor, aldermen, sheriffs, and the several companies "in their formalities with stately pageants," met the procession at London, and the streets through which the nation's triumph passed were decorated with the richest tapestries, with a profusion of plate, silks, and furniture, exhibited as demonstrative of the wealth of the inhabitants; and quantities of bows, arrows, shields, helmets, coats of mail, swords, and spears, were exposed in the balconies, windows, and shops, impressing strongly the idea of the power and martial character of the English. The cavalcade lasted from three in the morning till noon. Notwithstanding these incentives to military ardour, with which it might have been supposed the people would have been stimulated—at a time, too, when the advantages accruing to the nation from the use of the long-bow were so illustriously exemplified in the fields of *Cressy* and *Poictiers*, when the glory of the English archers was in its zenith—it strikes us as a great anomaly to find that the pursuits of various useless, dishonest, and unlawful games, as hurling of iron bars, stones, and wood, of hand-ball, foot-ball, bandy-ball, and *cambuck* or cock-fighting, almost engrossed the popular pastime; so much so, as to occasion Edward to send a letter of complaint upon the subject to the sheriffs of London, declaring that the skill in shooting with arrows was almost totally laid aside, and that in a short time the realm was likely to become destitute of archers; commanding them to prevent the prevailing idle practices, and to see that the leisure time upon holidays was spent in recreations with bows; in furtherance of which, a penalty was ordered in 1349 to be inflicted on offenders, by imprisonment during the King's pleasure. In the immediately succeeding reigns the renewal ot similar orders was found necessary. In the sixteenth century heavy complaints were made respecting the disuse of

[illegible] must [illegible]

[illegible] streets [illegible]

[illegible] with the greatest [illegible]

[illegible] of the inhabitants [illegible]

[illegible] of the power [illegible]

[illegible] evidence [illegible]

[illegible] might have been [illegible]

[illegible] been [illegible]

[illegible] and [illegible]

[illegible] from the [illegible]

[illegible]

the long bow, especially in the vicinity of London; and Stow informs us, that before this time it was customary at Bartholomew-tide for the Lord Mayor, with the Sheriffs and Aldermen, to go into the fields at Finsbury, where the citizens were assembled, and shoot at the standard with broad and flight arrows for games. In the reign of Henry the Eighth, however, a revival of this manly sport had taken place; and at a great archery meeting at Windsor, a citizen of London, named Barlow, an inhabitant of Shoreditch, joined the archers and surpassed all the assembly in skill, at which his Majesty was so much pleased, that he jocosely gave him the title of ***Duke of Shoreditch***, a distinguishing honour which the captain of the London archers retained for a considerable time afterwards. In 1583, during the reign of Elizabeth, a grand archery match was held in London, the ***Duke of Shoreditch*** summoning a suit of nominal nobility under the titles of ***marquis*** of Clerkenwell, of Barlow, of Islington, of Hoxton, of Shacklewell, earl of Pancras, &c. The companies proceeded in pompous march from Merchant-tailors' hall, consisting of ***three thousand*** archers, as Strype says, "oddly habited," nine hundred and forty-two wearing chains of gold. They passed through Broad-street, the residence of their captain, thence into Moorfields, and thence to Smithfield, where having performed several evolutions, they shot at a target for honour. A similar meeting was made by the London archers in 1682, in the reign of Charles the Second, the King himself being present. But the close of the seventeenth century legislative interference failed in keeping alive the popular feeling in favour of the bow, and its use gradually became discontinued, owing, in great measure, to the various enclosures made in the neighbourhood of London, thus depriving the citizens of room sufficient for the exercise, and in part, from the general adoption of the musket. Fashion in more modern times has, however, prevented the total extinction of the noble craft of the bow; and honourable instances of skill in archery have been exhibited by the company of "Toxophilites," and other societies of Bowmen and *Bowwomen*; many of our fair countrywomen, in later days, having "twanged the yew" with as unerring skill as their eyes have shot forth darts from Cupid's quiver; while in no diversion does the position afford so favourable an opportunity of effectively displaying "the line of beauty" of the finely moulded form of woman's elegant figure.

Now that the population of London was becoming more dense, and the houses more thickly crowded together, few years elapsed without the City being visited with that dreadful scourge of humanity, the plague. The narrow streets, in which the current of air was either obstructed by architectural projections, or by signs across the street, together with the want of cleanliness, owing to the inefficient supply of water and the difficulty in preventing the accumulation of filth in the streets, did much to increase, if not to generate the distemper, which proved at various periods so fatal to the inhabitants of the metropolis. In the middle ages, the churchyards groaned with the accumulation of bones of the dead, piled up and exposed to the air, which they contributed to corrupt; the streets were filled with garbage and filth, which no exercise of authority seems to have been able to force the inhabitants to remove; the sewers, which generally ran above ground, were in a neglected state; while the dirty, sluttish habits within doors corresponded with the filthiness of the streets without. In 1348, during the rejoicings for Edward the Third's conquest of Calais, a disastrous pestilence, which was said to have spread from India over all the western countries, reached England, destroying immense numbers of inhabitants; and it was computed that in London not more than one in ten survived. The usual places of sepulture not being large enough to receive the bodies, several humane individuals were induced to purchase grounds for burial; and in one enclosure appropriated by Sir Walter Maury, comprising thirteen acres, there were buried 50,000. The reduction which took place in the price of provisions from the consequent falling off in the consumption deserves note; for instance, a horse previously worth 40s. sold at 6s. 8d., a best ox at 4s., do. cow 1s., a best heifer or steer 6d., a wether sheep, 4d., an ewe 3d., and a lamb 2d., a best hog 5d., and a stone of wool was not worth more than 9d. Wines also were sold at very low prices, Gascony obtaining only 4d., and Rhenish 6d. per gallon. Wheat suffered, likewise, considerable fluctuations in its value throughout the reign of Edward, either from scarcity of money, owing to the exhaustion of the nation's resources, chiefly in prosecution of the Scottish war, or from dearths occasioned by failure in the crops, or the ravages of the plague causing the supply to exceed the demand. Thus we find in 1335, wheat realized the enormous sum of 40s. per quarter, while in the succeeding year it is quoted at 2s.; and again in 1359, 1369, and 1370, selling "at the excessive prices" of 24s. and 26s. 8d. per quarter. These sudden alterations in the currencies of the staple commodity of life would lead to the conclusion that ruinous losses must have been sustained by the agriculturists of the day; and it is therefore necessary, in order to form a just estimation of the outlay of the grower, that the value of land should be specified, which we are enabled to do from Bishop Fleetwood's "Chronicon Preciosum," wherein it appears that eighty acres of arable land were worth 20s. per annum, or 3d. per acre, meadow-land being let at 4d., and pasture 1d. per acre.

As early as the year 1361 the prevalence of the plague was attributed to the want of cleanliness in the streets of the City, fears being entertained that the disease which raged that year in France might be communicated to London, or revived by the putrid blood and entrails of beasts which the butchers used to throw into the streets. Edward, by way of precaution, issued a command to the mayor and sheriffs, stating that from these practices "abominable and most filthy stinks proceeded, sicknesses and many other evils having happened to such as had abode in the City or resorted thereto;" and that in future no animals should be slaughtered nearer London than the town of *Stratford* on the one part, and the town of *Knightsbridge* on the other. Three hundred years later, in the eventful periods of 1625 and 1665, the plague was still attributed to the want of cleanliness, and the tracts of those times teem with complaints on the subject. "Let not carcasses of horses, dogs, cats, and other animals lye rotting and poisoning the air as they have done in More and Finsbury-fields and elsewhere round the citie, whence arise unsavory stenches, and these fœtid smells are the maintaining cause of the contagion." In the succeeding year, 1666, occurred the "great fire" of London, which, though devastating in its progress, causing misery and ruin at once dreadful and appalling, was yet ultimately productive of more beneficial effects than any conflagration recorded in history. Indeed, it is the opinion of many able writers of the day that the fire was the "one thing needed" radically to exterminate the disease, as there is strong reason for believing that for some centuries the City was not before this period wholly free from infection. It is not, therefore, too much to infer, that had it not been for this calamity, London might much longer have suffered from the pestilence. Instead of narrow dirty streets, however, without any free circulation of air, a new city arose improved, in all the conveniences of life. This would not have occurred for ages in the regular course of events.

It is needless reciting the melancholy detail of each particular year,

> "When Contagion with mephitic breath
> And wither'd Famine urg'd the work of death;"

yet, perhaps, a brief description of the last plague which passed with pestiferous blast over the devoted walls of London, while it affords a faint picture of those previous awful visitations to which the City was subjected, may render us the more thankful, that in this our day, we can daily walk the streets of the metropolis without the dread of inhaling air pregnant with deadly infection. It was towards the close of the year 1664 that the plague first broke out in Long-acre, when two or three persons dying suddenly, the frightened neighbours took the alarm and removed into the City, whither they are supposed unfortunately to have carried the infection. There, from the denseness of the population, it gathered strength, and its ravages rapidly augmented. A frost which set in in December, and continued three months, suspended its dire effects; but at the close of February, 1665, the thaw commencing, the plague began again to increase, and when it was found that several parishes were infected, the magistrates issued an order that every house visited with the contagion should be shut up, and marked with a red cross bearing the inscription, "Lord, have mercy upon us," none of the inmates being allowed egress. This impolitic measure was attended with most distressing consequences; for, though the extension of the infection may have been thus partially checked, yet whole families were sacrificed, who might have escaped had they been allowed to quit the house on the first appearance of the disease. In the months of May, June, July, it continued with more or less power, until in August and September it quickened into horrible activity, sweeping away 4,000, 8,000, and even 12,000 souls in one week; and at its height of fatality 4,000 perished in one night. All business was paralysed; the minister often received the stroke of death in the exercise of his sacred office; the physician, finding no assistance in his own antidotes, died while administering them to others; the very bells seemed hoarse with tolling; and the dead were now no longer numbered, for the parish clerks and sextons perished in the execution of their office. In the parish of Stepney alone, 116 sextons, gravediggers, and carters employed in removing the bodies, died in one year. Those moving sepulchres, the "dead carts," continually traversed the streets, while the appalling cry, "Bring out your dead," thrilled through every human frame within whom the spark of life still lingered. Then it was that parents, husbands, wives, and children saw all that was dear to them thrown with a pitchfork into a cart, like the offal of the slaughter-house, to be conveyed without the walls, and flung into one promiscuous heap. In the last week of September, this human scourge mitigated its fell attaks, at which time upwards of 10,000 houses were deserted; and, according to Defoe, 100,000 victims were offered as human sacrifices to the want of cleanliness, conveniences, and bad construction of the streets and houses.

Even the survivors in this year of desolation would have perished of famine but for the charitable contributions of the affluent. The money subscribed is said, each week, to have amounted to 100,000*l.*, to which Charles the Second gave 1,000*l.*; in the parish of Cripplegate alone, the disbursements to the poor amounted to 17,000*l.* a-week. The conduct of the magistracy redounded infinitely to their honour, and Darwin has justly lauded, in verse, the heroic devotion of Sir John Laurence, "London's Generous Mayor." Space will not permit us to detail, even in the most cursory manner, the numerous anecdotes of the most "heart-rending miseries and

C. Marshall J. C. Bentley

trials" with which the people of any nation were ever visited; we shall, therefore, conclude our mournful narrative of this epoch in the calamities of the City with the traditionary account of a narrow escape of a poor *Scotch piper*, whose remembrance has been immortalized by that great sculptor, *Cibber*, in a statue well known in Tottenham-court-road, representing a Highland piper with his dog and keg of liquor by his side. It is to be premised, that many were the instances in which, the stupor of disease having been mistaken for the sleep of death, the sufferer was buried beneath a mass of the dead; and sometimes bodies, yet warm and breathing, met the same fate. Reverting, however, to the *piper*, it appears, he was accustomed usually to stand at the bottom of Holborn-hill, near St. Andrew's church. Having one day met some of his countrymen and drank too freely, he was glad to find repose on the steps of the church. The nightly "dead cart" passing by during his slumbers, one of the men hesitated not in putting his fork into the piper's belt, and transferring him from a bed of stone to one of death. The piper's faithful dog attempted to prevent the forcible capture of his master; but, unable to succeed, he determined not to forsake him, and, leaping into the cart, began to howl most piteously over the body. The jolting of the cart and moans of the dog aroused the piper from his lethargy, who instinctively turning to his pipes, struck up one of his native spirit stirring pibrochs, to the great terror of the drivers, who fancied their cart haunted "with ghosts and goblins, or spirits damned;" until lights having been procured, the piper was released from his deadly company, and his narrow escape was communicated by one of his benefactors, who employed Cibber to execute a statue of him.

Richard the Second, in 1377, unfortunately ascended the throne at too early an age, being only eleven years old, for the City to anticipate much solid or permanent benefit to result to their mercantile and corporate interest during his rule, unless the youthful Monarch had been gifted with more than usual strength of mind and philosophical reasoning far beyond his years, to have rendered him proof against the multiform temptations arising from pleasures, which the possession of apparently unbounded riches rendered subservient to his will. Had he escaped this *Scylla* of the regal state, the *Charybdis* which awaited him was more likely to wreck his prudent intentions, created by the adulation of courtiers, who so adulterate the stream through which the clear waters from the fountains of truth have to flow, that they reach royalty divested of all their purity, and have been so perverted from their simple and straight current, that it requires an acuteness of judgment, and highly reflective organization hardly to be hoped for, to enable the human mind to penetrate the illusive veil thus artfully thrown over actions and things. This perception of facts through a false medium, seeing "through a glass darkly," has been too often the bane of those who are immaturely impressed with the feeling and knowledge that they have only *to will, to have*. A portion, however, of the first years of his reign was marked by traits of decision and firmness of conduct, which led to more favourab predictions than his after actions realized. Unlike his amiable father, the Black Prince, he grew up rash and inconsiderate, irritating his friends into estrangement, and exciting his enemies to rebellious opposition; even the citizens, infected by the manners of the Court, were often tumultuous, inconsistent, and irregular in their proceedings. One of the King's first acts was his reconciliation of the Duke of Lancaster with the City, after which his Majesty made his grand entrance from *Sheen* (*Richmond*) into London, and for which the most magnificent preparations were made; exhibiting at once

CUMBERLAND TERRACE,

REGENT'S PARK

the prodigality as well as the fanciful but not inelegant character of the pageantry and entertainments of the day. The cavalcade, when it reached Cheapside, stopped opposite a large conduit erected in the form of a castle, from which flowed white and purple streams of wine. Four beautiful girls, as *Hebes*, about the age of the King, supplied the Sovereign and nobility with wine in golden goblets, throwing gilt flowers on the King's head, and scattering *Danae* showers of florins among the populace.—Again, when the King favoured the City with his presence, he was escorted by four hundred of the citizens, in superb dresses, to London-bridge, where he was presented with a stately courser, richly trapped with golden brocade, and his Queen with a white palfry with furniture equally splendid. His arrival was greeted by thousands of joyous citizens; the houses by which he passed were decorated with cloths of gold, silver, and silks; the conduits ran with the choicest wines, and at every step costly gifts were heaped on the Royal personages. At the standard in Cheapside was a splendid pageant, on which stood a boy, personifying an angel, who offered the King wine in a golden cup, and placed on his head a rich crown of gold, "most curiously garnished with precious stones and pearls of great value, and the same on the head of the Queen;" after which he was given two gilt silver basins, each containing a thousand gold nobles, together with a curious picture of the Trinity, valued at 800*l*., a gilt silver table for an altar, worth a thousand marks, besides other presents of great value.

These exhibitions were not only profuse and extravagant, idly dissipating immense sums in vain ostentation, but extremely impolitic, as impressing the Court and nobility with the belief, that the wealth of the citizens was like an inexhaustible mine from whence resources could be drawn at pleasure. If, therefore, loans of money were refused to the

Royal demand, the denial was supposed to proceed not from inability, but requiring only a high pressure system to force a reluctant compliance. In fact, these civic shows reflect little credit on the wisdom or foresight of the citizens of yore; and the extortions and amercements to which they were subjected from the Crown, were encouraged by their own imprudence and ostentation.

In the second year of the King's reign, a subsidy was granted by Parliament to cover the expenses incurred in the wars carried on in France and Flanders, by which all men were assessed according to their several qualities or stations in life, and which assumed the name of the "*poll-tax:*" tradesmen, mechanics, &c., with their wives and children, were taxed at *fourpence* per head; all persons, in fact, above fifteen years of age; or, according to *Fabian*, fourteen years. On this occasion the Lord Mayor was rated as an *earl* at four pounds, and the aldermen as *barons* at two pounds each; which would imply that the epithet of "*Right Honourable*" had been already attached to the mayoralty. Exclusively of the onerous nature of this new imposition, the mode of collection became the crying grievance of the land, the Government agents resorting to the most brutal and indecent behaviour towards the female portion of the lower classes in endeavouring to ascertain their age. The excitement of the people became at length so violent, that on one of the collectors having rudely treated the daughter of a man named *Wat Hilliard*, by profession a *Tyler*, known afterwards as "*Wat Tyler*," ressdent at Dartford, in Kent, the father became so irritated, that he knocked out the fellow's brains, and, to save himself from prosecution, easily persuaded the populace to rise in his defence, and endeavour to extricate themselves from the heavy yoke of taxation under which they had so long groaned. Hence arose, in 1381, the most dangerous rebellion that ever threatened England, and which shook the pillars of the throne to their very foundation; its suppression proving as miraculous as its rise and progress had been unprecedentedly rapid and foreboding. On the arrival of the rebels at Maidstone, they released from prison a fanatic priest named *John Ball*, who had been excommunicated, and confined for his seditious preachings, and was a fit instrument to co-operate with the factious insurgent, *Wat Tyler*. A congenial spirit to the text which he adopted from an old proverb,

> "When *Adam* delv'd, and *Eve* span,
> Who was then a *gentleman*,"

at once exemplifies the specious principles of *equality* which he instilled into his hearers; and from such tenets, the results which followed may be readily conceived. The rebel army encamped on Blackheath 100,000 strong, and on the King refusing to come at their bidding and hear their demands, they marched to London, vowing destruction to the nobility, and especially the members of the legal profession, committing numerous acts of incendiarism and murder. Admittance was gained into the City, and the work of devastation commenced. One of the divisions of the forces, under the command of Wat Tyler, was posted about West Smithfield, and terms were offered by the King similar to those which had been acceded to by the Essex division. These, however, were not satisfactory to the rebellious chief, who was in consequence invited to conference with the King at *Smithfield*, to which place he marched his confederates, consisting of from twenty to thirty thousand. The moment *Wat Tyler* caught sight of the King, in Smithfield, he left his companions, whom he ordered to halt, "and setting spurs to his horse stopped not till he touched the croupier of the King's horse," whom he rudely accosted; and his general demeanour was so insolent and overbearing, that the King's attendants suggested the propriety of having him arrested. In order to put this bold design into execution in the face of a hostile force which outnumbered the Royal party, as hundreds to units, the Lord Mayor WALWORTH, as magistrate of the jurisdiction, was ordered to execute it. This, on the impetus of the moment, he dauntlessly performed, by striking Tyler heavily on the head with his sword, causing the traitor to stagger and fall from his horse, who was soon despatched by the attendants, and the body thrown into the Hospital of St. Bartholomew. At the sight of their chieftain's death, the rebels furiously exclaimed, "Our captain is murdered, let us revenge his death," and immediately bent their bows. The King, with an extraordinary presence of mind in a youth of fifteen, boldly dashed forward with his horse, crying out, "*What, my friends! will you kill your King? Be not troubled for the loss of your leader, I will be your captain, and grant what you desire.*" This heroic conduct seems to have awed the rebels into temporary submission, and they passively followed the King to St. George's-fields. In the meantime, the mayor and alderman *Philpot*, assisted by aldermen *Brembre* and *Laund*, raised on the moment one thousand citizens completely armed, and sent them so expeditiously, under the guidance of Sir Robert Knowles, to the King's assistance, that the rebels threw down their arms and sued for mercy. *Jack Straw*, who was second in command, previously to his execution confessed, that it had been resolved by him and his accomplices to sack and burn the City on the evening of the very day in which Wat Tyler was killed, and to have murdered all the nobility and principal citizens. We have thus minutely recounted this insurrection, so celebrated in English history, as it places the gallant behaviour of the London citizens in a brilliant light, reflecting on them a blaze of glory which will gild their memory to the latest posterity. The Lord Mayor, *William Walworth*, with the aldermen *Philpot*, *Brembre*, and *Laund*, were meritoriously knighted, and the Mayor was further rewarded with a fee farm-rent of 100*l.* per annum, and the other aldermen with 40*l.* annually, and Sir William Walworth's memory has been perpetuated in the name of a suburban village which gave him birth.

An erroneous opinion has become prevalent that the dagger, represented in the City armorial bearings, was granted as an honorary distinction by Richard in commemoration of the heroic action of the Mayor; but it appears that in the fourth year of the King's reign, and a year previous to the insurrection, it was agreed and ordained, at a full assembly in the upper chamber of Guildhall, that the ancient seal of office being deemed too small and unbecoming the dignity of the City, a new one should be adopted, "made in a more masterly manner, in which, besides the images of *St. Peter* and *St. Paul*, was placed the shield of the arms of the said city well engraved, supported by two lions, and with two more on each side of the arms, and two niches containing two angels, between whom, over the images of the apostles, sate the image of the Virgin Mary." The *cross* and *sword* are therefore to be considered emblematical of St. Paul, and not the *dagger* of Sir William Walworth.

While descanting on the characters of the different civic dignitaries of this epoch, we must not omit eulogizing that of *Sir John Philpot*. This brave and worthy citizen fitted out a fleet at his own expense, which he manned with a thousand able seamen, taking the command himself, in order to check the piracies of a Scotch adventurer named *Mercer*, who had for some time considerably harassed the coasting trade, and captured several merchantmen. After a severe engagement, Mercer was defeated, and most of his vessels captured by the victorious Londoner. Again, when the Government sent a powerful fleet and army to the assistance of the Duke of Bretagne against France, Sir John, then Lord Mayor, hired a considerable number of ships, and redeemed the armour and arms of upwards of a thousand soldiers, which they had been obliged to pawn to procure the necessaries of life. He also caused the City ditch to be cleansed, and rated each householder only at the small sum of *fivepence*. We have specified this sum, in order to show the wages given to a labourer at that time, which was the amount paid by each householder. In fact, Sir John appears to have been for many years "the pillar of the City," "the head, heart, and hand of London." His unflinching integrity in Parliament in defending the rights of his fellow-citizens, and averting the threatened innovation of their privileges, added to his indefatigable zeal in its internal good government, fully exemplified that its welfare was cherished as the dearest object of his existence.

Sir William Walworth was succeeded in the mayoralty by alderman Northampton, whose character forms a striking contrast with that of the brave and patriotic Sir John Philpot; for, though the promoter of some beneficial regulations, yet the violence of his disposition led him into seditious outrages, which ultimately caused the confiscation of his property and his perpetual imprisonment. He, succeeded, however, in a great measure, in curbing the licentiousness and immorality too prevalent among citizens; though, for his *practical ethics*, he incurred the displeasure of the clergy, who looked upon his interference as an innovation of their authority. The same motives, however, instigated him as those which induced the magistrates at a later period of the reign to take the punishment of the various immoral transgressions into their own hands, in consequence of the negligence and partiality of the clergy and spiritual courts, "who connived at licentiousness for a bribe."

[illegible] the [illegible]

[illegible] and redeemed the [illegible] soldiers, which [illegible] [illegible] necessaries of [illegible] [illegible] licensed, and [illegible] of *free-passes*. We [illegible] the wages given to a [illegible] the amount paid by [illegible] for many years the [illegible] [illegible] in the ancient [illegible] the rights [illegible] [illegible] [illegible] [illegible] of his own [illegible].

[illegible] W[illegible] was succeeded [illegible] [illegible] brave and patriotic [illegible]; [illegible] [illegible] [illegible] He succeeded, however, in a [illegible] the licentiousness and immorality [illegible] [illegible], though, for his [illegible], [illegible] of the clergy, who looked upon [illegible] of [illegible]. The [illegible] him as those which [illegible] [illegible] [illegible] of the reign to take the [illegible] [illegible] to aggressions from their own [illegible] of the negligence and partiality of [illegible] [illegible] who connived at directions [illegible] for a [illegible]

THE UPPER POOL.

In 1383 a gleam of joy burst forth amidst the gloom and oppression which were rising on the horizon of the City's prospects: Richard, at the recommendation of his Parliament, confirmed all former charters and grants, professing to hold inviolate the rights and liberties of the citizens. But, notwithstanding this solemn contract, the Constable of the Tower shortly afterwards succeeded in establishing his right of dues on certain commodities entering the port of London; such as possession of all craft found adrift between London-bridge and Gravesend, all swans and stray animals floating past the Tower, &c., which proved a constant subject of irritation even so late as the reign of James the First, when the custom was abrogated. About this time Richard fixed the prices of Rhenish, Gascoigne, and Spanish wines at 6*d.* per gallon in London and other towns, and if sent into the country, the price was not to be raised more than a halfpenny per gallon for every fifty miles of land-carriage. In 1386 the walls had become considerably dilapidated, and houses on the exterior were built contiguous to them. On an anticipated invasion from France by Charles the Sixth, the walls were ordered to be repaired, the houses pulled down, and the ditch cleansed; but on the alarm subsiding, the work of reparation was discontinued.

The extravagance of the King was now becoming unbounded, and his Court was unrivalled in splendour. He is said to have maintained six thousand persons daily in his palace; some authorities enumerate them at ten thousand. His whole establishment of *cooks*, at the different Royal residences, is reported to have been two thousand; and some appeared to have been deeply versed in the *gastronomic art*, as is instanced in a curious work entitled the "Forme of Cury," compiled about 1390 by the master-cooks of this luxurious monarch, in which are preserved recipes for the most exquisite dishes of the age. In order to obtain resources to meet his enormous expenses, infringements, as usual, were made on the privileges of the citizens under the most frivolous pretexts; remonstrances were construed into presumption and unwarrantable questioning of the supreme pleasure and authority of the Crown, and mulcts and extortions ensued, even to the forcing some of the eminent citizens to sign and seal blank papers, which were afterwards filled up with sums that were found suitable to the convenience of the Court. Such is a specimen of the "good olden times," which ought to make the citizens reckon, beyond all price, the constitutional liberty they now enjoy. At this crisis of the nation, we behold the London merchants standing forth in bold relief in this dreary picture of the people's wrongs, stern and inflexible as mediators, not only for their brother citizens, but between the kingdom's grievances and the oppressive acts of a vicious Government. *Sir Simon Sudbury*, with a deputation of London and provincial citizens, sought an audience of the King at Windsor, and represented, in nervous but respectful language, the gross abuses under which his subjects laboured, begging the speedy summoning of a Parliament to redress the evils. The King at first gave an evasive answer, which called forth the following spirited ebullition of a frank remonstrance:—" With humble submission to his Majesty, justice was never less practised in England than at present, and that by the subtle management of certain persons it was impossible for him to come at the truth of things, seeing the ministers found it their interest to conceal from him the management of his affairs; in consideration of which they (the citizens) did not think it consistent with their interest, nor that of the kingdom, to wait the meeting of Parliament, seeing a speedier remedy might be applied, by calling to account those individuals who had plundered and embezzled the public treasure, and to inquire how these immense sums, raised for nine years past, had been applied; and that all those who could not discharge themselves honourably, and had misbehaved themselves in the administration of public affairs, should stand to the judgment of Parliament and have substituted in their stead men of worth and probity." The King, surprised at the confident tone and character of this speech, turned for advice to his uncles and brother, the Duke of York, and other nobles, who all declared, that they saw nought unreasonable in this demand of the commonalty of his realms, and a Parliament was, in consequence, appointed to meet at Westminster to inquire into the state of the nation. In order, however, to avoid this Parliamentary investigation, the King, urged by his two designing and unprincipled favourites, Robert De Vere, created Duke of Ireland, and Michael de la Pole, Earl of Suffolk, and Chancellor, removed the Court to Bristol. These two minions, unsatisfied with the influence they already possessed, and fearful that they would not totally engross the Royal ear during the life of the King's uncle, Thomas, Duke of Gloucester, who had deservedly obtained the confidence of many of the citizens, entered into a conspiracy to assassinate the Duke and other parties of eminence attached to his person. To this purpose, they hinted the subject to Alderman Exton, then Mayor, suggesting the feasibility of the plan, by inviting the Duke and his friends to sup at the house of Sir Nicholas Brembre, the late Mayor, who had filled the office two successive years,* and

* A striking instance of the influence which the principal, or as they were termed, "the great companies," had now obtained in the government of the City, appears in their compelling, in 1385, the return for two successive years of Sir Nicholas Brembre, *Grocer*, as Mayor of London, in opposition to the whole of the freemen. This curious civic incident is thus recorded in the "Chronicle of London. "Also this yere Sir Nicholl

who sided with the conspirators; it being suggested that when the wine had circulated freely, the Duke and the whole of his company might be readily despatched. This traitorous knight, Sir Nicholas, on the success of the plot was to have been created Duke of London, but instead of this honorary *elevation*, he was soon afterwards *exalted* on a gallows at Tyburn. Alderman Exton, in silent astonishment, listened to the proposal, but revolting at so foul a deed, immediately informed the Duke of Gloucester, which led to an open rupture between the Court party and the Duke and citizens. De Vere was despatched by the King to Wales to raise a Welsh army to reduce the Londoners, and his Royal relatives, to submission. He soon succeeded in mustering a force of 15,000 men, at the head of which he marched towards the metropolis. The Londoners, however, were not supine; they also assembled a considerable army, which, under the guidance of the Duke of Gloucester, marched to Oxford, where they met the King's troops, whom they completely routed. This perfidious attempt against the lives and liberties of the inhabitants of London, lost Richard the affections of the citizens, and laid the foundation of those commotions which deprived him of his sceptre and life; and he acquired too late the fatal knowledge, how dangerous to the stability of his throne was the open hostility of the citizens of London.

About 1389, the number of British merchants trading to, and residing in the ports of Prussia and other hanse-towns, had so greatly augmented, and the ramifications of the com-

Brembre was chosen Maire agene, be the said craftes and by men of the contre at Harowe, and the contre there aboughte, and *not be free eleccion of the Citee of London, as it ourth to be:* and the oolde halle was stuffed with men of armes overe even, be ordinaunce and assente of Sir N. Brembre for to chose hym Maire on the morowe: and so he was."

[illegible] being suggested that [illegible] the [illegible] [illegible] dispatched. [illegible]

[illegible] of the plot was to have [illegible] instead of the [illegible] was *exalted* on a gallows at [illegible] [illegible] so [illegible] immediately [illegible] which led to an open [illegible] and [illegible] [illegible] King to Wales to raise a [illegible] Lords [illegible] his royal relatives. [illegible] He soon succeeded in mustering a force of [illegible] at the head of [illegible] he marched towards the metropolis. The Lords [illegible] however, were not supine; they [illegible] army, which, under the guidance [illegible] marched to Oxford, where they [illegible] completely routed. This [illegible] the lives and liberties of the [illegible] the affections of the citizens [illegible] of those commotions which deprived [illegible] and life; and he acquired too late the fatal [illegible] dangerous to the security of his throne was [illegible] citizens of London.

[illegible] of [illegible] arising to, [illegible] of Persia and other [illegible] and the ramifications of the con-

[illegible]

WOOLWICH.

mercial proceedings of London had become so extensive, that Richard confirmed the election of ***John Babys***, merchant of London, to be governor of all the merchants of England in the foreign "lands, places, and dominions specified;" an honourable office which was nearly similar to that which bears the more modern designation of consul-general. In 1391 a dearth occurring, and wheat advancing to **16*s*. 8*d*.** per quarter, the Mayor, Adam Bamme, and other aldermen, by their prompt and charitable conduct, attained a high degree of popularity, by subscribing a sum of money and taking from the "Orphans' Fund" two thousand marks, with which they purchased corn abroad; and this seasonable importation effectually relieved the wants of the poor.* In 1394 the graziers resorting to Smithfield complained to the Privy Council of the extortion of the City officers, who, in many instances, demanded from them a toll of every ***third beast*** they brought to market. The Mayor and Sheriffs were summoned to answer the allegations, and a discontinuance of the imposition was ordered.

At the close of the previous and commencement of the present reign, we begin to discern a separation of the wealthier from the more indigent guilds, or such as sent most members to the Common Council and paid the highest ***fermes;*** namely, the Merchant Tailors, Vintners, Skinners, Fishmongers, Mercers, Grocers, Goldsmiths, Drapers, and such others as may be assumed constituted the "THIRTEEN MYS-

* Stow and Fuller eulogize also Sir Stephen Brown, who, during a great dearth in his mayoralty in 1438, chaitably relieved the wants of the poor citizens, by sending ships, at his own expense, to Danzig, which returned laden with *rye*, and which soon depressed grain to reasonable rates. "He is beheld as one of the first merchants who, during a want of corn, showed the Londoners the way to the barn-door, prompted by charity, not covetousness, to this adventure."

TERIES," and which, from the time of Richard the Second, we always find alluded to with some epithet implying *superiority*. Though evidently of less public importance in the earlier stages of society than the Weavers, Saddlers, Bakers, and the guilds previously alluded to, the fraternities above-named, as luxury and commerce advanced, comprised the chief mercantile staple and manufacturing interests of the kingdom, at the same time that they had enrolled among their body the principal citizens.

Having now arrived at the period in which the companies may be said to have become fully established, as the enrolment of their charters was made imperative by Richard the Second, we have enumerated the forty-eight "several mysteries" from which the common-councilmen were first chosen; and though the *thirteen mysteries* were not then specified, yet, in all probability, they comprised the present "twelve great companies," which we have inserted in italics among the subjoined list. The order in which they stand denotes their rank of precedency in our times; a knotty point of etiquette, which led to much animosity and dispute, and remained unsettled till the reign of Henry the Eighth.

Mercers, incorporated 1393,
Grossers, or *Grocers*, do. 1345,
Drapers, do. 1439,
Fishmongers,* do. 1536,
Goldsmiths, do. 1392,
Skinners, do. 1327,
Tailors, or *Merchant Tailors*, incorporated 1466,
Haberdashers, do. 1447,
Salters, do. 1558,
Ironmongers, do. 1462,
Vintners, do. 1437,

* The dealers in fish consisted originally of salt-fish and stock-fishmongers; the former were incorporated in 1433 and the latter in 1569, but the division proving prejudicial to the trade, they were united and incorporated in the reign of Henry the Eighth, 1536.

Clothworkers, incorp. 1482,
Saddlers,
Weavers,
Tapestry Weavers,
Leathersellers,
Founders,
Joiners,
Chandlers,
Fullers,
Curriers,
Freemasons,
Brewers,
Fletchers,*
Bakers,
Girdlers,
Stainers,
Braziers,
Cappers,
Pewterers,
Ale Brewers.
Hatters,
Smiths,
Horners,
Masons,
Leather-dressers,
Armorers,
Butchers,
Cutlers,
Spurriers,
Plummers,
Wax Chandlers,
Barbers,
Painters,
Tanners,
Pouchmakers,
Woodsawyers, and Dealers,
Pinners.

It may be observed, that from these "*twelve companies*" the Lord Mayor was for centuries *exclusively* chosen. None of the lists of Lord Mayors, in the ancient histories of London, afford a single instance to the contrary, from *Fitzalwin* to *Sir Robert Wilmot*. Only the wardens of these "great companies" were allowed to attend the Lord Mayor, as chief-butler at coronations. The "twelve" alone (with the single exception of the armourers), had the honour of enrolling the Sovereign amongst their members, and generally entertaining foreign princes and ambassadors: they took precedence in all civic triumphs; they occupied the chief standings in all State processions through the City; they alone of the companies

* Bowyers and Fletchers are, reaoectively, manufacturers of bows and arrows

contributed to repair the City walls; and lastly (not to mention various other proofs which might be adduced), they were the companies who were always the most largely assessed in all levies for the Government or the City. The common opinion, therefore, that the Lord Mayor must be a member of one of these companies, is indisputably founded on prescriptive right and usage. It was in 1742, that Sir Robert Wilmot, just mentioned, was sworn Lord Mayor, notwithstanding that he was not so qualified, and that upon the advice of counsel, who said there was no law for it. His lordship was of the Coopers' Company, and would have been translated to the Clothworkers' (which is one of the twelve), but his admission being carried only by a small majority, and they, at the same time, refusing him their hall, he resolved to give them no farther trouble. It is now understood, that being free of one of the twelve companies is only necessary to qualify the Lord Mayor for President of the Irish Society.

It is but candid, in conclusion, to remark that, notwithstanding the ancient rank of the "twelve companies," many of the others are, on various accounts, of equal or superior importance. The *Weavers* and *Sadlers* claim precedence as to antiquity; the *Stationers*, besides their growing wealth and extensive concerns, rank high as a rich, commercial, and working company. The *Dyers* once took precedence of the clothworkers. The *Brewers* are distinguished for their ancient and very curious records; and yield on that point, perhaps, only to the *Leathersellers*, who, at their elegant modern hall in St. Helen's-place, have some matchless charters, as regards embellishment, and the most ornamentally written "wardens' accounts" of any extant. Various others might be included in this list as equally worthy of observation.—*Herbert's History of the Twelve Companies.*

[illegible] (not [illegible] [illegible]), they [illegible] possessed [illegible] [illegible] Mayor [illegible] [illegible] pre- [illegible] in 1712 [illegible] several Lord Mayors [illegible] [illegible], and that [illegible] was [illegible] [illegible] would have been [illegible] (one of the twelve), [illegible] carried [illegible] by a small majority, and [illegible] be resolved [illegible] is now [illegible] [illegible] of the [illegible]

[illegible] to with- [illegible] of [illegible] company [illegible] accounts, of [illegible] superior [illegible] and [illegible] Stationers, [illegible] high [illegible] continued. The *Dyers* [illegible] precedence of [illegible] *Brewers* [illegible] for their [illegible] point, [illegible], who, at their elegant [illegible] [illegible] [illegible] Various [illegible] of the *Livery Companies.*

Having displayed somewhat in detail such important events as are connected with the early history of our great metropolis, it now becomes necessary to sketch with a more rapid pen the successive scenes which may lead to a contemporaneous period. London, as she has hitherto been seen, stands forth as the mighty heart of a mighty empire; but, her pre-eminent greatness, her glory as the first city of the first nation of the earth, has yet to be shown.

Richard the Second, having rendered himself odious to his subjects, Henry, Duke of Hereford, son of John of Gaunt, late Duke of Lancaster, was invited to ascend the throne of England; and the person of the unfortunate monarch having been seized, Henry was crowned on the 13th of October, 1399, in Westminster Abbey. On the discovery soon afterwards of a plot by certain of the nobility to assassinate King Henry, Richard was sent from the castle of Leeds, in Kent, to that of Pontefract, in Yorkshire, where he was murdered in his chamber by Sir Piers Exton, and a gang of assistant ruffians.

Henry the Fourth, on the day of his coronation, was attended from the Tower of London to Westminster, by the mayor and aldermen; and the King, to evince his great affection towards the citizens, caused all the blank charters that had been extorted from them in the late reign, to be burnt at the standard in Cheapside. Certain statutes of Edward the Third, which were deemed rather oppressive, were also repealed; an extension of privilege to merchants, relative to the package of goods, was granted; and the provision-markets, especially those for fish, were subjected to various salutary regulations.

Henry, though crowned, was not yet firmly seated on his throne. A little before Christmas, a conspiracy was formed by the Abbot of Westminster, in which, besides the Dukes of Albemarle, Surrey, and Exeter, the Earls of Gloucester and Salisbury, and others, the King's own son was implicated. In crushing this conspiracy, or rather in quelling the rebellion to which it gave rise, the citizens of London rendered excellent service to their Sovereign; and, in return, they were favoured in the following year (1401) with a new charter, which conferred upon the corporation and their successors for ever, the custody of Newgate and Ludgate, and of all the gates and posterns in the City, with various other privileges. In this same year, the prison called the Tun, in Cornhill, was converted into a cistern or conduit for Tyburn water: on one side of it was erected a cage, with a pair of stocks over it, for the punishment of night-walkers; also a pillory for the exhibition of cheating bakers and thievish millers.

About the year 1404, the woollen-manufacture was rapidly becoming the staple of the country; and a law was passed that all woollen cloths made in London should have a leaden seal affixed to each piece to distinguish them from those of inferior texture, and prevent imposition in the sale. Two years afterwards, an English mercantile company, denominated "The Brotherhood of St. Thomas à Beckett," which had been established towards the close of the thirteenth century, received a charter of confirmation, under which it long flourished.

The year 1407 is memorable for a dreadful and destructive plague which raged in London, and carried off thirty thousand of its inhabitants; by which corn became so cheap that wheat was sold at three shillings and fourpence the quarter. Six years afterwards, it was sold at sixteen shillings the quarter.

In 1410, two of the King's sons, the princes Thomas and John, were engaged in so serious a tumult in Eastcheap, that the Mayor, Sheriffs, and other citizens, found it necessary to repair to the spot. The case was investigated by commissioners, and the King was satisfied that the citizens had acted with a most laudable spirit.

It was in March, this year, that John Bradly, or Badly, a tailor, and follower of the doctrines of Wicklyffe, was convicted before Thomas, Archbishop of Canterbury, of heresy, and burnt to ashes in a cask in Smithfield. Henry, Prince of Wales, was present at the execution, and would have saved him; but the Prince's offer was resolutely rejected by the determined martyr.

Amongst other remarkable events of this reign, may be mentioned the erection of the Guildhall, by Sir Thomas Knowles, Lord Mayor, in 1411; and the rebuilding of a market-house, called the Stocks, on the site of the present Mansion House.

Henry the Fifth, soon after his accession to the throne, achieved the glorious victory of Agincourt. On Lord Mayor's day, 1415, Nicholas Watton was on his way to Westminster to qualify himself for the office of Mayor, when he received the news of this event by a King's messenger. Returning from Westminster, accompanied by the Bishop of Winchester, the Lord High Chancellor, &c., he repaired to St. Paul's cathedral, where Te Deum was sung with great solemnity. On the day following, a pompous and solemn procession was performed by the Queen, nobility, clergy, mayor, aldermen, and the several corporations of the City, on foot, from St. Paul's to Westminster, where the assemblage made a great oblation at the shrine of St. Edward, and then returned to the City in triumph. On his Majesty's return from France, with numbers of the French nobility as his prisoners, he was met on Blackheath by the Mayor, Aldermen, and Sheriffs of London in their robes, attended by three hundred of the principal citizens, mounted on stately horses richly accoutred. On that day the City conduits ran with various sorts of wine for the entertainment of the populace; and altogether the procession and triumph were of a description never surpassed for magnificence in London. The expense of the expedition to France, however, had been so enormous, that, in addition to the sum granted by Parliament, the King found himself obliged to pawn his crown to the Bishop of Winchester for twenty thousand marks, and his jewels to the citizens of London, for one thousand.

The reign of Henry the Fifth was a flourishing period for the City. A new gate was built leading to the waste in Finsbury-manor, since called Moorfields; Holborn was then first paved; and lanterns were first hung out for illuminating the streets by night, for the convenience and safety of the citizens. In 1419, Sir Simon Eyre built Leadenhall at his own expense, and gave it to the City to be used as a public granary against a time of scarcity.

The following anecdote forms a curious but rather painful illustration of the manners of the period. Inflamed, as it is said, by an ancient grudge respecting precedence, the ladies Grange and Trussel never met without a quarrel ensuing. The church itself was not proof against their violence. Being in a pew in the church of St. Dunstan's-in-the-East, they so imperiously vied for superiority, and became so shamefully outrageous, that their husbands, the Lord Grange and Mr. Trussel, became engaged in the quarrel. To revenge the presumed indignity offered to each other's wife, they drew their swords; and, refusing to listen to any terms of accommodation, they in the affray killed Thomas Petwarden, a fishmonger, and wounded several other persons. They were both, in consequence, apprehended, and committed to the Poultry Compter. Soon afterwards, they were excommunicated by the Archbishop of Canterbury, in St. Paul's Church, and by his order, in all the parish churches in

London: nor were they absolved till due submission had been made both to the church in which the murder was committed, and to the widow of Mr. Petwarden. After due inquisition, made into the affair, by the Archbishop of Canterbury, Lord Grange and his lady were convicted as the culpable parties.

A more gracious act was that of Sir Robert Chichly, Lord Mayor, who, by his will, appointed that, annually, on his birthday, a sufficient dinner should be given to two thousand four hundred poor citizens, with twopence to each in money.

On the demise of Henry the Fifth (August 31, 1422), his son, then only eight months old, was raised to the throne as Henry the Sixth, under the protectorship of his uncles, the Dukes of Gloucester and Bedford; and, on the 14th of November following, he was carried on his mother's lap, in an open chair, through the City in great state, to the Parliament of Westminster, where his accession was duly recognized. Thus, at the commencement of his reign, appearances were eminently auspicious, until a dangerous quarrel occurred between the Duke of Gloucester, Protector, and the turbulent Bishop of Winchester, afterwards Cardinal Beaufort, which had nearly proved fatal to the City, and involved the whole nation in blood. The Protector having received intelligence of the bishop's design to surprise the City of London, while the citizens should be engaged in feasting on the Lord Mayor's night (1426), he held a secret conference with John de Coventry, the Mayor; and, by the active exertions of that officer, the bishop's faction was, on the following morning, repelled in its attempt to force the City, from Southwark, and the insurrection was quelled without the effusion of blood. However, as it was found impracticable to effect a reconciliation between the Protector and the bishop, the Duke of Bedford, Regent of France, and brother of the protector, came over to England with the view of interposing his good offices. The mayor and aldermen, members of the nobility, and many of the more distinguished citizens, met him in state at Merton, and conducted him to and through the City to Westminster. On the day following, they presented him with a thousand marks in gold, in two silver-gilt basins.

About this time water conduits were first erected at Billingsgate, Paul's Wharf, and St. Giles's, Cripplegate, for supplying those neighbourhoods with water. In after times, it became customary, upon great occasions, to inscribe the City conduits with moral couplets; such, for instance, as

"Life is a drop, a sparkle, a span,
A bubble: yet how proude is man."

In 1426, Sir John Rainwell, then Mayor, having detected great malpractices amongst the Lombard merchants, in the adulteration of their wines, caused a hundred and fifty butts of the commodity to be staved in the kennels. It is said to have "emitted such a very noxious smell, that it infected the air to a great degree." Sir John gave certain lands and tenements for the payment of Parliamentary taxes, for the relief of the poor in the wards of Aldgate, Bishopsgate, and Dowgate.

The citizens appear to have forgotten the outrages which they had experienced at the hands of the proud Bishop of Winchester; as, on the return of that prelate from France, in the character of cardinal, they met him on his approach to London, and conducted him in great state to his palace in Southwark.

Feudal tyranny may be said to have received its death-blow in the metropolis in the year 1428. The express law of Edward the Confessor, entitling London to the privilege of conferring liberty on *servants (i. e. slaves)* who should have resided for a year and a day in the City unreclaimed by their

[illegible] ers of the [illegible] citizens, and [illegible] and though [illegible] not pre- [illegible] two [illegible]

[illegible] were [illegible] Wars and the Gates [illegible] for [illegible] wall water. [illegible] great occasion, to [illegible]

[illegible]

[illegible] Roosevelt, [illegible] having detected [illegible] the [illegible] It is said to [illegible] the [illegible] certain lands and [illegible] taxes, for [illegible] of Aldgate, Bishopsgate, and

[illegible] from France, [illegible] great [illegible]

[illegible] to have received its death [illegible] law of [illegible] shares) [illegible]

lords, was solemnly recognized and confirmed, and extended to all other cities, walled boroughs, and castles in the realm. An odious statute, imposed in the reign of Henry the Fourth, enacted, "That no person whatever, not possessed of land to the annual amount of twenty shillings, should be at liberty to put out a child or children as apprentice to any trade; and the tradesman taking such unqualified person as an apprentice to any trade was subjected to a grievous penalty. This was repealed.

In the same year, the stately palace called Baynard's Castle was destroyed by fire; but it was soon afterwards rebuilt in a more magnificent style by "the good Duke Humphrey of Gloucester."*

* Castle Baynard, whence the ward or aldermanry in which it was situated took its name, was one of the two castles built on the west-end of the City with walls and ramparts, as mentioned by Fitzstephen. It received its denomination from Ralph Baynard, a follower of William the Conqueror, who, at the general survey, possessed many other lordships in England. His descendant, Henry Baynard, having taken part with Helias, Earl of Mayne, who endeavoured to rob Henry the First of his Norman possessions, that Monarch confiscated Baynard's lordships, and deprived him of his barony, which he bestowed on Robert Fitz-Richard, grandson of Gilbert, Earl of Clare, who gave to him also the barony of Dunmow, in Essex. (For an interesting incident connected with the history of this castle, *vide* page 83.) The Fitz-Richard or Fitz-Walter family continued in high honour and reputation till the reign of Henry the Sixth, when the male branch having become extinct, Anne, the daughter and heiress, married into the Ratcliffe family, in which the title of Fitz-Walter was revived. In right of the castle, this family held the office of castellan and standard-bearer of the City of London. How the castle came into the hands of the Crown, has not been ascertained. On the death of Humphrey, Duke of Gloucester, by whom it was rebuilt after its destruction by fire, it was granted by Henry the Sixth to his cousin Richard, Duke of York, who lodged here during the convention of the great men of the kingdom, preparatory to the civil wars which followed. It was in this castle that Edward, Duke of York assumed

On the 21st of February, 1431, Henry the Sixth, returning from having been crowned at Paris, was met at Blackheath by the Mayor and Corporation of London, in a grand procession of state, and conducted by them to the City, where he was received and entertained in a style of the utmost pomp and magnificence. On this occasion, the City was decorated with costly silks and carpets; and on the bridge and streets through which the cavalcade passed, were seen a variety of gorgeous pageants, with persons representing the Loves, Graces, and Sciences. These, by their studied orations and minstrelsy, contributed largely to the splendour and excitement of the scene. Two days afterwards, the Mayor and aldermen attended the young King at Westminster, and presented him with a golden basket containing 1,000*l.* in nobles.

At this period, water was conducted from Tyburn to the Standard in Cheapside, at the expense of Sir John Wells, the late Mayor.

In 1434, so early as the 24th of November, a great frost

the title and dignity of King, in 1460. Richard the Third assumed the same dignities in Baynard Castle; and there it was that he received his minion Buckingham, by whom he was afterwards deserted. The castle was substantially repaired by Henry the Seventh, who converted it from a fortress to a palace; frequently resided within its walls, and hence made several of his solemn progresses. At a subsequent period it was the residence of Sir William Sydney, chamberlain and steward to Edward the Sixth. Here the "bloody Queen Mary" maintained her right to the Crown of England, and hence her partizans issued to proclaim her title. The castle was at that time the residence and property of William Herbert, Earl of Pembroke, a particular favourite of Mary's. Queen Elizabeth did that Earl the honour to sup with him; after which she went upon the water to show herself to the people. The last inhabitants of the castle were the Earls of Shrewsbury and their families, who resided in it till it again became a prey to the flames in the conflagration of 1666. It gives the name to the most wealthy and respectable ward in the City of London.

C. Marshall. J. Henshall.

set in, and continued till the 10th of February following, whereby the Thames was so intensely frozen, that all sorts of merchandize and provisions brought into the mouth of the river were unladen and brought by land to the City. The preceding autumn had been remarkably wet; and, in consequence, the corn was greatly damaged, a dearth ensued, and wheat was sold at the excessive rate of 1*l.* 6*s.* 8*d.* per quarter. Four years afterwards, the harvest again suffered so much by storms of wind and rain, that wheat once more, in London, reached the same enormous price; and in many parts of the country the poor were reduced to the necessity of making bread from fern-roots and ivy-berries. Speedy relief, however, was obtained by the exertions of Stephen Brown, the Mayor, in sending ships to Prussia for a supply of rye.

Philip, Duke of Burgundy, having perfidiously broken his alliance with the English, many of his unoffending subjects were, in 1435, murdered by the Londoners. In the following year, favouring his new ally, the French King, he commenced the seige of Calais; when the citizens of London distinguished themselves not only by getting ready their quota of troops within the time prescribed, but also by maintaining them at their own expense. On the arrival of the English force in the neighbourhood of Calais, the Burgundians, intimidated, raised the siege, and precipitately fled.

Philip Malpas, one of the sheriffs in 1440, proved a munificent benefactor to the City. He left, by his will, 124*l.* for the relief of poor prisoners; and every year, for five years, 400 shirts and shifts, 40 pairs of sheets, and 150 gowns of frieze to the poor. To 500 poor people in London 6*s.* 8*d.* each; to poor maids in marriage 100 marks; to the repair of highways 100 marks; 20 marks a-year for a graduate to preach; and 20*l.* to preachers at the Spital on the three

Easter holydays. In these charities, which were truly great at the time, he was imitated by Robert Large, Mayor in the same year, who gave 200*l.* to his parish church of St. Olave's, in Surrey; 25*l*, to St. Margaret's, Lothbury; 20*l.* to the poor; 100 marks to the bridge; 200 marks towards the vaulting over the water-course of Wallbrook; to poor maids in marriage, 100 marks; to poor householders, 100 marks, &c.

The ignorance and superstitious feeling of the times are shown by the following incident. In 1440, Sir Richard Wick, Vicar of Hermetsworth, in Essex, was burnt on Tower-hill for his reputed heretical opinions. Regarded by the people as a pious and holy man, the vicar of Barking Church, in that neighbourhood, a fraudulent and covetous priest, embraced the opportunity to impose upon the credulous multitude. Mixing ashes with the powder of aromatic spices, he secretly strewed them over the place where the martyr had been sacrificed, and then industriously reported the pretended miracle of the fragrancy of the dust. This immediately produced the effect required; the people in crowds hurried from all parts to the place of execution; and, finding the scent of the ashes in accordance with the report, they tumultuously arraigned the justice of the judges, for condemning a holy man. By the address and management of the crafty priest, the people were inadvertently led into idolatry; great numbers resorted to the spot, invoked the departed as a saint, and profusely offered at his shrine large sums of money, waxen images, &c. This farcical proceeding was kept up for about a week, to the no small profit of the priest, when, by an order from the Government, the Mayor and aldermen apprehended the author of the fraud, and many of his dupes, and committed them to prison.

In 1441, the beautiful cross which had been erected at

tne western end of Cheapside, or, as it was then called, West-cheap, by King Edward the First, in pious and affectionate remembrance of his beloved Queen Eleanor, in the year 1290, having fallen into decay, John Hatherly, the Mayor, applied to the King for permission " to re-edify the same in a more beautiful manner, by way of ornament to the City." Upon the exact size of this cross (demolished in 1581), a standard for the protection of the public in crossing the end of Cheapside has recently been erected. The first stone was laid on the 28th of May, 1838, by Mr. Westwood, the deputy of the north-side of the Ward of Farringdon Within. It is a plain shaft of granite, slender and tasteless in form, and too small for the area of which it forms the centre.* In digging for its foundation some antique remains were discovered.

Margaret, daughter of Rayner, Duke of Anjou, and titular King of Sicily, Naples, and Jerusalem, newly espoused to King Henry, was, on her way to London, 1445, met at Blackheath by the Mayor, corporation, and chief citizens, and conducted into the City with a degree of pomp and splendour almost equal to that with which her royal husband had been received on his return from having been crowned at Paris. Some time afterwards the King made the Queen a present of ten pounds per annum out of the profits arising from the *ripæ reginæ*, or Queen Hithe, in Thames-street.

The union of Henry with Margaret of Anjou was far from proving a happy event for the country. The imbecility of the King soon became notorious; the Queen and her minions

* The following inscription, placed in a glass vessel, was laid under the basement-stone:—" Farringdon Ward Within, North side. The first stone of this standard, erected by the Honourable the Commissioners of Sewers and Pavements, for the protection of the public, was laid on Monday, the 28th day of May, 1838, by Robert Westwood, Deputy. The Right Worshipful Thomas Kelly, Esq., Alderman."

usurped all power and authority; unusual discontent and tumult prevailed. Margaret, with Cardinal Beaufort, and the Dukes of Somerset, Suffolk, and Buckingham, had succeeded in accomplishing the ruin and death of that worthy and patriotic nobleman, the Duke of Gloucester. In revenge, the people of Kent had seized and beheaded the Queen's favourite, the Duke of Suffolk. Margaret's rage became boundless, and led the way to an insurrection so formidable as to shake the kingdom to its very centre. The Duke of York regarded this as a favourable time for making an effort to obtain the Crown. Having sounded the inclinations of the people, he found a suitable tool in the person of Jack Cade, a ruffianly Irishman, who, for his crimes, had been compelled to flee from his country. Nor from his own country alone; for, in the preceding year he had murdered a woman in a state of pregnancy, in England. For this offence he took sanctuary in a church, but having, through the interest of friends, obtained leave to transport himself, he went over to France. His restless spirit, however, induced a speedy return to his country, when he became known to the Duke of York. He is said to have borne a strong personal resemblance to John Mortimer, a prince of the blood, of the family of March, who was beheaded in the early part of the reign. Assuming to be Mortimer himself, Jack Cade went into Kent, where, under the pretext of reforming abuses in the Government, and of liberating the people from all taxation, he soon found himself at the head of an extensive rabblement force, with which he marched back towards London. At Blackheath he formed an encampment for a month, and established a regular communication with certain disaffected parties in the City. Horses, arms, and money, and a daily accession of force were thus obtained. The King marched against him with an army of fifteen thousand men.

C. Marshall. J. C. Varrall.

[illegible]

The Royal force was led into ambush in the neighbourhood of Seven Oaks, and utterly defeated with great loss. Flushed with success, Cade again set out for London. At Blackheath he was met by the Archbishop of Canterbury and the Duke of Buckingham, who, in the King's name, demanded his surrender. This he refused, unless Henry would come to him in person and grant all his demands. On the receipt of this intelligence, the King and Queen retired to Kenilworth Castle, leaving no troops in London but those in garrison at the Tower. Cade, upon advice of the King's flight, marched for London, and fixed his head-quarters in the White Hart Inn, Southwark. All was confusion in the City. Most of the members of the Lord Mayor's council summoned upon the emergency, were for the immediate admission of Cade; but Robert Horne, alderman and fishmonger, strenuously opposed his reception. So enraged were the rebels at this opposition, that to pacify them the Mayor was not only obliged to send Horne to Newgate, but to open the City-gates and admit them. Cade immediately issued a proclamation strictly commanding all his followers not to molest or offer any violence to the citizens, nor extort anything from them without payment upon pain of death. In his march through Cannon-street, he struck London-stone with his sword, exclaiming, " Now is Mortimer Lord of this City." He returned at night to his quarters in Southwark. Next day he caused the Lord Saye, High Treasurer of England, to be apprehended and arrainged before the Lord Mayor and Judges at Guildhall. On his refusal to plead, and insisting upon his right of peerage, Cade caused him to be taken from the bar, and instantly led to the standard in Cheapside. There, without allowing him time for confession, he had him beheaded: his head, fixed upon a spear, was carried before the rebels in triumph, and his body, at a horse's tail, was drawn through the City, hanged upon a gibbet, and afterwards quartered. Sir James Cromer, the late Chancellor's son-in-law, and sheriff of the county of Kent, was subjected to a similar fate at Mile-end. His head, placed upon a pole, was, with that of Lord Saye, carried before Cade through the principal streets of the City, the sanguinary rebel making them, in mockery, kiss each other in every street. Cade, with the view of enriching himself, now plundered many of the chief merchants of the City. The wives and daughters of the citizens were also exposed to the brutal assaults of his rabble. These evils speedily wrought their own cure. Cade having marched into Southwark for the night, it was unanimously resolved to shut the gates and oppose his return. Attempting to force his passage over the bridge, a desperate battle, with great loss of life on both sides, ensued. In defence of the drawbridge, Sir Mathew Gough, Lieutenant of the Tower, Alderman Sutton, and many of the brave citizens, were either killed or drowned. Greatly discouraged and weakened by his loss, Cade was obliged to recruit his army with the prisoners of the King's Bench and Marshalsea. With the view of prevailing upon the people to return to their respective homes, a general pardon was now offered. This produced so sudden and wonderful an effect, that before daylight, Cade was deserted by most of his followers and left to shift for himself. Not daring to wait for the succours promised by the partisans of the Duke of York, he fled in disguise into the woody part of Sussex. A proclamation was issued by Government, offering a reward of one thousand marks for his capture dead or alive. Cade was discovered lurking in a garden at Hothfield, by Alexander Eden, or Iden, a Kentish gentleman, who, in his attempt to seize him, killed him in fight. He then put his corpse into a cart and conveyed it to London, where he received the proffered

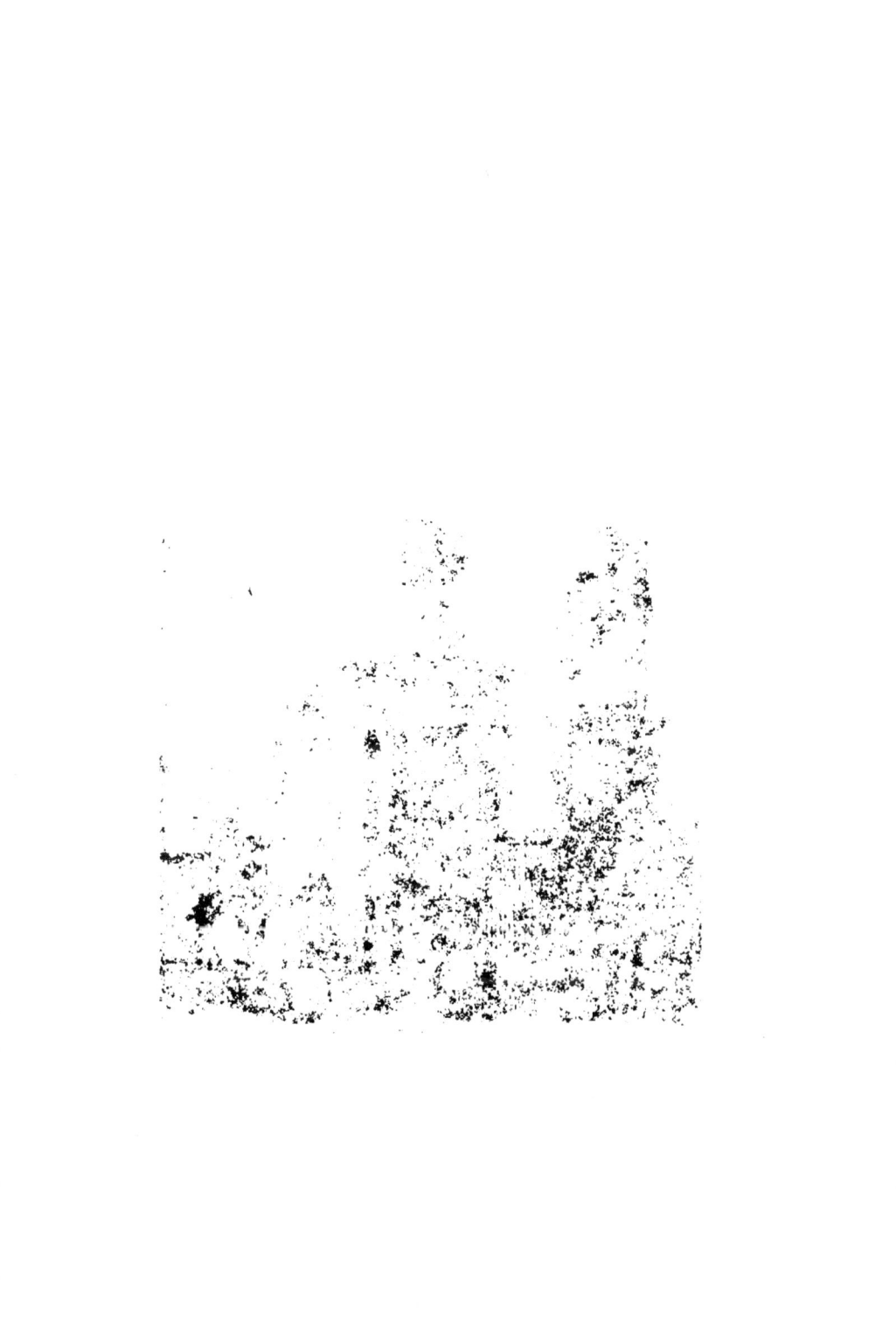

[illegible] City, [illegible] a gibbet, and afterwards Sir James Cromer, [illegible] Chancellor [illegible] of the county of Kent, was subjected [illegible]. His head, placed upon a pole, [illegible] carried before Cade through the [illegible] the sanguinary rebel making [illegible] each other in every street. Cade, [illegible] himself, now plundered many of the [illegible] City. The wives and daughters of [illegible] were [illegible] exposed to the brutal assaults of his rabble, [illegible] speedily wrought their own cure. Cade having [illegible] into Southwark for the night, it was unanimously resolved to shut the [illegible] and oppose his return. Attempting to force his passage over the bridge, a desperate [illegible], with great loss of [illegible] on both sides, ensued. In defence of [illegible] Sir Mathew Gough, Lieutenant of the Tower, Alderman [illegible], and many of the brave citizens, were either killed or drowned. Greatly discouraged [illegible] by [illegible], Cade was obliged to recruit his [illegible] the prisoners of the King's Bench and Marshalsea. [illegible] calling upon the people to return to their [illegible] a general pardon was now offered. The [illegible] wonderful an effect that [illegible] deserted by most of his followers and [illegible] to wait for the [illegible] of the Duke of York, [illegible] in [illegible] of Sussex. [illegible] reward of [illegible] alive. [illegible] by [illegible] Eden, of [illegible] who, in his attempt to seize him. [illegible] protected

Eng^d by I. Woods

ST. MARTIN'S CHURCH

AND

CHARING CROSS.

reward. Thus, through the bravery and gallant deportment of the citizens of London, a dangerous rebellion was suppressed with slight comparative loss. In consideration of the service performed by the citizens on this trying occasion, Sir Godfrey Fielding, the Mayor, was, in 1452, appointed one of his Majesty's Privy Councillors.

In 1454, John Norman, having been chosen Mayor, changed the custom of riding to Westminster on the day of inauguration to that of proceeding thither by water. His example of building a stately barge at his own expense was followed by the several companies of the City, and the barges, all splendidly adorned and majestically floating on the stream, formed a striking aquatic spectacle. The watermen, to whom the change proved highly advantageous, were so delighted that they framed a song in praise of the new Mayor, commencing with the words, "Row thy boat, Norman, row to thy leman." The Lord Mayor's procession by water has continued to the present time. Through the influence of the bishops and clergy, numerous public schools were, in the course of the reign of Henry the Sixth, established in different parts of London. The alleged object of this was, "to check and suppress other smaller schools set up by illiterate men, who did the youth more harm than good.

The contests which had long subsisted between the clergy and laity, arising out of the power given to the curates of the City to levy certain offerings or rates, were finally and amicably adjusted in the year 1453.

From the defective state of the City police at this period, tumults were almost incessantly occurring in the streets. On one occasion, in a broil between the students of the Inns of Court and the inhabitants of Fleet-street, the Queen's attorney was killed; and, in consequence, the principals of Furnival's, Clifford's, and Barnard's-inns were committed prisoners to Hertford Castle, and Alderman Taylor and others were committed to the Castle of Windsor.

After a long succession of civil disturbances in various parts of the kingdom, the imbecile Henry was deposed; the Earl of March, the eldest son of the Duke of York, was unanimously chosen King in his stead, under the title of Edward the Fourth; and on the 5th of March, 1461, he was proclaimed at the usual places in the City. On the same day, the new Sovereign dined at Baynard's Castle, and continued there till his army was ready to march in pursuit of his predecessor, who had fled into the north and assembled an army of sixty thousand men. How lightly human life is held by the rulers of semi-civilized states, may be estimated by the seriously-related story, that during King Edward the Fourth's stay at Baynard's Castle, " he caused Walter Walker, an eminent grocer in Cheapside, to be apprehended and tried for a few harmless words innocently spoken by him, viz., that he would make his son heir to the Crown, inoffensively meaning his own house, which had the Crown for its sign, for which *sanguinary crime* he was beheaded in Smithfield on the eighth day of his reign." A few months afterwards, a servant of the King's household had one of his hands cut off at the Standard in Cheapside for striking a man within the Palace at Westminster.

In the second year of his reign, King Edward, to evince his gratitude to the citizens of London for the many great and signal services done to him, granted them a new charter, confirming all their former liberties and free customs, and investing them with many important additional privileges.

In 1463, the Lord Mayor distinguished himself by insisting upon his right of precedency in the City. On a call of new Sergeants-at-Law, an entertainment was given by them at Ely House, Holborn, to which the Mayor and Corporation were invited. Upon their entrance it was perceived that Baron Ruthen, the Lord High Treasurer, had assumed the seat of honour at table. The Lord Mayor insisted that at all times and upon all occasions he, as the King's representative, and in honour of his principal and Sovereign, was entitled to the pre-eminence, or most honourable place of all subjects of what denomination soever, within the City and liberties thereof. Lord Ruthen, however, refused to surrender his seat, and the Mayor and citizens, in consequence, withdrew from the hall and returned to the City. There they were sumptuously entertained by the chief magistrate.

On the night before the coronation of Queen Elizabeth, in 1465, Thomas Cook, the then Lord Mayor, had the honour of being installed a Knight of the Bath in the Tower of London. Shortly after the expiration of his mayoralty, Sir Thomas Cook, with others, was impeached of the crime of high treason. He was, in the first instance, admitted to bail, but afterwards he was arrested, committed to the Tower, his goods seized, and his wife consigned to the custody of the new Mayor. Upon his trial at Guildhall, Sir Thomas was honourably acquitted; but, through the cupidity of his prosecutors, he was detained a close prisoner till he had purchased his liberty at the exorbitant price of eight thousand pounds to the King, eight hundred marks to the Queen, and the sacrifice of immense property embezzled by the servants of his enemies, who had obtained possession of all his estates.

About this time, an alderman, for offensive language to the Mayor, and for his obstinacy in refusing to remove the noisome carcass of a dog from before his door, was fined by the Court of Aldermen in the sum of fifty pounds.

An amusing illustration of the manners of the period (1468), presents itself in the mode of punishment inflicted on some of the London jury who had been found guilty of receiving bribes. They were sentenced to ride from Newgate to Cornhill with paper mitres upon their head; having been some time exposed, they returned in the same manner.

The Earl of Warwick having succeeded in effecting the release of King Henry from the Tower of London, where he had endured a confinement of more than six years, Henry was restored to the Crown, and Edward was declared a usurper, and with his brother, the Duke of Gloucester, attainted by Parliament in the winter of 1471. At that period the Parliament sat at St. Paul's. Violent proceedings were so much dreaded by the Lord Mayor, John Stockton, that to avoid participating in them he feigned illness, and Sir Thomas Cook (admitted to his seat and restored to his estates), sat for a considerable time as his *locum tenens.* The sanguinary conflicts which ensued were at length terminated by the death of the unfortunate Henry, and the consequent undisputed possession of the throne by Edward the Fourth.

In 1472, there being only one pair of stocks in London, the Mayor caused stocks to be erected in every ward for the more effectual punishment of vagrants; and in the following year he endeavoured to clear the City and liberties of disorderly women by means of corporal punishment and indecent exposure.

It is due to the memory of William Caxton, citizen and mercer, and to the noble and invaluable art of typography, to place his name upon record as the first English printer. Caxton, a native of Kent, was born in the year 1410. Having served his time as a mercer, he went abroad as agent to the Mercers' Company, and afterwards was taken into the suite of Margaret of York, wife of the Duke of Burgundy. Whilst residing in Flanders, he acquired a knowledge of the art of printing, and translated and printed in that country the

"Recuyell of the History of Troy." Returning to England in 1472, he brought with him this and other printed books as specimens of his skill, and in the year following, under the patronage of Thomas Milling, Abbot of Westminster, he established a press in the Almonry, where he produced, in 1474, a little book translated from the French, called the Game at Chess. This is the first book ever printed in England.

Indefatigable in application, Caxton printed and published about fifty works, some of them large volumes, and many of them his own productions. He died in 1491.

From the autumn of 1475 to the winter of 1476, a pestilence raged in London by which an incredible number of people died. During the prevalence of this calamity, Sir Bartholomew James, the Mayor, while at his devotion in St. Paul's church, imagined himself to be insulted by Robert Byfield, one of the sheriffs. His Lordship complained to the Court of Aldermen, by which Court the sheriff was subjected to the fine of fifty pounds, to be appropriated towards the repairs of the City conduits. In 1480, the Lord Mayor and court of Aldermen fined a person named Robert Deynis twenty pounds, for presuming to marry an orphan in the City without their license.

King Edward, in 1481, obtained a loan of five thousand marks from the City; in return for which he, in the following year, gave the Mayor and Corporation a grand hunting-match in Waltham Forest. Amongst other things, he also sent two hares, six bucks, and a tun of wine for the entertainment of the Lady Mayoress and the wives of the aldermen and chief citizens.

The death of Edward the Fourth (1483)—the assumption of the Protectorate by Richard, Duke of Gloucester—his usurpation of the Crown, and alleged murder of the young

King, Edward the Fifth, and his brother, in the Tower—and his death on Bosworth-field—are matter of general rather than of local history, unless it were upon a more extended scale than the present.

Henry, Earl of Richmond, proclaimed King by his victorious army on the 22nd of August, 1485, was met at Highgate five days afterwards, by the Lord Mayor and aldermen in state, and conducted into the City. It was about the 11th of October following that that dreadful distemper denominated the sweating sickness, first began to rage in London. Amongst the incredible numbers who were rapidly carried off by this terrific scourge were the new Mayor, Thomas Hyde, and his immediate successor Sir William Stokker, and one f the sheriffs; so that, in this year, the City had three mayors and three sheriffs. So strict were the citizens at this period, to exclude all foreign interest, that, in the mayoralty of Nicholas Exton (1456) it was renewed and confirmed, by a clause in the oath prescribed to every freeman at the time he was made free, that he should " take none apprentice, but if he be free-born, that is to say, no bondman's son, nor the son of any alien." Two years afterwards, very salutary regulations were passed (and it would be well could they be renewed) prohibiting, under penalties, the slaughter of cattle within the walls of the City.

Henry the Seventh, who, throughout his reign, extorted large sums from the City, in the form of loans, benevolences, &c., gave a grand Christmas banquet to the Mayor and Corporation, at Westminster, in 1493. On this occasion, he conferred the honour of knighthood on Ralph Austry, the Mayor.

In 1498, many beautiful gardens at Finsbury were converted into a spacious field for the use of the London archers, or, trained-bands. Portions of this site are now occupied by

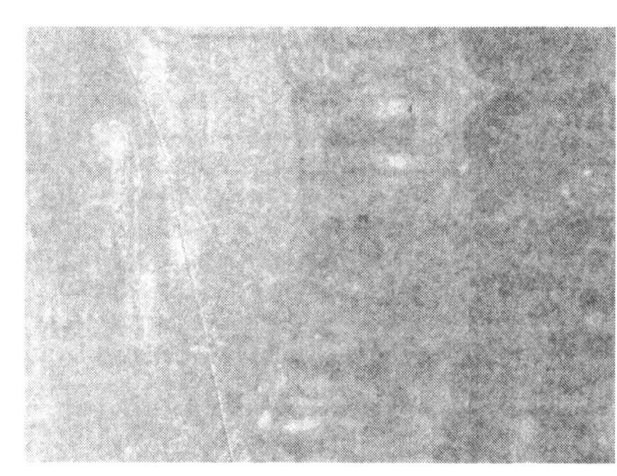

what is termed the Artillery-ground, and by an extensive burial-place for Dissenters.

The prices of provisions, at successive periods, are not without interest. In the year of the sweating sickness, such was the dearth that wheat was sold at 24*s.* the quarter; in 1493, it had fallen to 4*s.*, and pickled herrings might be purchased at 3*s.* 4*d.* per barrel; in 1499, wheat was at the same low price, wine was sold at 10*s.* per hogshead, and bay-salt at 4*d.* per bushel. The consumption of the City must have been soon afterwards reduced; as, in 1500, from 20,000 to 30,000 of its inhabitants were carried off by the plague.

Amongst the improvements of the metropolis, in the reign of Henry the Seventh, it may be mentioned that, in 1502, Fleet-ditch, the remains of the old river of Wells, was scoured down to the Thames; so that it was rendered navigable for large boats, laden with fuel, fish, &c., up to Old-bourne, or Holborn-bridge. Excepting as a common-sewer, all traces of this old river" are now extinct. About the same time, Houndsditch, which, till then, had been a noisome receptacle of carrion and all sorts of filth, was carried up and paved over.*

* Edric, the Saxon thane, who assassinated his Sovereign, Edmund Ironside, after losing him a battle by treachery, was drawn by the heels from Baynard's Castle through the City, and thrown into Houndsditch, by command of King Canute, after he had been tormented to death by burning torches.—Brayley's *Londiniana*, vol. iv., p. 35. From time immemorial, Houndsditch appears to have been inhabited by much the same class of people as at present; Jews, pawnbrokers, usurers, dealers in old clothes, &c. Stow observes that, "towards the street, were some small cottages, of two stories high, and little garden plots backward, for poor bedrid people, for in that street dwelt none other, builded by some prior of the Holy Trinity, to whom that ground belonged." Anthony Munday, in his additions to Stow, speaks of the "unconscionable broking usurers, a base kind of vermin," who had crept into Houndsditch, and were both the "discredit of the age, and of the place where they are suffered to live."

Although London, in common with every other part of the kingdom, suffered lamentably from extortion during the tyrannical reign of Henry the Eighth, many important improvements were effected. Not only did the City indulge itself in all the pageantry of splendid and expensive spectacles, according to the taste of the age, but due attention was paid to the arts and sciences, and to the general comfort and elegancies of life. Henry's first public act, that of committing Empson and Dudley, the tools of his predecessor, for illicitly furnishing his coffers, to the Tower of London, was eminently calculated to induce popularity. These wholesale plunderers of the people were afterwards condemned and attainted by Parliament, and beheaded upon Tower-hill. Two days after the King's accession, all beggars, not belonging to the City, were banished, and compelled to seek relief from their respective parishes. On St. John's eve, 1510, Henry, in the habit and arms of one of the yeomen of his guard, came into the City to witness the setting of the City-watch; one of the most interesting and magnificent processions of those times, and, excepting that it was at night, not slightly resembling the festival of *Corpus Christi* as celebrated in all Roman Catholic towns of the Continent. So delighted was he with the spectacle, that, on the St. Peter's night following, accompanied by his Royal consort, and attended by the principal nobility, he returned to the City, and in Cheapside was again a spectator of the show.

Sir William Fitz-William was, in 1510, disfranchised becaused he refused to serve the office of sheriff. On the fall of Cardinal Wolsey, his former master, this gentleman gave him kind entertainment at his country-house. The King demanded how he durst entertain so great an enemy to the State. His answer, was, that he had not contemptuously nor wilfully done it, but because he had been his master, and partly the maker of his fortune. Pleased with his answer, the King said he had himself too few such servants: he immediately knighted him, and afterwards made him a Privy Councillor. Sir William, at his death, left many large sums for charitable purposes; and to the King he bequeathed his great ship with all her tackles and his collar of the Garter, with his best George set with diamonds. He was Knight of the Order of the Garter, Lord-Keeper of the King's Privy Seal, and Chancellor of the Duchy of Lancaster.

Roger Achilly rendered his mayoralty, in 1511, remarkable by storing Leadenhall, the City-granary, with every sort of grain. He also caused Moorfields to be levelled, and the passage to the adjoining villages rendered more commodious, by raising causeways and building bridges as might be required. In the following year, the sheriffs of London and Middlesex were, for the first time, empowered by Parliament to empannel jurors for the City courts. In 1514, a tumultuous mob from the City broke down all the fences in the neighbourhood of Islington, Hoxton, and Shoreditch, on pretence that their inhabitants had debarred them from their usual exercises in the fields; and also that when any of them attempted to divert themselves with shooting, their bows and arrows were seized, and destroyed before their eyes, and they themselves were indicted for trespasses. The King's Commissioners severely reprimanded the Mayor and alderman for neglect of duty on this occasion.

In 1517, a new tribunal was established by the Common Council under the denomination of the Court of Conscience. The act of the Council appointed "that the Lord Mayor and aldermen for the time being shall monthly assign and appoint two aldermen and four discreet commoners to sit at Guildhall, in a judicial manner, twice a-week, viz., on Wednesdays and Saturdays; there to hear and determine all matters brought before them between party and party (being citizens and freemen of London), in all cases where the due debt or damage does not exceed forty shillings." This act was passed as an experiment for two years; but its effects were found so beneficial that it was afterwards extended from time to time, and at length rendered perpetual by Parliamentary authority in the first year of James the First.

The May-day of 1515, was rendered memorable in the City of London by a serious tumult, which broke out chiefly, in the first instance, amongst the artificers and apprentices, against strangers who were permitted to send their wares and to exercise handicrafts in the City, " to the great hindrance and impoverishing of the King's liege people." Many lives were lost in the affray, and the day was ever afterwards distinguished as " Evil May-day." Mayings and May-games, with the ceremony of setting up a May-pole in Leadenhall-street, were less frequently celebrated after this insurrection. It was about this time that London was again grievously afflicted with the sweating sickness, which, as it was peculiar to England and to Englishmen, in foreign parts was termed Sudor Anglicus, or the English sweat. In 1521, another infectious distemper raged in the City and swept off numbers of the population.

Henry, in the tenth year of his reign, granted the citizens of London a charter for removing the sessions of the peace from St. Martin's-le-Grand to Guildhall. He also granted a charter of incorporation to the physicians. In the same year, the common ditch between Aldgate and the Postern next the Tower-ditch, was cleansed at an expense of 95*l*. 3*s*. 4*d*. The payments indicate the cost of labour at this period: the chief ditcher sevenpence per diem; the second ditcher sixpence;

TWICKENHAM AIT

the other ditchers fivepence; and labourers, or vagabonds as they were then termed, one penny *per diem* each, and meat and drink at the City's charge.

In 1531, one of the greatest entertainments recorded in the annals of London was given in the Bishop of Ely's palace in Holborn, for five days in succession. The occasion was that of eleven gentlemen of the law being promoted to the dignity of the coif. There were present at this feast, the King, Queen, Foreign Ministers, Lord Mayor, Judges, Master of the Rolls, Aldermen of the City, Masters of Chancery, Sergeants-at-Law, principal Merchants of London, many knights and esquires, and a certain number of citizens, members of the chief companies. Making due allowance for the difference between the value of money then and at the present period, and also for the difference between the size and weight of cattle then and now, the reader may be enabled, from the subjoined list (which is only *part* of the bill of fare), to form some estimate of the nature, cost, and extent of this entertainment.

	£.	s.	d.
Twenty-four large oxen, each at	1	6	8
The carcass of a large ox	1	4	0
One hundred sheep, each at	0	2	10
Fifty-one calves, each at	0	4	8
Thirty-four hogs, each at	0	3	8
Ninety-one pigs, each at	0	0	6
Ten dozen capons of Greece, each dozen at .	0	1	8
Nine dozen and a half of Kentish capons, each at	0	1	0
Nineteen dozen of common capons, each at .	0	0	6
Seven dozen and nine of grouse or heath-cocks, each at	0	0	8

	£.	s.	d.
Fourteen dozen and eight common cocks, each at	0	0	3
The best pullets, at	0	0	2½
Common ditto, at	0	0	2
Thirty-seven dozen of pigeons, each dozen at .	0	0	10
Three hundred and forty dozen of larks, each dozen at	0	0	5

This subject demands a little further illustration. It is stated, upon the authority of Anderson's "History of Commerce," that, at the period above referred to, the number of butchers, in London and the suburbs, did not exceed eighty. Upon an average, each butcher killed nine oxen per week; which, multiplied by forty-six (the number of weeks in a year during which meat was eaten, none being consumed during Lent) gives 33,120 as the total annual consumption of oxen in London. In round numbers the carcasses at present consumed in a year are about—

Oxen, 110,000	Calves, 50,000
Sheep, 770,000	Swine, 250,000
Lambs, 250,000	

This constitutes an average amount of 1,738,303 cwt., and produces a sum of 10,000,000*l*. to the agriculturist.* In

* It must be remembered also, that a large quantity of meat now arrives in London ready slaughtered, not only in steam-vessels from Scotland and Ireland, but in carts from the provinces. This quantity is increasing, and may, perhaps, be estimated at one fourth of the whole consumption. A further increase will result from the arrangements made with the different railroads.

In addition to meat must be taken into account poultry, fish, bread, butter, cheese, eggs, milk, vegetables, &c. The first of these is estimated to amount annually, in value, to 85,000*l*.; to which must be added, game.

addition to the vast increase of numbers must be taken into consideration the immense increase of weight in all cattle, which has been more than doubled, even within the last century and a-half. About the year 1700, the average weight of the oxen sold in the London market was 370lbs.; of calves, 50lbs.; of sheep, 28lbs.; and of lambs, 18lbs.: the present average

pigeons, rabbits, &c., amounting to as much in price, though the supply is less in quantity than the product of the farm-yard.

London is supplied with fish chiefly from the two wholesale markets of Billingsgate and Hungerford. From Billingsgate, by far the larger of the two, the following has been recently given as the division of 120,000 tons of fish in a single year:—

Fresh salmon . . .	45,446	Haddock	90,604
Turbot	87,558	Mackarel	482,492
Cod	444,138	Lobster	3,076,700
Herring	3,366,400	Whiting	1,954,600
Maid, Plaice, Skate, Sprat & Sole (bshls)	115,215	Eel (cwt.)	1,500
		Crab	500,000

It is generally considered that the article of FISH is by far too dear before coming to the consumer; and that this wholesome part of our animal food might, with proper management, be had generally at a much lower price: as a proof of what may be done that way, those fishmongers who are content with moderate profits, and offer their commodity at a reasonable price, all command immense business.

With bread and flour, it requires about 1,000,000 quarters of wheat per annum to supply the metropolis. Of butter, the annual consumption is estimated at 21,000,000lbs., of cheese, 26,000,000lbs. With milk, the town is supplied by upwards of 10,000 cows, supposed to yield a daily average of nine quarts each, making a total of 8,212,500 gallons annually: producing to the wholesale dealers a sum of 400,000*l.*; on which the retail dealers are considered to lay a profit of cent. per cent., exclusive of what they realise by the addition of water *ad libitum*. Of eggs, including those from France, Holland, Ireland, Scotland, &c., in addition to the produce of our own country, the consumption is incredible. The fruit and vegetables, brought to the London markets, from the gardens in the vicinity of the metropolis (exclusively of the produce of Kent, Surrey, and the more distant counties), are thought to amount in annual value to upwards of 1 000,000*l.* sterling.

weight is, of oxen, 800lbs.; of calves, 140lbs.; of sheep, 80lbs.; and of lambs, 50lbs.

The philosophic mind will be yet more deeply impressed with a sense of the growing greatness of the metropolis, when it is brought to view, that London, formerly contained within a circumference of two miles, now occupies a surface of eighteen square miles, within a supposed circumference of thirty miles. Taken in its largest extent, London is understood to contain from 10,000 to 12,000 streets, squares, lanes, courts, &c.; 156,000 houses and public edifices; and from 1,500,000, to 2,000,000 of people.

In 1544, " by reason of a great mortality among the cattle, occasioned by great rains in the preceding season, meat rose to such an excessive price, that mutton was sold at 2*s*. 4*d*. the quarter, and a lamb at 3*s*. 4*d*." In consequence, the Lord Mayor and Council made a sumptuary law for preventing luxurious eating.* By this law it was, amongst other things, enacted that, " neither the Mayor, aldermen, nor sheriffs, should buy any cranes, swans, or bustards, upon penalty for every fowl so bought, of the sum of 20*s*." About the same time, coal, bought at Newcastle for 2*s*. 2*d*. per chaldron, was sold in the City at 4*s*.

King Henry, in the year 1532, and again in 1539, caused a general muster of the citizens, from the age of sixteen to that of sixty, to the extent of 15,000 men, to be made at Mile-end; with an account of the weapons, armour, and other military accoutrements belonging to the City. In the first instance, the citizens assembled early in the morning: before nine, they commenced their march through the City to Westminster; went round St. James's-park; passed down Holborn, and thence to Leadenhall, where they separated at five o'clock. This procession, which occupied more than eight hours, appears to have been of a very imposing character.

* *Vide* page 88.

[illegible] 8d. [illegible]

[illegible] the metropolis [illegible] London [illegible]

[illegible] in its largest extent, London [illegible] from 10,000 to 12,000 streets, [illegible] houses [illegible] different [illegible] 1,500,000 [illegible]

In 1[illegible] dearness [illegible] the preceding season, meat [illegible] was sold at 2s. 4d. [illegible] In consequence, the Lord [illegible] Mayor [illegible] [illegible] was [illegible] [illegible] the Market [illegible] [illegible] quarter [illegible] About [illegible] bought at Newgate for 2s. 2d. per stone, was [illegible]

[illegible] the year 1782 and [illegible] 1789, [illegible] [illegible] sixteen [illegible] of 15,000 men [illegible] [illegible] armour, and other [illegible] [illegible] the City. In the first [illegible] [illegible] the [illegible] [illegible] through the City to [illegible] [illegible] than eight hours, appears [illegible] [illegible] been of a [illegible] character.

* [illegible]

WEST INDIA DOCK.

IMPORT

Still more splendid, however, was the pageant by which, in 1533, Queen Anne Boleyn (descended from Godfrey Boleyn, or Bolaine, Lord Mayor of London in 1457) was, upon her coronation, conducted by the Mayor and all the City companies from Greenwich, by water, to the Tower; and thence, by land, to St. Paul's, and afterwards to Westminster. In gorgeous pomp and stately magnificence, it would be difficult to imagine this joyous procession surpassed. Within three years afterwards, the hapless Queen terminated her brief career of loyalty upon the green within the Tower; where, at the behest of a sanguinary tyrant, "who never spared man in his anger nor woman in his lust," her blood flowed at the stroke of the executioner!

In the course of his reign, which terminated in 1547, the Strand, Holborn, Whitechapel, and most of the other chief thoroughfares of the metropolis, were paved. Water was also conveyed into the City in additional streams from Hampstead, Marylebone, Hackney, Muswell-hill, and the springs of Agnes le Clair, Hoxton.

During the brief reign of Edward the Sixth many salutary regulations were effected, and numerous benefits were conferred upon the City. By a new charter, its right and title to the jurisdiction of the borough of Southwark was confirmed. To prevent injurious combinations between the butchers and graziers, the prices of cattle, through the different seasons, were fixed by law; as were also the prices of various other provisions. The company of Hanseatic, or German merchants, generally termed merchants of the Still-yard, having engrossed nearly the whole trade of the kingdom, was dissolved, and trade was thrown open. Christ's Hospital, commonly called the Blue Coat School, was founded by Edward the Sixth for the "innocent and fatherless."*

* This noble institution consisted at first of a grammar-school for boys,

It may not be deemed unworthy of notice, that, on her return from France, through England, in 1550, after the demise of her husband, the ill-fated Mary Queen of Scots was sumptuously entertained at the Bishop of London's palace, by the Mayor and citizens, for four days successively. On her departure, she was attended by the chief nobility in a style of extraordinary magnificence. The Duke of Northumberland had in Cheapside one hundred men on horseback, armed with javelins; of whom forty were dressed in black velvet, with velvet hats and feathers, and golden chains about their necks: next to them were ranged one hundred and twenty horsemen belonging to the Earl of Pembroke, with javelins, hats and feathers; then one hundred gentlemen and yeomen belonging to the Lord Treasurer, with javelins; the procession closing with three bodies of horse extending from the end of Gutter-lane, in Cheapside, to Birchin-lane, in Cornhill. The Queen of Scots was attended by all the nobility to Shoreditch Church, and thence conducted by the sheriffs of London to Waltham.

and a separate school for girls. By Charles the Second it was further endowed with 1,000*l.* to found a school for the instruction of forty boys in mathematics and navigation. A second mathematical school for thirty-six boys was subsequently founded by Mr. Travers. There are now on the foundation nearly 1,200 children. The Mayor and Corporation are guardians of the institution. The building, occupying the site of the ancient order of Franciscians, founded in 1225, is very irregular. The ancient cloisters, serving as a place of recreation for the boys in wet weather, have been lately replaced by new ones, the masonry of which is remarkably fine. The south-front, opening to Newgate-street, is ornamented with Doric pilasters, and a statue of the royal founder. A new and commodious hall, of the Tudor style of architecture, and forming a beautiful feature in the public eye, has lately been built from designs by John Shaw, Esq. Several of the wards, and other portions of the structure, have been rebuilt in a style admirably corresponding with the more ancient parts of the edifice. The revenues of the Hospital are very considerable. The annual expenditure amounts to 30,000*l.*

As related to the City of London, the most remarkable incident in the reign of Queen Mary was the rebellion originated in Kent by Sir Thomas Wyatt. To oppose his force, on its march to attack the City, five hundred men were confided to the command of Alexander Brett, an experienced officer. At Rochester, however, Brett harangued his men, and succeeded in carrying them over to the rebel army. In consequence, many of the chief officers of the Duke of Norfolk's force fled in terror, and their ordnance, ammunition, and equipage, fell into the hands of Wyatt. London was thus thrown into a state of the utmost consternation. At length, after a series of successes, Wyatt was compelled to surrender, and his crime was expiated under the axe on Tower-hill.

At this period, taverns and places of similar resort had so perniciously increased in number, that it became expedient to restrict them by law. It was accordingly enacted, that the number of retailers of wine within the City and liberties of London should not exceed forty, nor those of Westminster three. French wines were then sold, duty free, at 8d. per gallon, and other wines in proportion.

Upon the demise of Queen Mary (1558), her sister the Princess Elizabeth was proclaimed Queen of London, with the usual solemnities, heightened by the extraordinary and heartfelt joy which was experienced on the occasion. On the 14th of January, 1559, she rode through the City to Westminster in state, in the most pompous manner. At the upper end of Cheapside, she was presented by the Recorder with a thousand marks in gold in a purse of crimson velvet, richly embroidered, as a sincere testimony of the unfeigned love and respect of the citizens towards her Majesty. In July following, the twelve principal corporations of London sent out twelve companies, consisting of fourteen hundred men, of whom eight hundred were pike-men in bright armour, to be reviewed in Greenwich-park before the Queen.

The year 1561 was memorable from the circumstance of the steeple of St. Paul's Church, and a great part of the building, being destroyed by lightning. And the same year the plague committed great ravages in the City.

In 1566, Sir Thomas Gresham, a merchant and citizen of London, proposed to the corporation that if they would find a convenient site, he would erect, at his own cost, a commodious edifice or bourse, for the accommodation of merchants. A fine building was accordingly opened in November, 1567. It was originally called the Bourse, but, on the visit of the Queen Elizabeth and her Court to the City on the 23d of January, 1570, when her Majesty dined with Sir Thomas, at his mansion in Bishopsgate-street, she caused it to be publicly proclaimed as the Royal Exchange. At his death, Sir Thomas Gresham beqeathed it to his widow, and after her decease, to the Mayor and citizens of London, and to the Mercers' Company; directing the rents to be expended in the support of lectures on the sciences. This building was destroyed by the great fire of 1666, and was quickly rebuilt nearly upon its former site, with statues of the Kings, and of Sir Thomas Grosham, at an expense of nearly 100,000*l*. Sir Christopher Wren, or, according to some accounts, Mr. Edward Jerman, was the architect. It was opened on the 28th of September, 1669, only three years after the destruction of the original building. A few years since, it was substantially repaired, and a new clock-tower was erected from the designs, and under the superintendence of George Smith, Esq., architect to the Mercers' Company, at the joint expense of that company and the Corporation of London. This edifice was destined to experience the fate of its predecessor. On the night of the 10th of January, 1838, a fire broke out in

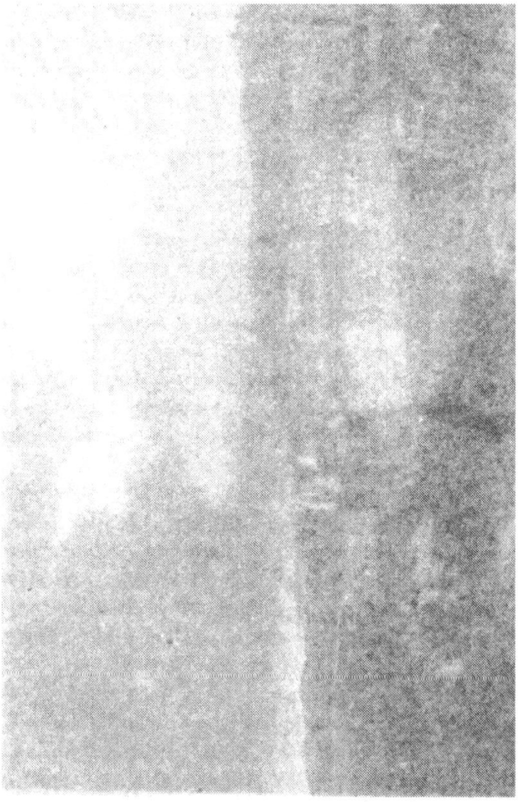

Lloyd's Coffee-room, at the north-east corner of the building, opposite the Bank of England. A considerable time elapsed before the requisite assistance for arresting the progress of the flames could be obtained; and the consequence was the entire destruction of one of the noblest monuments of British wealth and mercantile power.

The Gresham Lectures, endowed by Sir Thomas, were formerly delivered in one of the rooms in the Royal Exchange. Since the fire, they have been delivered in the theatre of the City of London School, a new and handsome structure, occupying the site of Honey-lane-market, in the rear of the houses facing Bow Church, in Cheapside.*

* It will be only anticipating the order of time to state, that the first stone of this school was laid by Lord Brougham, on the 21st of October, 1835, and that it was opened in February, 1837. The design was by James Bunstone Bunning, Esq., architect to the Foundling Hospital. It is an imposing building, in the style of the Elizabethan age, the principal windows and entrance being of an earlier period, and more enriched character. Excepting the chief portion of the centre compartment, of the principal front, which is nearly all of stone, it is executed in white brick with stone dressings. The porch of the centre is novel, and the entrance to the interior is by a splendid hall. The school contains nine class-rooms and a library, rooms for the masters, a theatre for lectures, apartments for the secretaries, offices for the servants, &c. John Carpenter, the original founder of the school, was town-clerk of London in the reigns of Henry the Fifth and Henry the Sixth. By his will he gave and devised to the City of London the sum of nineteen pounds ten shillings per annum, arising from houses in the City; directing the same to be expended in the education of four sons of freemen of London. By the improved value of property, the present clear annual income of the estate is not less than nine hundred pounds. The state of the charity was investigated in 1833, and the City afterwards obtained an Act of Parliament for establishing the present school. The candidates for admission are the sons of freemen of the City, or householders therein. Four scholarships have been founded on the suggestion of Carpenter's will, upon a certificate of merit from the head master. Four boys are educated, boarded,

The first public lottery in England was drawn at the west-gate of St. Paul's Cathedral, in 1569. The drawing commenced on the 11th of January, and continued, without ceasing, day and night, till the 6th of May following.

At the Midsummer following, the pompous cavalcade of the City marching watch was discontinued on account of its enormous expense; and in lieu thereof a system of night police was established, which was continued until within these few years.

The poulterers of London having by combination greatly enhanced the prices of poultry, the Corporation settled the prices according to the following table:—

	£.	s.	d.		£.	s.	d.
The best goose at. .	0	1	0	The best woodcock .	0	0	5
The best wild mallard	0	0	5	The green plover .	0	0	3
The best capon, at .	0	1	0	Pigeons, per dozen .	0	1	0
The second sort . .	0	0	10	Blackbirds, ditto . .	0	0	10
The best hen . . .	0	0	7	Rabbits, each . . .	0	0	3
The best chickens, each	0	0	3	The best eggs, five for	0	0	1
An inferior sort . .	0	0	1½	The best butter, per pound.	0	0	3

Other regulations respecting costume are not less curious. Luxury having made great inroads amongst the chief citizens of London, they had become so extravagant in dress, that in the year 1579 the Queen found it necessary to issue a proclamation against excess of apparel, gold chains, and cloaks, the last of which were worn of such length that they reached to the heels. By the same proclamation, the length of daggers was limited to twelve inches clear of the hilts; and

and clothed, and receive the sum of one hundred pounds each towards their advancement. The instruction given is of a high character. An annual public examination takes place, at which prizes are distributed. There is a head master, and twelve others in the various departments; and, as they are allowed to receive pupils, the number is upwards of five hundred.

[illegible] at the [illegible]

[illegible] drawing [illegible]

[illegible] without [illegible]

[illegible] the [illegible]

[illegible] a [illegible] police was [illegible] within these few years. [illegible] settled [illegible]

[illegible]

[illegible] costume [illegible] great [illegible] the chief citizens [illegible] so extra[illegible] that in [illegible] found [illegible] to [illegible] a pro[illegible] and [illegible] of such length that they reached [illegible] same [illegible] the length of [illegible]

[illegible] the sum of one hundred [illegible] towards [illegible] instruction given [illegible] An [illegible] public [illegible] place, at which prizes are distributed. [illegible] and twelve others in [illegible] departments; [illegible] allowed to [illegible] pupils, the number is upwards of five

J. Salmon, del. T. Woods, sc.

VIEW IN ST. JAMES'S PARK.

three feet only was allowed for the length of swords. Three years afterwards, the apprentices of London, encouraged by the example of their superiors, had reached such an excess in their style of apparel, that the Lord Mayor and Common Council found it necessary to enact:—

"That from thenceforth no apprentice whatsoever should presume, 1. To wear any apparel but what he receives from his master. 2. To wear no hat within the City and liberty thereof, nor anything in stead thereof, than a woollen cap, without any silk in or about the same. 3. To wear no ruffles, cuffs, loose collar, nor other thing than a ruff at the collar, and that only of a yard and a-half long. 4. To wear no doublets but what were made of canvas, fustian, sack-cloth, English leather, or woollen-cloth, and without being enriched with any manner of gold, silver, or silk. 5. To wear no other coloured cloth or kersey, in hose or stockings, than white, blue, or russet. 6 To wear little breeches, of the same stuffs as the doublets, and without being stitched, laced, or bordered. 7. To wear a plain upper coat of cloth or leather, without pinking, stitching, edging, or silk about it. 8. To wear no other surtout than a cloth gown or cloak lined or faced with cloth, cotton, or baize, with a fixed round collar without stitching, guarding, lace, or silk. 9. To wear no pumps, slippers, nor shoes but of English leather, without being pinked, edged, or stitched, nor girdles nor garters other than of crewel, woollen, thread, or leather, without being garnished. 10. To wear no sword, dagger, or other weapon but a knife; nor a ring, jewel of gold, nor silver, nor silk, in any part of his apparel, on pain of being punished at the discretion of the master for the first offence; to be publicly whipped at the hall of his company for a second offence; and to serve six months longer than specified in his indenture for a third offence."

It was further enacted, "That no apprentice should frequent or go to any dancing, fencing, or musical schools, nor keep any chest, press, or other place for keeping of apparel or goods, but in his master's house, under the penalties aforesaid."

It is remarkable with what facility the City appears to have been able to raise vast bodies of men in cases of emergency. On the first rumour of a Spanish invasion in 1585, the several Corporations sent a handsome body of five hundred men into the field, completely armed, at their own expense. Soon afterwards, the same companies fitted out a considerable body of soldiers, who were sent to the assistance of the Dutch against the Spaniards. In 1587, the threat of Spanish invasion still operating *in terrorem*, ten thousand men were raised in the City. The armada having been dispersed, apprehensions were yet entertained of future attacks, and, in 1596, the Lord Mayor and aldermen while at church received a message from the Queen, commanding them forthwith to raise a certain number of able-bodied men, fit for immediate service. On this warlike mission, they instantly left the church: before eight at night they had pressed a thousand men, and with an unparalleled expedition they completely fitted them with martial accoutrements before the next morning. This little army, raised as it were by magic, disappeared as suddenly: intended to proceed to Dover to assist the French against the Spaniards in defence of Calais, it was dismissed before it had been full four-and-twenty hours assembled. Soon afterwards, the same number of men were impressed in the churches of the City during the time of Divine service. They were immediately armed and sent off towards Dover to embark for France, but in consequence of intelligence of the reduction of Calais, they were countermanded and came home about a week after their departure. On many occasions the citizens also raised a considerable naval force.

At the summer sessions in 1585, there were discovered to be in London, Westminster, Southwark, and the suburbs, no fewer than eighteen houses for the lodging and entertaining of thieves of all descriptions. "Among the rest," observes Maitland, "they found out one Wotton, a gentleman born, and sometime a merchant of good credit, but fallen by time into decay. This man kept an ale-house, at Smart's Key near Billingsgate, and after, for some misdemeanour put down, he reared up a new trade of life; and in the same house he procured all the cut-purses about the City to repair to his house. There was a school-house set up to learn young boys to cut purses. Two devices were hung up, one was a pocket and another was a purse: the pocket had in it certain counters, and was hung about with hawk's-bells, and over the top did hang a little sacring-bell; the purse had silver in it: and he that could take out a counter without any noise was allowed to be a public *foyster:* and he that could take a piece of silver out of the purse without noise of any of the bells, was adjudged a judicial *nypper*, according to their terms of art. A *foyster* was a pick-pocket, a *nypper* was a pick-purse or cut-purse."

It was in the year 1585, that the first instance appears upon record of the custom of the Lord Mayor's nominating sheriffs by drinking to persons considered qualified for the execution of that office.

Queen Elizabeth having terminated a long and glorious reign in the year 1603, was immediately succeeded by James the First, who was proclaimed King in the City on the 24th of March, with every demonstration of joy.

Notwithstanding the short-sighted policy of the pedant King, who appears to have been incessantly haunted by the idea that the metropolis had outgrown itself, and that restrictive measures were necessary to prevent its further excess, many local improvements were effected in the course of his inglorious career. Sir Hugh Myddleton completed his admirable scheme of supplying the City with water by means of the New River; the footpaths of the principal streets were, for the first time, paved with flag-stones; Spitalfields began to be covered with houses; a large pond in the vicinity of Smithfield was filled up, and transformed into thoroughfares under the names of Cow, Chick, Hosier, and other lanes; the extensive fields and gardens of the grand priory of St. John of Jerusalem, and of a convent to the north of Clerkenwell-green, were built upon; Holborn gradually stretched away westward till it formed a junction with the village of St. Giles-in-the-Fields; and twelve new public granaries were erected at Bridewell, sufficiently capacious to hold six thousand quarters of corn, to be sold to the poor at prime cost in case of dearth or famine. The Levant or Turkey Company were incorporated under a perpetual charter, by the designation of the Merchants of England trading to the Levant seas; the London and Liverpool merchants went on successfully, and unrivalled, in their Greenland fishery; and the Merchants Adventurers' Company —those of the Staple, the Russia, and the East India Companies—made a progress so vast in the respective branches of their commerce, that, in the year 1613, the money paid for exports and imports in London alone amounted to 109,572*l*. 18*s*. 4*d*.—nearly thrice as much as all the other ports of England paid in the same year.

The monastery of the Carthusian Friars, near Smithfield, having been granted, on the suppression of the order, to the Earl of Suffolk, Mr. Thomas Sutton, in 1612, purchased it of that noble family for the sum of 13,000*l*. and laid out 7,000*l*. more in repairs and improvements, intending to render it at once a seminary of literature, and an asylum for decayed merchants, &c.; he also endowed it with lands, producing, at that time, 4,490*l*. a-year. This excellent institution, now inaccurately known by the name of the Charter House, has given education to some of the first schools of our time, and is in a very flourishing state.

In the year following, Sir Baptist Hicks (afterwards created Viscount Campden), one of the justices of the peace for the county of Middlesex, at his own expence built a sessions-house for the accommodation of the magistracy, at the bottom of St. John-street. This was called Hicks's Hall, in honour of the founder; and, for many years, it constituted the point from which distances on that line of road were measured.

It was about the year 1617, that several of the bishops applied to the King for leave for the people to amuse themselves on Sundays. James, willing to indulge the prelates in their requests, as well as the people in their pleasures, caused certain rules to be drawn up and published, under the royal sanction, entitled, ***The Book of Sports;*** with a positive injunction to the several parochial incumbents to read the same in their respective churches, upon pain of the King's displeasure. Many of them, proving refractory, were suspended and imprisoned. The Lord Mayor, despite of the Royal licence, caused the King's carriages to be stopped, as they were passing through the City on a Sunday in the time of Divine service. For a time, these proceedings induced an ill feeling between the Court and the City, but it speedily subsided.

The reign of the unfortunate Charles the First commenced inauspiciously. In its first year, the plague raged most destructively in London and its suburbs; carrying off 35,417 persons—about one-third of the inhabitants.

Without entering into particulars, which want of space precludes, it may be remarked, that, from the commencement of his reign, Charles and the City were at variance. Disputes arose in relation to ship-money, loans, and other grievances. The City was deprived of some advantages gained in the proceding reign, and amerced in 50,000*l*. The citizens, taking part with the Parliament against the King, strengthened their City with forts, joined by a line of communication, formed by a rampart of earth, which completely surrounded London Westminster, and Southwark.

Shortly after Charles's execution, Sir Abraham Reynardson, then Lord Mayor, refusing to proclaim the abolition of monarchy, was degraded from his office, and imprisoned, and a new Mayor chosen in his room.

In 1657, the Lord Mayor assisted at the inauguration of Cromwell; but, after the death of that usurper, the City joined with General Monk in bringing about the restoration. On the 29th of May, 1660, the Lord Mayor and Aldermen went out and met Charles the Second in St. George's-fields.

At the close of this, and commencement of the following year (1661), London became the theatre of an extraordinary insurrection, originating with a small number of wild, desperate, and sanguinary enthusiasts, called "Fifth-Monarchy Men." From the appearance of certain dangerous symptoms, Colonel Overton, Major Wild, Cornet Day, and other principal members of the sect, had been arrested. This proceeding so incensed their confederates, that, assembling in their meeting-house in Swan-alley, Coleman-street, on the evening of Sunday, the 6th of January, about sixty in number, well armed, they broke into open rebellion, under the conduct of their preacher, Thomas Venner, a cooper. Possessed with the fanatical notions, "that no weapon formed against them should prosper, not a hair of their heads be touched—that one should chase a thousand, and two put ten thousand to flight"—their design was to erect a Fifth Monarchy for the personal reign of Jesus Christ upon earth. In their "Declaration," entitled, "A Door of Hope opened," they affirmed, "That they would never sheath their swords, till Babylon (as they called Monarchy) became a hissing and a curse; and there be left neither remnant, son, n — nephew: that, wner.

Drawn by Hablot Browne from a Sketch by E. Garland. Engraved by J. Woods

LIMEHOUSE CHURCH

they had led captivity captive in England, they would go into France, Spain, Germany, &c., and rather die than take the wicked oaths of supremacy and allegiance: that they would not make any leagues with monarchies, but would rise up against the carnal, to possess the gate, or the world, to bind their kings in chains, and their nobles in fetters of iron."

Having read their proclamation, they marched to St. Paul's church-yard, and declaring for King Jesus, they killed a man who declared for King Charles. Sir Richard Brown, the Lord Mayor, receiving intelligence of this, hastened with a party of the trained-bands to suppress the riot. The rebels, however, fell upon his force with an impulse of infatuation so incredible, that it was speedily routed. Marching, without opposition, towards Bishopsgate, and through Whitecross-street, they re-entered the City at Cripplegate. Learning that a party of horse was in pursuit of them, they thence retreated as far as Beech-lane; where, being opposed, they killed a constable, and proceeded to Caen-wood, in the neighbourhood of Hampstead. There they reposed for the night. Next day they were dispossessed of the wood by a military force, and some of them taken prisoners. The day after, they rallied again and returned to London, when they divided themselves into two parties, one marching towards Leadenhall, the other to Haberdasher's Hall, in Maiden-lane, with the view of surprising the Lord Mayor. The former were pursued by the trained-bands, and, after an obstinate resistance, dispersed in Eastcheap. The latter, headed by Venner, missed the Lord Mayor, and passed into Wood-street, where they encountered the trained-bands, and also a party of the horse-guards, who had come to their assistance. A desperate battle ensued; and the rebels continued fighting till Venner was dangerously wounded and taken, and two others of their preachers and fiercest combatants were killed. A retreat toward Cripplegate was then commenced; the rear firing in good order upon the troops in pursuits. More effectually to prevent the advance of the military, Colonel Cox, their commanding officer, posted ten men in a neighbouring alehouse, which they defended with great energy till it was surrounded and entered on all sides, and seven of the rebels killed. The quelling of this desperate commotion, though on so small a scale, cost the lives of twenty of the King's troops, besides several of the trained-bands and others. Of the rebels, about twenty men were killed and fourteen taken; eleven of whom were afterwards tried, convicted, and executed; and thus terminated a petty insurrection, which, for a few days, assumed a formidable aspect.

In 1663, the King granted the City a confirmation of all its ancient charters, privileges, liberties, rights, and customs; and the citizens in return advanced considerable sums of money towards carrying on the war with Holland, for which they received the thanks of both Houses of Parliament. An extraordinary mark of his Majesty's favour towards the City of London was his confirmation of the Irish estates in the province of Ulster to the citizens, of which they had been violently deprived by an arbitrary decree of the Star Chamber during his father's reign. By this tenure the City of London and the several companies concerned are still in the enjoyment of these estates.

The metropolis was now to experience calamities of the most disastrous nature. Scarcely, as it may be said, had the sword of civil war been sheathed, than heaven in its dispensation destroyed its inhabitants by pestilence, to the extent of a hundred thousand persons, in the awful year 1665;* and in the following year its entire surface was desolated by fire. Whether it be considered with reference to its immediate

* For particulars relating to the plague of the year 1665, *vide* page 127.

effects or to its remote consequences, the latter was one of the most important events that ever occurred in London. The conflagration of 1666 broke out about one o'clock in the morning of Sunday, the 2d of September; being impelled by strong winds it raged with irresistible fury, nor was it entirely mastered until the fifth day after it began. It originated in the house of one Farryner, the King's baker, in Pudding-lane, near New Fish-street-hill, and within ten houses of Lower Thames-street, into which it spread within a short time; nearly all the contiguous buildings being of timber, and lath and plaster, and the whole neighbourhood consisting of little else than close passages, and narrow lanes and alleys. Its ravages were at length stayed at the Temple church, near Holborn-bridge, Pie-corner, Aldersgate, Cripplegate, near the end of Coleman-street, at the end of Basinghall-street, by the Postern, at the upper end of Bishopsgate-street, Leadenhall-street, at the Standard in Cornhill, at the church in Fen-church-street, near Clothworkers' Hall, in Mincing-lane, at the middle of Park-lane, and at the Tower-dock. The destructive fury of this conflagration was never, perhaps, exceeded in any part of the world, by any fire originating in accident. Within the walls it consumed nearly five-sixths of the whole City, and without the walls it cleared a space almost as extensive as the one-sixth part left unburnt within. Hardly a single building that came within the range of the flames was left standing. Public edifices, churches, and dwelling-houses, were involved in one common fate; and, making due allowance for irregularities, the fire may be said to have extended its ravages over a space of ground equal to an oblong square of a mile and a half in length, and half a mile in breadth. In the summary account of this tremendous devastation, given in one of the inscriptions on the Monument, and which was drawn up from the reports of the surveyors appointed after the fire, it is stated that the ruins of the City were four hundred and thirty-six acres (viz., three hundred and seventy-three within the walls, and sixty-three without the walls, but within the liberties); that of the six-and-twenty wards, it utterly destroyed fifteen, and left eight others shattered and half burnt; and that it consumed eighty-nine churches, four of the City-gates, Guildhall, many public structures, hospitals, schools, libraries, a great number of stately edifices, thirteen thousand two hundred dwelling-houses, and four hundred streets. The aggregate loss of property sustained on this occasion has been roughly estimated at from seven to upwards of ten millions sterling. Whether this calamity were the effect of accident or design, is a question that has been productive of much controversy; but there are many circumstances upon record which combine to enforce a belief that the fire had been preconcerted by the Papists. Fortunately, however, amidst all the confusion and multiplied dangers which arose from the fire, it does not appear that more than six persons lost their lives.

Great exertions were made both by Government and individuals to re-edify the City, and the Parliament, acting on the King's proclamation, passed an Act for regulating the buildings and expediting the work. While this was in progress, various temporary edifices were raised for the public accommodation, both with respect to Divine worship and to general business. Gresham College, which had escaped the flames, was converted into an Exchange and Guildhall, and the Royal Society, founded only two or three years before, removed its sittings to Arundel House. The affairs of the Custom House were transacted in Mark-lane; the business of the Excise-office was carried on in Southampton-fields, near Bedford House; the General Post-office was removed to Brydges-street, Covent-garden; the offices of Doctors'-commons, were

[illegible] fire, it is stated that the ruins of [illegible] and thirty-six acres [illegible] within the walls, and sixty-three [illegible] within the liberties; that of the six- [illegible] fifteen, and [illegible] eight [illegible]; and that it consumed [illegible] City-gates, Guildhall, many public [illegible] schools, libraries, a great number of [illegible] thousand two hundred dwelling-houses, [illegible] streets. The aggregate loss of property [illegible] on [illegible] occasion has been roughly estimated at from [illegible] of ten millions sterling. Whether this calamity [illegible] is a question that has been [illegible] of much controversy; but there are many circum- [illegible] combine to enforce a belief that the fire had been [illegible] by the Papists. Fortunately however, amidst all the [illegible] and multiplied dangers which [illegible] fire, [illegible] does not appear that more than six persons [illegible].

[illegible] both by Government and [illegible] the Parliament, acting on the [illegible] passed an Act for regulating the buildings [illegible]. While this was in progress, various [illegible] were [illegible] for the public accommodation [illegible] to Divine worship and to general business. [illegible] had escaped the flames, was con- [illegible] and Guildhall, and the Royal [illegible] three years before, removed its [illegible]. The officers of the Custom House [illegible] Mark-lane; the business of the Excise- [illegible] in Southampton [illegible] Bedford [illegible] was removed to Bridge- [illegible] of Doctors'-commons [illegible]

held at Exeter House, in the Strand; and the King's wardrobe was consigned from Puddle-wharf to York-buildings. For a time, the inhabitants were chiefly lodged in huts raised in Finsbury and Moorfields, in Smithfield, and on all the open spaces in the vicinity of the metropolis.

Amongst the several plans that were proposed for the restoration of the capital, were three which acquired much celebrity: the first was designed by Dr., afterwards Sir Christopher Wren, surveyor-general and principal architect for rebuilding the whole City; the second by Mr., afterwards Sir John Evelyn; the third by Dr. Newcourt, father of Richard Newcourt, author of the "Repertorium, or Ecclesiastical History of the diocese of London." Neither of these plans, however, "could be adopted in practice, though every person was convinced of the advantages that would eventually result; for the jealousies of the citizens, lest they should be too far removed from the sites of their old residences, proved to be insuperable, and very few would recede from their claims to particular spots. From that cause the opportunity was lost of rendering this metropolis the most magnificent of any in the world. Still, however, much was effected; avenues were widened, declivities raised, and obstacles removed. And although all was not done that might have been executed, under the influence of other feelings, the entire City (with the exception of the churches and larger public buildings) was rebuilt within little more than four years, and in a style of far greater splendour and regularity, and infinitely more commodious and healthful than the ancient capital." One of the great advantages of this change was the total extermination of the plague, which has never since made its appearance in London.*

* The fullest particulars of the fire of London are to be found in Lord Clarendon's "History of his own Life;" in the Diaries of Evelyn

The Monument, on Fish-street-hill, erected by Sir Christopher Wren, to commemorate the fire of 1666, was commenced in 1671, and finished in 1677. It is fluted, of the Doric order, and stands on a massy pedestal forty feet high. This column exceeds in height the famous pillars of Trajan and Antoninus at Rome, and contains upwards of twenty thousand square feet of Portland-stone. At different times four persons have committed suicide by precipitating themselves from the top of this column,—the last a young lady, in September, 1839.

James the Second ascended a throne (1685) upon which he was unworthy to sit. His enmity against the City of London was never effaced; and though he restored a charter of which he had been the means of depriving the citizens, it was pusillanimity alone that impelled his conduct. The sacrifice of Alderman Cornish, alleged to have been implicated in the Rye-house plot, was an act of cold-blooded revenge, inexcusable as it was base. Another act of his tyranny was the commitment of the seven bishops to the Tower. The power of the Papist was for a brief period in the ascendant. James, however, saw when too late that the popular resentment was more than mere popular clamour; and in the deep discontent of his people, he beheld the fatal errors he had committed, and would have retracted the steps he had taken in favour of Papal jurisdiction. His concessions were as mean as his tyranny had been excessive. On his abdication of the throne which he had disgraced, about thirty of the peers and bishops then in town (being the only remaining authority in the State) met at Guildhall; and after a short consultation with the Lord Mayor and aldermen, it was resolved to adhere to the Prince of Orange, subsequently

and Pepys; in a tract, entitled, "God's Terrible Advice to the City, by Plague and Fire," by the Rev. T. Vincent, a Non-conformist divine; in Malcolm's "Londinium Redivivum," &c. There is also an ably-condensed view of the subject, to which we have been indebted in the above sketch, in Brayley's "Londiniana," vol. i., page 148, *et seq.*

proclaimed King as William the Third, with his consort, Mary the Second, the daughter of James.

In the year 1687, the City had been greatly enriched, and its population increased, by the settlement of between thirteen and fourteen thousand French Protestants, who, driven by persecution from their native home, sought an asylum in this country of civil and religious liberty. These children of peaceful industry took up their abode chiefly in Spitalfields and the parts adjacent.

In the reign of William and Mary, certain places of supposed privilege from arrest in the City were suppressed: that in the Minories; those in and near Fleet-street, as Salisbury-court, Whitefriars, Ram-alley, and Mitre-court; in Holborn, Full-wood's-rents, and Baldwin's-gardens, in Gray's-inn-lane; the Savoy, in the Strand; in Southwark, Montague-close, Deadman's-place, the Clink, and the Mint.

King William, who had survived his consort, dying in 1702, the Princess Anne, daughter of the late King James, and consort of his Royal Highness George, Prince of Denmark, succeeded to the crown, to the universal delight of the nation. During the preceding reign, she had suffered many petty persecutions from the King, her brother-in-law, who, whatever he might be as a ruler, had little that was amiable in his character as a man. Consequent upon the several splendid victories achieved by the Duke of Marlborough, the Queen, in testimony of her gratitude to the Almighty, for his great and glorious success, visited St. Paul's church in solemn procession. On the humble request of the citizens of London, all the standards and colours taken by the British troops at the battle of Ramillies, were presented to the City by order of her Majesty. In this reign an order was given for building fifty new churches, which greatly improved the appearance of the metropolis.*

* It may be worth while to mention, if only in a note, that, at the com-

On the death of her Majesty Queen Anne (1714), George Lewis, the eldest son of Ernest Augustus, Duke and Elector

mencement of the eighteenth century, the village of St. Marylebone was almost a mile distant from any part of London, the nearest street being Old Bond-street, which then hardly extended to the present Clifford-street. Soon after the accession of George the First, New Bond-street arose, with other streets in the immediate neighbourhood, and the houses in Berkeley-square and its vicinity. Hanover-square and Cavendish-square were open fields in the year 1716. They were built about the beginning of the reign of George the Second, at which time the houses arose on the north-side of Oxford-street, which then first took the name. The neighbourhood of Cavendish-square and Oxford-market, Holles-street, Margaret-street, Vere-street, &c., are of the same date; and the grounds for Harley, Wigmore, and Mortimer-streets, were laid out, the village and church of Marylebone being still separated from them all by fields. At the same time the Legislature ordered the erection of the three parishes of St. George, Bloomsbury, St Anne, Limehouse, and St. Paul, Deptford; London having then extended further in the last quarter than in any other, by reason of the trade on the river.

After the year 1737, the west end of the town was improved by the addition of Grosvenor-square and its neighbourhood. Anticipating time, it may be added, that the increase of the metropolis on all sides was in proportion to the length of the reign of George the Third. The vacant space near Marylebone was filled in; Southwark became a mass of houses united with Westminster; and new towns, rather than suburbs, appeared in all quarters; some with the names of towns, as Camden-town and Somers-town; to which have been added, since the death of that Prince, Portland-town, and a large half of Paddington, now almost joined with Kilburn. Then, again, the whole of the extensive space from Goodman's-fields to Stepney, over Whitechapel-road to Shadwell, has been covered with closely-compacted habitations. The London, the St. Katherine's, and the East and West India Docks, have been constructed, and the space to Hackney, Bethnal-green, and Mile end, built upon. The neighbourhood of the respective new churches in Marylebone and the Regent's-park, presents a succession of noble mansions.

Public convenience and the improved state of society called for enlarged thoroughfares; and crowded districts have been converted into noble streets, lined with costly residences. Such was the origin of the architectural

[illegible] Queen Anne (1714). George [illegible] of Ernest Augustus, Duke and Elector [illegible]

[illegible] the village of St. Marylebone was [illegible] of London, the nearest [illegible] being [illegible] extended [illegible] street. [illegible] of George the First, New [illegible] street [illegible] neighbourhood, and the houses [illegible] Hanover-square and Cavendish-square [illegible] year 17[illegible]. They were built about the beginning [illegible] the Seventh, at which time the houses arose on [illegible] first took the name. The [illegible] Cavendish-square [illegible] Holles-street, [illegible] same date; and the grounds [illegible] were [illegible], the village [illegible] of Marylebone [illegible] separated from them all by fields. At the same time the [illegible] ordered the erection of the three [illegible] St. Anne, Limehouse, and St. Paul, Deptford [illegible] have [illegible] extended [illegible] in the last quarter [illegible] of the [illegible] on the river.

[illegible] 1737 [illegible] west end of the town was improved by the [illegible] square and its neighbourhood. Anticipating time, [illegible] the metropolis on all sides was in [illegible] of George the Third. The vacant [illegible] was filled in; Southwark [illegible] a mass of houses [illegible], and new towns, rather than suburbs, appeared [illegible] with the names of [illegible] Camden-town and [illegible] the death of that Prince, [illegible] of Islington, now almost joined with [illegible] the space [illegible] Goodman's-[illegible] to Shadwell, has been covered [illegible] close [illegible] upon. The [illegible] Marylebone and the [illegible] park, [illegible] succession of noble mansions.

[illegible] state of society called for enlarged [illegible] districts have been converted into noble [illegible]

of Brunswick Lunenburg, by the Princess Sophia, youngest daughter of Frederick, Elector Palatine of the Rhine, and

improvements in the vicinity of Pall-mall; and a magnificent line of streets, including Regent-street and the Quadrant, leading from St. James's Park to the Regent's Park. A stately range of elegant houses has been formed on the site of Carlton Palace; dividing which, in the centre, his late Majesty William the Fourth, on ascending the throne, commanded a way to be broken into the park, and a fine flight of steps to be constructed for the accommodation of the public. At this point is a monument—a column of pale red granite, one hundred and fifty feet in height—erected to the memory of the late Duke of York. The column, ascended by a spiral staircase, is surmounted by a bronze statue of his Royal Highness.

Exeter Change, and the line of old houses down the north side of the Strand, have been removed, the streets widened, and many improvements made, while others are still in progress. That fine edifice, St. Martin's church, now open to the view of the public, forms part of the eastern side of a spacious opening named Trafalgar-square; on the northern side of which is an unworthy structure, denominated the National Gallery of the Fine Arts; and in the centre of which is to be erected a public monument to the memory of Nelson.

Fleet-market has been removed; and the opening now forms a wide and airy street, leading to Holborn-bridge, and which, it is expected, will, at no distant period, be carried on to Islington. Covent-garden-market has undergone an entire change, and is now not an object of commerce only, but of curiosity and interest. The new Hungerford-market, at the south-western extremity of the Strand, is finished, and proves a formidable competitor, not only to Billingsgate-market, but to that of Covent-garden.

The New Post-office, St. Martin's-le-Grand, has long been in full activity; the Colosseum, and St. Katherine's Hospital, in the Regent's-park, are objects of considerable interest; and the Zoological Gardens, much enlarged, and considerably enriched by the liberality of their late Majesties, George the Fourth and William the Fourth, have become eminently attractive.

The New Palace at Pimlico (Buckingham House remodelled at an enormous expense, and with lamentable deficiency of taste and judgment) is, from its having been made the chief residence of her present Majesty, Queen Victoria, and from the surrounding improvements, likely to become the centre of the Court end of the town. Belgrave-square, eclipsing in

Elizabeth, eldest daughter of James the First, succeeded to the throne of Britain. His Majesty, accompanied by his eldest son, Prince George, arrived in England, and made his public entry into London on the 20th of September. He was received at St. Margaret's-hill, Southwark, by the Lord Mayor, aldermen, sheriffs, and officers of the City, in whose name Sir Peter King, Recorder, addressed him in a congratulatory speech, and the King was received with every mark of public satisfaction. In this reign of thirteen years there is little of importance to record specifically relating to the City of London. In 1716, the "Mug-house riot," instigated by a low Jacobite rabble, was suppressed by the execution of five of the ringleaders, in front of a house which they had nearly demolished in Salisbury-court, Fleet-street. The same year, owing to a long-continued drought, the fresh stream of the Thames was reduced so low, that, by the intervention of a violent wind at west-south-west, the bed of the river became so dry that many thousands of people passed it on foot, both above and below London-bridge. Of all the affairs of the time, however, the South Sea bubble, as it was termed, was the most extraordinary. The sums of money proposed to be raised by this and about one hundred and sixty other joint stock speculations, besides numbers which perished in embryo, amounted to 300,000,000*l.* The lowest of the shares of any of them advanced above *cent. per cent.*; and most of them above 400*l. per cent.* A sum amounting to 2,014,000*l*, was confiscated from the estates of those who were principally concerned in the South Sea transaction alone, towards making good the damage sustained.*

magnificence all the other squares of the metropolis, is in its immediate neighbourhood; besides others which, though handsome, are of minor note.—Vide Lacey's New Picture of London, and also Lacey's Stranger's Guide through London.

* In a list preserved of one hundred and fifty-six of the projected

The reign of George the Second, commencing in 1727, and closing in 1760, was scarcely more prolific in incident, so far as the metropolis was concerned, than that of his predecessor. The Londoners, however, most loyally distinguished themselves in their efforts against the cause of the Pretender. Large subscriptions were raised; the most substantial citizens entered into associations, armed themselves, learned the military exercise, and tendered their services; the lawyers of the Middle Temple formed themselves into a regiment; the trained-bands were reviewed by the King; and the promoters of order and the Protestant succession seemed united in repelling the invader of the Government and Constitution.

Numerous improvements and salutary regulations were at this period effected. In 1751, an Act was passed for regulating the commencement of the year, and correcting the calendar;* by which, amongst other changes, the annual admission of the Lord Mayor was altered to the 8th of November, and the solemnity of swearing him in at the Court

companies (some of which were actually incorporated) are the following, and several others equally ridiculous and unfit to be named:—for a flying-engine—for feeding hogs—for making iron with pit-coal—for curing the gout and stone—for transmuting quicksilver into a malleable metal—for an air-pump for the brain—for an insurance against divorces—for making butter from beech-trees—for making deal-boards from saw-dust—for japanning of shoes—for a scheme by which to teach wise men to cast nativities, &c.

* It was by this statute enacted, "That the year should, for the future, begin on the 1st of January; and that the eleven intermediate or nominal days, between the 2d and 14th of September, 1752, should, for that year, be omitted; so that the day which would otherwise have been called the 3rd of September, was dated the 14th." By this correction, the equinoxes and solstices happen nearly on the same nominal days on which they fell at the Council of Nice, in the year 325.

of Exchequer, in Westminster, to the day following. Through a noble stand, made by the citizens, Sir Robert Walpole's artful scheme for extending a general excise throughout the kingdom was subjected to a signal defeat. Amongst other regulations, the City gates were pulled down. Aldgate was sold for 177*l.* 10*s.*; Cripplegate for 91*l.*; and Ludgate for 148*l.*; to be taken down and removed by the purchaser within a limited time. The precinct of Blackfriars, which, from the dissolution of its monastery by Henry the Eighth, had claimed a privilege of exemption from the jurisdiction of the City, was, by a decision of the Court of King's Bench, declared unentitled to the pretended exemption. Fleet-ditch, from Blackfriars to Holborn-bridge, long a serious nuisance to the public, was arched over; a pavement was formed, and a market erected upon it. A general reform of the London prisons was effected in this reign; considerable improvements were adopted in the mode of watching and lighting the streets of the City; and laudable exertions were repeatedly made for the suppression of liquor-shops, masquerades, and other immoral and mischievous nuisances.

The reign of George the Second was remarkable for the number of its new and important undertakings and establishments. Westminster-bridge was begun and finished—the Mansion House* was built—the Society of Antiquaries was formed—and the British Museum, the Foundling, and the Small-pox Hospitals, were founded.

The defective state of the police, and the superstitious notions which prevailed amongst the people, are curiously

* The Mansion House was built from a plan by George Dance, architect, at an expense of 42,638*l.* 18*s.* 8*d.* The chief corner-stone of the structure was laid on the 25th of October, 1739, by the Lord Mayor, Micaijah Perry, Esq. It was not completed till 1753.

C. Marshall. C. Mottram.

illustrated by two circumstances which it is expedient briefly to record. In 1728, London and Westminster was infested by street-robbers to an almost incredible extent. On one occasion, they formed a design to rob the Queen in St. Paul's churchyard, as she was privately returning from supper in the City to St. James's; and the attempt was not made, only from the circumstance, that the villains were at the time busily engaged in robbing Sir Gilbert Heathcote, an alderman of London, on his return, in his chariot from the House of Commons, her Majesty's coach actually passing at the moment! However, by the adoption of rigorous measures, this crying evil was soon put down.

In the month of August, 1754, two large and strange birds were seen perched, one on the cross and the other on the pine-apple of St. Paul's cathedral. Some thought they were eagles, others said they were cormorants. On the firing of a gun from the gallery, they flew away. "See! see!" exclaimed the gazers, "how the Spaniards fly away at the firing of a gun; nothing else will bring the Dons to reason!" This incident was turned to good account by the authorities. The necessities of the State, at this time, requiring a fleet to be suddenly manned, a live turkey was placed on the top of the Monument. This proved highly attractive—an idle mob was assembled—and the press-gangs, lying in wait, made prize of many who answered their purpose.

George the Third's extended reign of sixty years commenced auspiciously; but it involved long periods of expensive warfare and consequent national privation—enemies inevitably of grand improvements, public or private. The present history, however, now draws so near towards its close, that a few leading dates and indications must stand in lieu of detailed records and descriptions.

His Majesty, with his Royal consort, the Princess Charlotte

of Mecklenburgh, was crowned, with due solemnity, in Westminster Abbey, on the 22d of September, 1761. A general peace ensued in 1763. In the autumn of 1768, Christian the Seventh, King of Denmark, who had married the Princess Carolina Matilda, his Majesty's younger sister, paid a visit to the Royal Family of England, and, amongst numerous other honous paid him, he was splendidly entertained at dinner, by the Lord Mayor, on the 23rd of September. At the usual period of election, in 1769, William Beckford, Esq., of Font-hill, was chosen Lord Mayor, for the second time, for the ensuing year. This gentleman, by his strenuous assertion of the rights and privileges of the City, in opposition to the views of the Court, gave great offence to the latter. There is a marble tablet to his memory, in Guildhall, representing him robed, and in the act of delivering a remonstrance to the King on the 23d of May, 1770. The memorable "No Popery" riots of 1780, in which between four hundred and five hundred people were killed and wounded, were followed by a change of Ministry in 1781; and, in 1783, peace was concluded with France, Spain, Holland, and America, and the Shelburne Ministry was compelled to resign. In 1789, his Majesty's recovery from a long and severe mental affliction was celebrated (April 26) by a procession of the Royal Family, attended by the two Houses of Parliament, to St. Paul's Cathedral to return thanks to Almighty God. The war of the French revolution, dooming millions to death, soon afterwards broke out, and was finally terminated only by the victory of Waterloo, achieved by Wellington on the 18th of June, 1815. For three great naval battles fought and gained by the Lords Howe, St. Vincent, and Duncan, the King, Queen, Royal Family, and Parliament, went in procession to St. Paul's to return thanks, on the 19th of Dec., 1797. A brilliant general illumination followed. The peace, or "hollow armed truce of Amiens," was proclaimed in 1801; but hostilities soon afterwards recommenced, and a threatened invasion by France called forth a patriotic volunteer spirit in the kingdom. In London and Westminster alone, and the parishes immediately adjacent, the number of effective volunteers amounted to 27,077. This appears by the general orders which were issued from the Horse Guards, after the volunteer reviews by his Majesty in Hyde-park. A jubilee, in celebration of the King's entrance on the fiftieth year of his reign, was held on the 25th of October, 1809. In February, 1811, the Prince of Wales was invested with the Regency; on which occasion he soon afterwards gave a grand *fête* to a company of two thousand persons at Carlton House. Consequent upon the abdication of Napoleon Buonaparte as Emperor of France, and the accession of Louis XVIII. to the throne of that kingdom, London was visited, in the summer of 1814, by a concourse of illustrious visitors, in number and rank surpassing any former example. At the head of those distinguished foreigners were the Emperor Alexander of Russia, and his sister the Duchess of Oldenburgh, and the King of Prussia with his sons. The splendour of their reception and the public festivities induced by their presence, were unprecedented. On the 9th of June the Sovereigns and Princes were received in state at Carlton House; and on the 18th, they were sumptuously entertained by the Mayor and Corporation of London at Guildhall. On the 7th of the following month, the Prince Regent went in solemn state to St. Paul's, to return thanks for the restoration of peace. On the 9th, the Duke of Wellington was entertained at Guildhall in the same magnificent manner that had been displayed when the Royal guests were present. All these gratifying exhibitions proved to be, in some measure, premature. The security of France was again endangered, and the peace of Europe disturbed, by the escape of Buonaparte from Elba, and his sudden reappearance in arms. However, the triumph of Waterloo terminated, in a few days, his Imperial career; and the narrow boundaries of St. Helena became the resting-place of a spirit in whose eyes thrones had been but toys, and to whom the destinies of empires were familiar and subservient things.

From the reign of George the Third, which finally closed on the 29th of January, 1820, is dated the foundation of the Royal Academy of Arts, the annual exhibitions of which were held at Somerset House, in the Strand, till 1837. In this reign also were built the bridges of Waterloo, Blackfriars, Southwark, and Vauxhall.* By the introduction of gas, in 1807, a noble improvement was effected in the illuminations of streets and houses.

His Majesty, George the Fourth, was crowned in Westminster Abbey, on the 19th of July, 1820. On this occasion, the old crown of Edward the Confessor was used. The procession from Westminster Hall to the Abbey was georgeous beyond all precedent. At six in the evening, three hundred noble persons, besides the Royal Family, sat down to a sumptuous dinner in the Hall; the theatres were thrown open to the public; and illuminations and fireworks met the fascinated eye in every direction.

As King, with all the forms of Royalty, his Majesty's reign was brief. He expired on the 26th of June, 1830; and was succeeded by his next brother, William the Fourth, who, with his Royal consort, Queen Adelaide, was crowned on the 8th of September, 1832. From the advanced age and infirmity of the Sovereign, his coronation was of a less ostentatious character than that of his predecessor.

On the 9th of November, 1830, their Majesties intended to

* *Vide* page 69.

[illegible] by the corpse of Buonaparte [illegible]

[illegible] St. Helena [illegible]

[illegible] were [illegible] and

[illegible] the Trench [illegible] finally closed [illegible] the [illegible] exhibitions of which were [illegible] in the Strand [illegible] 18[illegible]. In this [illegible] also were built the bridges of Waterloo, Blackfriars, [illegible] and Vauxhall. By the introduction of gas [illegible] 18[illegible] [illegible] improvement was effected in the illumination of streets and houses.

His Majesty, George the Fourth, was crowned in Westminster Abbey, on the 19th of July, 1820. On this occasion, the old Crown of Edward the Confessor was used. The procession [illegible] Westminster Hall to the Abbey was gorgeous beyond [illegible] in the evening, three hundred noble [illegible] Royal family, sat down to a sumptuous [illegible] the Hall; the theatres were thrown open to the [illegible] and fireworks met the fascinated eye [illegible]

[illegible] the former of [illegible] his Majesty's reign [illegible] the 26th of June, 1830, and was succeeded [illegible] brother, William the Fourth, who, with his Royal consort, Queen Adelaide, was crowned on the 8th of September, 18[illegible] [illegible] age and infirmity [illegible] sovereign, his coronation was of a less ostentatious [illegible] than that of his predecessor.

On the 5th of November, 1830, their Majesties intended to [illegible]

HAMPTON COURT

have honoured the Lord Mayor and Corporation of London with their presence at dinner in Guildhall, but were prevented doing so by the fear of a disturbance. The arrangements for this festival were similar to those adopted on the visit of the Foreign Princes in 1814.

The opening of the new London Bridge, on the 1st of August, 1831, was attended by their Majesties in state. The Royal Cortegé went by water, and never did the face of old Father Thames assume such gaiety of appearance. On the King's reaching the top of the landing-stairs, the sword and the keys of the City were tendered to him by the Lord Mayor; when his Majesty was pleased to return them, signifying that they should remain in his Lordship's hands. Adjacent to the site of the new Fishmongers's Hall (a magnificent structure replacing the old one, pulled down in favour of the approaches to the Bridge), was erected an elegant pavilion for the accommodation of their Majesties, the Royal suite, the civic authorities, and the more distinguished of the company. In this pavilion, the whole party afterwards partook of a princely collation.

Her Majesty, Queen Victoria, on the decease of her Royal uncle, June 20, 1837, ascended the throne. On the 9th of November ensuing, her Majesty proceeded in state to Guildhall, to dine with the Mayor and Corporation. The Queen was received at Temple Bar by the civic authorities; the day was regarded as a public national festival; at night, along the whole line of the returning procession, the illumination was general; and nothing could surpass in enthusiasm the joy and delight evinced by the people at large.

Her Majesty was crowned on the 28th of June, 1838; and excepting that no coronation banquet was given, the ceremony was of a splendid and imposing description. On no previous occasion was London so full of people,—the country was literally depopulated, and the day was considered in every respect as a national holiday; and few Sovereigns have arrived at the crown attended more universally with the fervent wishes of the people, for a long, prosperous, and happy reign.

The giant strides made by steam-power, both by the deserved encouragement given to Railroads, which intersect the kingdom in every direction likely to benefit commerce,—and the laudable enterprise of the various Steam-Navigation Companies in their efforts to afford every facility and comfort in this delightful and economical species of travelling, as also to render more binding the happy commercial union of Britain and America, by making a voyage across the Atlantic merely a "holyday-trip," will distinguish the years 1838-9, in our country's annals, especially as regards the City of London, that being the grand focus of all enterprise.

The absurd disputes between the City sticklers for exclusive right to build their "own Exchange," (i. e. at the expense of the country, by an extra duty on Coals), in their own *exquisite taste*, without reference to the Lords of the Treasury, was settled by the Building Committee yielding *graciously* to the power which they could not control.

The stern opposition of the City to the New Police Act was crowned with signal success, and they continue to enjoy, in the plenitude of their greatness, the privilege of selecting their own "thief-takers!"

The passing of the New Police Act (which greatly enlarged the power of that useful body) has produced the most beneficial effects upon the "morale" of the metropolis. Those frightful scenes of bestial drunkenness, and its concomitants, no longer desecrate the Sabbath, which, formerly, rendered the public highways impassable to the well-conducted—nor are the slumbers of the tired "useful" disturbed by the boisterous blaguardism of the drunken and the dissolute. Stealing knockers, and ringing bells, has ceased to be laughed at as fashionable frolics; and the fear of the treadmill has proved the best cure for these exuberances of aristocratic wit.

But, above all, the New Postage Act will incalculably promote civilization—the interchange of affection and sympathy will no longer be confined to the upper classes; and many an anxious parent's sorrowing heart will be lightened of its burthen by the "pot hooks and hangers" from a distant child—the unheeded "penny" will often bring consolation to the "bruised reed" of many who have drank deep of "sorrows cup." Mankind *must* become wiser and better by this increased communion of thought and sentiment.

A proposition has received the City's approval, for a splendid quay from London to Vauxhall. This, if carried into effect, will render the banks of Old Father Thames unrivalled for beauty and convenience, and approach a little towards the Parisian method of managing these matters. In 1839 great exertions were made to throw open the passages of all the bridges over the Thames—the doing away with such exactions must be considered as a great boon, not only by those who reside in the immediate neighbourhood of either side of the bridges, but also by those who have occasion to pass over them night and morning, in coming from and returning to their domiciles "beyond the City's smoke." Besides which, the improvements contemplated by Sir Mathew Wood's Act, will, when carried into effect, do much to add to the comfort and convenience of the Metropolis. This Act, includes, among other things, the continuing of Oxford St. to Holborn, direct by cutting off the angle at High St., St. Giles's—taking down the north side of Middle Row, Holborn—the continuation of Farringdon St. to Islington—widening the Strand from St. Mary's Church to St. Clement's—and a new street from St. Clement's Church, to Holborn,—in addition to other improvements both at the East and West ends of the town.

THE GREAT EXHIBITION, 1851.

THE PALACE OF GLASS.

It is quite unnecessary to enter into the particulars of the private history of the origin of the Crystal Palace. The first idea of this magnificent and stupendous pile originated in the mind of that indefatigable and scientific man, Mr. Paxton, of whom the Duke of Devonshire very truly said, " I never knew Mr. Paxton resolve to undertake what he did not fully accomplish." It is enough to say, that Mr. Paxton's plans were not laid before the Royal Commission until they had nearly, if not quite, decided upon the adoption of one out of the numerous specifications which had been presented to them. Such, however, were the advantages as well as the simplicity and unity of Mr Paxton's design, that it was eventually unanimously chosen, not only by the Building Committee, but by the Royal Commission.

We will now give a brief description of the building—this tremendous pile of transparency! It stands on the piece of ground, on the south side of Hyde Park, between the ride known as Rotten Row, and the Knightsbridge road; occupying eighteen acres of ground. It is full 1848 feet long, and is crossed by a transept of 108 feet high, inclosing a row of elm trees, and dividing the whole length into 948 feet on the one side, and 900 on the other. The entire structure is composed of glass and supports of iron, excepting the joists and flooring, which are of timber. The columns are similar throughout, and the same may be said of each of the sash-bars, and of each pane of glass. There are about 2,244 cast-iron girders, for supporting galleries and roof, besides 1,128 intermediate bearers or binders, 358 wrought iron trusses for supporting the roof, 34 miles of gutters for carrying water to the columns 205 miles of sash bars, and nearly 900,000 superficial feet of glass.

The total cubic contents of the building will be 33,000,000 feet; and the glass alone weighs upwards of 400 tons. The total amount of contract is £79,000; the contractors, Messrs. Fox, Henderson, & Co., retaining the materials. Should, however, the Commission keep possession of the Palace altogether, the cost will be £150,000. Not the least part of this astonishing enterprise is, that a palatial exhibition building providing a total exhibiting surface of eighteen acres, and affording space for *nine miles* of tables, should have been put up in about four months, at a cost of less than a penny farthing a cubic foot!

Commissions have been formed in almost every city and town in the United Kingdom, as well as in nearly every place of importance in the civilized world, in order to forward the objects of the Exhibition. Austria, Hungary, Spain, Turkey, France, America, Belgium, Russia, India, Persia, China, and numerous other countries, have made applications for space to be allotted them for goods intended for the Exhibition; and in some cases as many as 100,000 square feet have been agreed for.

The articles which will be exhibited are too numerous to be enumerated. The first section will comprise raw materials and produce. The next division will be that of machinery of all kinds. In this department the production of our own country will bear a most important part. It has justly been remarked, in reference to this section of the Exhibition, "That every one may be able to see how cloth is made for his clothes, leather for boots, linen for shirts, silk for gowns, ibbons and handkerchiefs; how lace is made; how a pin and needle, a button, a knife, a sheet of paper, a ball of thread, a nail, a screw, a pair of stockings are made; how a carpet is woven; how a jug, cup and saucer, and plate are turned and pressed, and the mode in which a spoon is beaten or cast. In addition to this, machinery will be exhibited in motion; the printing press will be seen in action; and every process, indeed, by which a lump of the rude metallic ore is converted into the delicate watch-spring, or into a pin or needle. Among the models of engineering structure will also be exhibited that of the Britannia-bridge, the plan of the Barage of the Nile, and the most important of the dockyards of the country."

In the third section, which includes fabrics, spun, or woven, from flax, hemp, and cotton, will be exhibited articles either plain, or figured, in the loom, as well as printed and coloured, such as linen, canvass, calico, lace, embroidery, and every variety of fancy work.

The manufacturers in metals will furnish a vast catalogue of articles, alike ornaments to the palace and to monarchs, as well as of utility to the cottage and its inmates.

Glass, porcelain, earthenware of all kinds; ivory, bone, horn, parchment, leather, shells, feathers; silks, satins, carpets, shawls, and a host of other articles from all quarters of the globe, will be exhibited.

We must now conclude our brief account of this "Great Industrial Building," by noticing some of the principal products which will be found in the fourth or last division of the articles for Exhibition:—"It includes those productions which tend to illustrate the taste and skill displayed in the application of human industry to the raw material in the productions of sculpture, models, and the fine arts. The subdivision of this section includes sc lpture, as a fine art, in metals, whether single or compound; in minerals, whether from marble, stones, gems, or clay, or in glass or porcelain in woods and other vegetable substances, and in such animal substances as ivory, bone, shells, and cameos. Die sinking,

TREASURY, WHITEHALL.

intaglios, and medals form the second division; architectural decorations, whether integral, in relief, or colour, or adventitious, as in stained glass and tapestry. The fourth division is that of mosaics and inlaid work in stones, tiles, vitrified materials, wood, or metal; the fifth, enamels or metals, china or glass; the sixth, materials and process applicable to the fine arts generally, such as fine-art printing, models of architecture, and topography; and anatomy will constitute the seventh and last division."

THE TREASURY

Is situated at St. James's Park, and is built of stone, and embraces the Tuscan, Doric, and Ionic orders of architecture. The north front faces the parade.

This place was, till lately, a brick building of the most gloomy, not to say tasteless kind. It has, however, assumed a very different character under the transforming hand of Mr. Barry; for now, indeed, it is a very splendid palatial façade, "within whose walls is lodged the moving principle of Britis authority—the power of the purse. And yet England's Treasury contrasts strangely with the school-boy notions of a Treasury that cling to us. Here are no ingots of gold and silver, no stores of jewels, no piled-up substantia wealth. Plainly-dressed men, with about as much small-change as may suffice for the expenses of the day in their pockets, go out and in. Scraps of paper are handed about with large sums written or engraved on them. The abstract idea of money inhabits the empty halls; the power of endowing men with a magnetic power of attracting gold to them after they issue from the doors is there—nothing more. It is like the chests full of sand which the Spanish Jews are said to have received in pawn from the Cid, and to have guarded with scrupulous care, believing they contained the hero's plate and jewels. The chests contained something better than gold—the Cid's "promise to pay;" and the Treasury contains something better still—the collective faith of the British nation. The unseen, remote wealth at the command of this vacant Treasury exceeds what eastern imagination piled up in the cavern opened to Aladdin. In this building is deposited the talisman that keeps together the social fabric of the empire."

THE NEW HOUSES OF PARLIAMENT.

On the 15th of October, 1834, the old Houses of Parliament were destroyed by fire, and six years afterwards the new Palace of Westminster was begun, from the designs of C. Barry, Esq. Much credit is due to this eminent architect for the great simplicity as well as beauty which characterizes the whole of his plan for the erection of this truly national edifice. The Central Hall is of an octagonal form, and is about seventy feet square; and it is through St. Stephen's Hall and Porch by which you reach it. There is a communication from this Hall, by a flight of steps, with Westminster Hall. This approach forms an object of great magnificence. A corridor from the north of the Central Hall leads to the Commons' Lobby and the House of Commons. There is also a corridor to the south, which conducts to the Peers' Lobby and the House of Peers. Victoria Hall, the Royal Gallery, and the Queen's Robing-room, are in a line with the House of Peers, though a little further to the north. Her Majesty's state entrance is at the south-west corner of the pile, in Abingdon-street.

There may be some difference of opinion as to which will be the most picturesque view of the New Palace. Some maintain that the west, or land-front, will ultimately be the

HOUSE OF LORDS

richest and most magnificent; while others contend that the river-front, on account of its magnitude, (covering, as it does, nearly a thousand feet in length,) will be by far the grandest object of attraction in the new pile. If the latter opinion is the correct one, it seems to be a matter of regret that so much exquisite work should be "wasted on the desert air" of the Thames! However, this complaint may prove too premature; for it must be borne in mind, that at present only *parts* of the whole intended structure are to be seen; and that it is impossible to judge correctly of the aspect of the *whole* of this magnificent edifice from any one of the points which have been mentioned. When completed, it will cover an area of nine statute acres.

The Great Tower will reach the gigantic elevation of three hundred and forty-six feet, and the building will be adorned with towers of lesser magnitude. There are fourteen halls, galleries, and vestibules; eight first-rate official mansions; libraries, waiting-rooms, dining-rooms, and clerks' offices in abundance; and eleven greater courts, and a score of minor openings, give light and air to the interior of this superb fabric. Its cubic contents are stated to exceed fifteen millions of feet, which is one-half greater than St. Paul's; and it comprises not less than between five and six hundred differen apartments.

We can only barely mention some of the rooms and apartments which the New Palace of Westminster will contain beyond those already referred to. The Prince's Chamber, so called, in order to preserve the remembrance of a former chamber, similarly named and located, in connection with the old House of Lords. This chamber is to be decorated with a series of portraits of kings, in oil, on a gold ground. The colours of the roof are blue and gold, wonderfully brilliant. Carvings are distributed over the walls in the greatest profusion. The chimney-piece is a gorgeous combination of colours and ornamental workmanship; furniture, fittings—all are on a scale of corresponding splendour.

The Norman Porch differs most refreshingly from every other architectural feature of the New Palace, although it beautifully harmonizes with them. A fine picturesque effect is obtained by looking through the arched depths of the porch on the right, across to the Guard Room, and its lobby beyond. There is to be painted in fresco Young Talbot defending his father in battle, and Isabella Douglas barring the door with her arm, to protect James I. of Scotland. There will also be a subject in fresco in the lobby, of St. Edward the Martyr, slain by the Danes. The Royal Staircase, although of chaste design, and pure magnificence, does not possess any ornaments except the windows, and slender shafts, and mouldings that ascend the walls, and run over the roof.

THE COAL EXCHANGE.

This building was erected in 1849, from the designs of the corporation architect, Mr. Bunning. It is situated in Lower Thames-street, near the Custom House; and in it is carried on one of our most stupendous and important trades. The visitor ascends the steps of a beautiful sort of round tower and passes through the folding swing-doors of the principal entrance. There is a space, or little vestibule, here, which forms the base of an iron well-staircase; at the very top of which is seen, through the coiling balustrades, a painting in the Rubens' style of colouring. Having arrived at the grand central market, we find ourselves in a circular area, boarded with oak planks of a light and dark hue. Around the floor of the area, at intervals, there are long desks of new polished oak, with ink-stands let into the wood, provided for the use of those persons who visit the building for the purpose of transacting business. There are also numerous private offices

[illegible] ... are, [illegible]

[illegible] ... gly from [illegible]

[illegible]

[illegible]

[illegible]

Rooms [illegible]

Young [illegible]

Douglas having [illegible]

Scotland. The [illegible]

of St. [illegible]

[illegible] by the [illegible]. The [illegible] staircase, [illegible] design, and [illegible] except the windows, [illegible] and [illegible] that [illegible] he was [illegible] the [illegible]

THE CO[illegible]

This building was [illegible] corporation architect, M[illegible] ... he ... ver ... ied ... most ... he ... ver ... ipa ... swi[illegible] ... spa[illegible] ... hich ... p on ... g in ... rand ... rded ... floor ... at intervals, [illegible] ... ished ... with ink-stands [illegible] ... e use ... persons [illegible] ... ose of ... business [illegible] ... offices

and recesses, which, for neatness and orderly appearance, do not exactly comport with the fanciful and emblematic pictures and designs which cover the panels of the wood-work that separates these offices.

Returning to the principal entrance, we ascend to the first gallery. Here the panels are all painted as below; the subject of most of them appears to be a colliery—that is, the works above ground, such as the little black house of the steam engine, with its long chain passing over the drum, and then over a wheel above the pit's mouth.

The second gallery, like the previous one, is of cast-iron. There is a picture of Newcastle on one side the semi-circle, with its iron bridge and railway combined, and its old stone bridge below; while on the other side is a picture of Durham, with its cathedral rising among the trees. Several other paintings are to be seen in this gallery,—such as that of a miner in his under-ground dress, and another of the same class of men with a Davy-lamp, &c.

The upper gallery contains at its entrance a painting of "Shields" on one side, and "Sunderland" on the other. The former is a very truthful and well-executed moonlight view of colliers on the river; and the latter, which is also a night-scene, attracts especial notice, in consequence of its faithful representation of Sunderland's one-arched bridge, which is so high above the water, that a collier can pass underneath without striking her topmasts. There are numerous paintings round the panels of this gallery also.

The building is faced throughout with Portland stone, and contains on the ground-floor, besides various other suites of offices, an area of upwards of four thousand superficial feet. The height from the floor to the top of the dome is about seventy feet.

Lightning Source UK Ltd.
Milton Keynes UK
UKHW020726240320
360792UK00008B/84

9 781342 457158